Political Economy and Public Finance

Political Economy and Public Finance

The Role of Political Economy in the Theory and Practice of Public Economics

Edited by

Stanley L. Winer

Canada Research Chair Professor in Public Policy, School of Public Policy and Administration, and Department of Economics, Carleton University, Ottawa, Canada

Hirofumi Shibata

President, Kanto-Gakuen University, Japan

IN ASSOCIATION WITH THE INTERNATIONAL INSTITUTE OF PUBLIC FINANCE

Edward Elgar
Cheltenham, UK • Northampton, MA, USA

Published by
Edward Elgar Publishing Limited
Glensanda House
Montpellier Parade
Cheltenham
Glos GL50 1UA
UK

Edward Elgar Publishing, Inc.
136 West Street
Suite 202
Northampton
Massachusetts 01060
USA

A catalogue record for this book
is available from the British Library

Library of Congress Cataloguing in Publication Data

Political economy and public finance: the role of political economy in
    the theory and practice of public economics / edited by Stanley L. Winer,
Hirofumi Shibata.
        p.   cm.
    Papers presented at the 57th IIPF Congress, held at Linz, Austria, August 2001.
    'In association with the International Institute of Public Finance.'
    Includes bibliographical references and index.
    1. Finance, Public—Congresses. I. Winer, Stanley L., 1947-   .
II. Shibata, Hirofumi, 1929-   . III. International Institute of Public Finance.
IV. Title.
HJ113.I73   2001
336—dc21   2002024582

ISBN 1 84376 073 8 (cased)
        1 84376 118 1 (paperback)

Printed and bound in Great Britain by Biddles Ltd, *www.biddles.co.uk*

Contents

v

Figures and tables

FIGURES

TABLES

Contributors

Robin Boadway, Queen's University, Kingston, Canada

Geoffrey Brennan, Research School of the Social Sciences, Australian National University, Canberra, Australia

Albert Breton, University of Toronto, Canada

Aníbal Cavaco Silva, Nova University of Lisbon and Portuguese Catholic University, Portugal

Walter Hettich, California State University, Fullerton, USA

Gebhard Kirchgässner, University of St Gallen, Swiss Institute of International Economics and Applied Economic Analysis and CESifo, Switzerland

Dennis C. Mueller, University of Vienna, Austria

William A. Niskanen, Chairman of the Cato Institute, Washington, DC, USA

Hirofumi Shibata, President, Kanto-Gakuen University, Tokyo, Japan

Eugene Smolensky, University of California, Berkeley, USA

Heinrich W. Ursprung, University of Konstanz, Germany

Frans van Winden, University of Amsterdam, The Netherlands

Stanley L. Winer, Carleton University, Ottawa, Canada

Donald Wittman, University of California, Santa Cruz, USA

Preface

The International Institute of Public Finance (IIPF) was founded in Paris in 1937. The goals of the Institute are to foster research on public finance and public economics, and to encourage the establishment of contacts and the exchange of opinions on related issues among persons of all nationalities.

Membership in the IIPF has grown steadily since its inception and today stands at approximately one thousand members from more than sixty countries. This membership includes both academics and public finance practitioners. Members come primarily from the universities, the public service and international organizations, and developing as well as developed countries are strongly represented. Many outstanding scholars have taken the presidency of the Institute in different periods, including Richard Musgrave, Fritz Neumark, Sir Alan Peacock and Carl Shoup.

The main activity of the Institute is its annual Congress, in which the IIPF promotes debates and exchanges of opinions on topics of common interest. With the exception of a few years during World War II, the Institute has organized an international conference every year since its inception. At each Congress, the IIPF aims to achieve high scholarly standards. The conferences encompass research and discussion on topics of practical relevance, on issues of implementation, as well as on matters of principle.

The IIPF also aims at the worldwide dissemination of the results of scholarly work and of practical experiences. The Congress programme committee selects, in collaboration with the journal editors, a number of congress papers for publication as a supplementary issue of the journal *International Tax and Public Finance*. It also occasionally publishes an additional selection of conference proceedings in book form.

The 57th IIPF Congress was held at Linz, Austria in late August 2001. Professor Stanley Winer of Carleton University, Ottawa chaired the Scientific Programme Committee, of which I was a member. The main theme addressed in several plenary sessions at this conference was 'The Role of Political Economy in the Theory and Practice of Public Finance'.

I wish to acknowledge the very valuable contributions of the following people offered in connection with publication of this volume, in addition to the authors and discussants: Professor Stanley Winer for his professional dedication in organizing the scientific programme for the Linz Congress and editing the papers presented herein; Professor Haruo Taniyama of the Institute of Tax and Management, Tokyo, who also attended the Linz Conference, for his generous financial support of this project; Friedrich Schneider, the local organizer of the conference, for excellent arrangements in Linz, and Dymphna Evans, Caroline Cornish and Matthew Pitman of Edward Elgar Publishing for their helpful editorial assistance.

Hirofumi Shibata
President, Kanto-Gakuen University
President, IIPF

1. Political economy and public finance: a brief introduction

Stanley L. Winer and Hirofumi Shibata

> It is costly to build a fence or to purchase a chain. It is possible to prove that the no-fence, no-chain solution is more efficient than either, provided that we model the behavior of our dog in such a way that he respects the boundaries of our property. As we put this example from personal experience, the exercise seems, and is, absurd. But is it really very different from that procedure which argues that tax structure X is more 'efficient' than tax structure Y provided that we model the behavior of government in such a way that it seeks only to further efficiency in revenue collection?
>
> Geoffrey Brennan and James Buchanan (1980, p. 193)

> If the economist were to accept any kind of 'political constraint' on the tax system as true constraints on economic policy, much of the prescriptive power of welfare analysis would clearly be lost.
>
> Agnar Sandmo (1984, p. 116)

The two quotes above illustrate the long-standing difference in perspectives that exists in the field of public economics, between those who think that the realities of collective choice must be formally acknowledged, and those who base their policy recommendations on the traditional social planning model of public policy in which political constraints do not play a formal role. The purpose of this book is to contribute to the dialogue between these two groups, in the belief that the future of both political economy and of normative public finance lies somewhere in between the two approaches.[1]

In this introductory chapter, we explain the structure of this book while also briefly introducing each of the chapters that are included in it. We note at the outset that the volume as a whole is not intended to provide a definitive account of every aspect of the vast territory that lies between public choice and public finance. The chapters included here are largely concerned with the contribution of political economy to public finance, rather than with why and how public finance can inform political economy. Moreover, it is fair to say that those who think that it is necessary to formally integrate a concern with political competition and political institutions into public economics are more heavily represented than are those who are less sanguine about the possibility of an integrated approach.

1

In some parts of the book, the chapters are organized as debates. Comments by the participants on each others' views are also included in several instances, and at times these comments are rather pointed. With one exception, the individual chapters were presented as invited plenary addresses at the 57th Conference of the International Institute of Public Finance in Austria during the last week of August 2001.[2]

The lack of integration of political economy and public finance is, perhaps, a surprising state of affairs. As Geoffrey Brennan and Walter Hettich both point out in their contributions, the political economy of public finance in the second half of the last century emerged from the earlier work on public finance by Knut Wicksell (1896), Eric Lindahl (1919) and others. These early public finance scholars were concerned with the role of collective choice in determining the allocation of public and private resources, a role they felt was central to both positive and normative analyses of public policy.

To be sure, over the past two decades or so, public finance academics and practitioners have gradually become more concerned with formal political economy when the issues at hand require an understanding of why governments do what they do, or of why the public sector is organized in the way that it is. So much so that the importance of political economy in understanding why public policy evolves as it does is now widely accepted. One can see this acceptance in the choice of recent Ph.D. dissertation topics, in the professional journals, and in the nature of the papers presented at international meetings such as the 57th Conference of the International Institute of Public Finance from which this book has emerged.

With respect to the specification of what constitutes good or better policy, and in the giving of advice to policy makers, however, there is much less agreement between students of political economy and traditional public finance scholars about how to proceed in either theory or practice. There is only limited consensus, too, among political economists, as readers of this volume will discover. For these reasons, the book has been designed to emphasize normative issues.

PART I: DOES PUBLIC FINANCE NEED POLITICAL ECONOMY?

Let us consider for the moment the standard or traditional approach to normative analysis in public economics. This approach adopts the perspective of a benevolent social planner who is concerned with Pareto efficiency, or who is more broadly concerned with both the allocation and distribution of resources as these are represented in a social welfare function. At first glance there appear to be several problems with this approach, among which are the following:

1. The information requirements for solving a social planning problem in practical contexts are large. In this respect, social planning suffers from the problems faced by a central planner. Consequently, it is standard practice in doing applied work to make use of simplified rules, such as tax neutrality instead of optimal taxation (with its complex blueprints), as a way of coping with the information problem. But these rules tend to be *ad hoc*, leaving a challenging gap between the formal theory and policy recommendations.

2. Social planning appears to be at odds with the classical solution to the information problem, which is to decentralize decision making. Since the information required to implement a social planning solution is substantial, should not more emphasis than is usual in the traditional approach be placed on the design and implementation of decentralized political processes, so as to economize on information and coordination costs?

3. Social planning usually takes no account of the consequences of the collective choice process itself for the allocation and distribution of resources. But public policies are necessarily *public*, and collective choice is not neutral in its effects for various reasons and may itself be an object of concern, suggesting that collective choice be formally integrated into any normative policy analysis.

4. Since the general equilibrium structure of the existing political process is not typically imposed on the solution of the planner's problem, there is no guarantee that an optimal social plan for the public finances is consistent with the equilibrium of an acceptable political process. This line of thought suggests restricting the policies that a social planner can advocate to a set that is consistent with acceptable restrictions on the collective choice process.

One might reasonably respond to the last statement in the spirit of the opening quote by Agnar Sandmo, as one can to most of the points raised, by arguing that by not taking political factors into account, it is possible to retain the ability to think of new and superior policies. An initial counter to this defense of the traditional social planning approach is that by implicitly taking political outcomes as bad when compared to some ideal counterfactual, we will always discover that policy has been corrupted by politics, and surely not all aspects of the policy process in a competitive political system are undesirable.

The volume begins with two extensive, affirmative answers to the question of whether normative public finance needs political economy. Geoffrey Brennan provides a general overview of the relationship between political economy and public finance, and then proceeds to focus on two matters he considers to be at the core of the question: first, whether it is necessary to include political constraints when doing normative analysis, an issue raised in points (3) and (4) above; and second, what objective is to be sought by the policy analyst.

On the first matter, Brennan is decidedly against the current practice in public economics which is to formally avoid incorporating political constraints into formal normative analysis. On the second matter, he is much closer to the social planning tradition than might be expected from one of the leading public choice theorists. He argues for carefully preserving a role for moral philosophy when doing normative public finance.

Brennan then applies his views to analyze the choice between fiscal policy and regulation as governing instruments. Here he raises doubts about the desirability of relying on regulation rather than fiscal policy when these instruments are substitutable.

Albert Breton argues for a political economy of public finance in quite a different manner. Breton focuses on the meaning and role of political competition, which he claims is an essential element of any internally consistent theory of public finance, whether positive or normative. His argument cuts across points (2), (3) and (4) raised earlier.

For Breton, political competition is not just about elections, but must be conceived of more generally as competition between centers of power, some of which are not elected. In this framework, he argues, institutional features of fiscal systems that are often considered negatively in traditional public finance, or even in some approaches to political economy, are seen differently. For example, interest groups help to reveal information about preferences, the struggle between centers of power results in links between spending and taxing that are stronger than those generally assumed in the standard approach to public finance and, as a result, the excess burden of taxation will generally differ from what it is in an apolitical model which assumes a complete separation between the two sides of the budget.

PART II   SHOULD COLLECTIVE CHOICE PLAY A ROLE IN THE STANDARD OF REFERENCE USED IN NORMATIVE PUBLIC FINANCE?

The chapters in the next two sections of the volume are motivated by the structure of neo-classical welfare economics. In the neo-classical approach, one begins with a standard of reference such as Pareto efficiency, and then asks under what conditions this standard will be achieved by an ideal allocation mechanism. The key result here is one of the crowning achievements of social science – the first theorem of welfare economics, also called the invisible hand theorem – which links the equilibrium of a competitive market and economic efficiency.

The next step in the neo-classical approach is to use an analysis of why this theorem fails as the basis for the design of public policy. This is the 'market failure' approach to policy analysis. Finally there is a third step, one not addressed in this book, that involves measuring the consequences for economic welfare of departures from the first-best, so as to know where to concentrate one's efforts to best effect. Benefit–cost analysis is an example of this third step, and the analogue in normative political economy remains to be developed.

Part II is directed towards the first step – the specification of a standard of reference – when collective choice is acknowledged. The debate spills over at various points to consider the same general issue that is taken up in Part I, though the discussion in Part II is somewhat more technical. There are two chapters in this part of the book, by Robin Boadway and Walter Hettich, as well as comments by them on each other's contribution. Comments on Boadway by William Niskanen and Geoffrey Brennan and a reply by Boadway are also included at the end of the section.

As we have noted earlier, no formal account is taken of collective choice or the political process in the traditional approach to welfare analysis. Politics is left outside the standard of reference employed in the analysis, as Sandmo reminds us, on the reasonable grounds that we need to think about how the outcome of the policy process can be improved. Only preferences, technology and endowments are used in defining the standard used to judge policy actions.

Robin Boadway argues that this approach to normative public economics remains appropriate and useful and, in contrast to Brennan, argues that it is not wise to allow formally for political feasibility constraints of various kinds in doing normative work. He thinks that the concept of political feasibility is an imprecise and malleable concept and, to further this argument, he includes in his chapter a critical review of two leading political economy models – the citizen candidate and probabilistic voting models – that might serve as a basis for incorporating such constraints. (The role of political feasibility in public finance returns in the comments on Boadway's chapter and in the chapter by Aníbal Cavaco Silva in Part IV.)

Boadway does not object to anyone raising political issues informally at the policy implementation stage, or even to other theorists including them in their work. But he sees the drafting of policy blueprints based on traditional welfare analysis as a vital part of the policy formation process. In this volume,

Boadway is the (very able) defender of the traditional approach to normative public finance.

Walter Hettich thinks that the standard of reference in normative work should be cognizant of the existence of collective choice. The main argument, which he develops at length, is that progress in normative public finance requires the development of a more complete welfare analysis that is so cognizant. In Hettich's view, this should begin with an understanding of how an ideal allocation, however defined, can be achieved as a political equilibrium – an invisible hand theorem for political markets – and then proceed with a corresponding theory of 'political market failure'. Measurement of departures from a first-best defined in the presence of collective choice is also required. He argues that such a complete, normative political economy, paralleling the structure of neo-classical welfare economics, is within our reach, and he illustrates some of his arguments with reference to the analysis of taxation.

Boadway and Hettich then turn to each other's argument in their comments. The comments on Boadway by Niskanen and Brennan follow. It is better if we do not risk spoiling the reader's enjoyment of this exchange by revealing details of it here.

PART III   WHAT IS A 'FAILURE' IN A NON-MARKET OR POLICY PROCESS?

The second step in the neo-classical approach to welfare economics involves the identification of political market or non-market failure. There has been a great deal of work on this topic in the last four decades, but it is still not clear what 'failure' means and whether and where it occurs. The two chapters in Part III, by Donald Wittman and William Niskanen, present opposing views about when the policy process fails. This part of the book is intended to be a more practical counterpart to the preceding debate between Boadway and Hettich.

Donald Wittman begins by tackling the view that pressure groups and political advertising distort the electoral process and result in inefficient outcomes. (The reader may want to compare and contrast this argument with that of Dennis Mueller in the next section.) Wittman argues that such conclusions are based on the view that uninformed voters are irrational. The argument here is informal, and readers may also wish to consult the technical counterpart to his chapter, part of which was presented at the IIPF Conference.[3]

Wittman also argues that political processes in all sorts of situations generally contain an invisible hand process. So much so that, in his view, we may rely on standard normative public finance to provide us with a predictive theory of what democratically elected governments actually do.

To say that William Niskanen takes a different view is an understatement. Niskanen thinks that government failure is an everyday occurrence, and is rooted in large measure in the same set of conditions as the failure of private markets. These conditions include asymmetric information, principal–agent problems, and insecure property rights. He sees the lack of effective constitutional limitations on the power of government as the most pressing contemporary issue to be faced in dealing with excessive and inefficient growth in the public sector, thereby adding a constitutional dimension to his vigorous defense of the standard approach to the theory of nonmarket failure.

Niskanen and Wittman then comment on each other's chapters. Perhaps Wittman could be said to be observing the half-full part of the democratic policy process, while Niskanen focuses (more usefully, he would say) on the half-empty part. Perhaps, but one suspects that the differences between them are more fundamental, involving the use of different standards of reference to judge observed policies. The debate here helps us to confront the question posed in the title of this section, even if it does not point the way towards consensus about how to identify policy failures in practice.

PART IV   WHAT HAVE WE LEARNED ABOUT THE THEORY AND PRACTICE OF PUBLIC FINANCE FROM THREE DECADES OF EMPIRICAL RESEARCH ON PUBLIC CHOICE?

After three or four decades of empirical research on public choice, it is appropriate to stand back and ask what follows for the theory and practice of public finance from this large body of positive empirical research. Part IV of the book thus includes three contributions that admirably survey the last three decades of empirical work on public choice in three important areas: the role of special interest groups and the size of government (by Dennis Mueller), the effects of fiscal institutions (by Gebhard Kirchgässner), and experimental work on collective action (by Frans van Winden).

Dennis Mueller focuses on the role of interest groups and redistribution in explaining differences in the size of government in the USA and Europe. He argues that the evidence suggests that we cannot understand this difference with recourse to normative arguments for redistribution, and that the explanation is to be found in understanding why special interest groups are more likely to be effective in Europe than in the USA. His explanation rests on differences between the operation of European parliamentary democracy under proportional representation and the operation of the US congressional system. (Here he necessarily deals with the identification of political failure and also crosses over into the territory of the next chapter, by Kirchgässner.) Unlike the other two chapters in this part, Mueller argues for a specific reform of the fiscal policy process, in this case to avoid the worst features of interest group politics. This proposal involves identification of policies that are primarily redistributive in nature, and restrictions on who may vote on such issues.

Gebhard Kirchgässner surveys the enormous volume of empirical work on fiscal institutions that has emerged over the last three decades. He considers (i) the role of constitutional and statutory fiscal limitations; (ii) budgetary procedures; (iii) fiscal outcomes in direct and representative democracies; and (iv) the relationship of federalism and the size of government. It is clear from his review that institutions matter, and that they do so in specific ways. As with all the chapters in this section, the detailed review of the literature he provides should prove valuable in consolidating and advancing research in the field.

Frans van Winden's assigned task is to deal with experimental work on collective action. He begins with contributions to theory that stem from the limited success in experimental work of the standard *homo economicus* model, and the apparent role of bounded rationality (cognition) and bounded reasoning (emotion). Van Winden also draws conclusions from the literature about what we have learned concerning the rationale for government intervention, the role of lobbying, and methods of encouraging collective action. For example, he argues that the rationale for collective action needs to be rethought, as in many cases government action is not required, and that lobbying should be seen as being important for informed policy making. The implications of these conclusions for Wittman's and Mueller's arguments remain to be developed.

PART V   A PRACTITIONER'S VIEW OF THE POLITICAL ECONOMY OF REDISTRIBUTION

No discussion of political economy and public finance is complete without consideration of the political economy of redistribution. Dennis Mueller's provocative chapter on this topic was introduced earlier. In addition, a public finance 'practitioner' was asked to give a different view of the political economy of redistribution. In Part V, Aníbal Cavaco Silva, who is both a professor of public finance and former prime minister of Portugal, presents his view of how a politician judges the political feasibility of a policy, generally defined by him as politicians' willingness to take policy actions to achieve desirable goals. While he does not address the issue of whether political constraints should be formally integrated into the underlying theory used to draw up policy blueprints, Cavaco Silva clearly advocates a greater concern among policy advisers with political feasibility. He then offers his view as to what sort of policy in the European Union towards income inequality is feasible in this sense, including greater targeting of transfer payments in order to finance more human capital formation.

The chapter is of heightened interest at least for two reasons: when he speaks of political feasibility, one recalls that he was the prime minister (interrupting his career as an academic) for much of a decade in the second half of the 1980s and the first half of the 1990s. But also, as Cavaco Silva notes, globalization and deeper economic integration in the European Union have led to a reduced concern with general income inequality and a greater emphasis on poverty policy, developments which Cavaco Silva thinks may be mistaken.

PART VI   WHERE DO WE GO FROM HERE?

Short contributions by two scholars, one specializing in public finance, and the other in public choice, conclude the volume. The assigned task here is to be both retrospective and prospective, and it is a difficult one. Eugene Smolensky, a policy-oriented public finance scholar, attempts to place the political economy work that was presented at the 57th IIPF Conference in a larger context, comparing European and American styles of work, and suggests a greater emphasis be placed on the evaluation of specific programs and on political or social engineering. Heinrich Ursprung presents his view of the current state of political economy. Finally, Stanley Winer offers his reflections on how these two perspectives relate to some of the broader issues addressed in the book.

NOTES

1. In this introduction, and generally in the volume, the terms 'public finance' and 'public economics' are used interchangeably. The term 'political economy' is also used interchangeably with 'public choice' here, though some authors included in this volume find it useful to distinguish between the public choice school of political economy associated most notably with James Buchanan and Gordon Tullock, and other approaches to the integration of economics and the study of political behavior and institutions.
2. The Conference was held in Linz, Austria, August 27–30, 2001. The Chair of the Scientific Committee was Stanley L. Winer of Carleton University. The chapter by Albert Breton included here (as Chapter 3) was presented as a contributed paper, and all other chapters were presented in plenary sessions. All have been revised for this volume. Further information about the IIPF is provided in the Preface.
3. Wittman's technical papers are found on his web page, the URL for which is given in the References.

REFERENCES

Brennan, Geoffrey and James Buchanan (1980), *The Power to Tax: Analytical Foundations of a Fiscal Constitution*, New York: Cambridge University Press.

Lindahl, Eric (1919), *Die Gerechtigkeit der Besteuerung*. Reprinted in part as 'Just Taxation: A Positive Solution' (transl. Elizabeth Henderson) in Richard Musgrave and Alan Peacock (eds), *Classics in the Theory of Public Finance*, New York: Macmillan, 1958.

Sandmo, Agnar (1984), 'Some Insights from the New Theory of Public Finance', *Empirica*, 2: 111–24.

Wicksell, Knut (1896). 'A New Principle of Just Taxation', in Richard Musgrave and Alan Peacock (eds), *Classics in the Theory of Public Finance*, New York: Macmillan, 1958.

PART I

Does Public Finance Need Political Economy?

2. Public finance, public choice and the political economy of regulation

Geoffrey Brennan

1. PREAMBLE

This chapter has two aims: first, to give a general overview of the relation between public choice and public finance; and second, to analyse a substantive issue – that of the role of regulation as a means of pursuing public policy goals.

The first task has been attempted before – by myself, Brennan (1999) among others. There are, for example, two papers by Buchanan (1975, 1979) bearing the titles 'Public Finance and Public Choice' and 'Public Choice and Public Finance'. And there is an entire compendium forthcoming shortly, under the editorship of Jurgen Backhaus and Richard Wagner, on the public choice approach to public economics.

Precisely because the territory here is so well traversed, I have tried to do something additional here – hence the second of my two ambitions. Consideration of the question of regulation will, I hope, illustrate some of the more general points made in the first half of the chapter. However, as will become apparent, I regard this issue, as viewed variously through the lens of public economics and public choice approaches, to be of considerable interest in its own right. Accordingly, although I want to take the opportunity in the course of the argument to make some general methodological points, that is a subsidiary purpose in the discussion as it stands.

2. PUBLIC CHOICE VERSUS PUBLIC FINANCE

Public choice theory – or 'rational actor political theory' or 'positive political economy' – as the movement presents itself today has several intellectual forebears and it is probably a mistake to claim predominance for any one of them. But at least one extremely influential strand – that associated with the Virginia School – arose *out of* public finance. Quite a number of the most influential early practitioners of public choice theory, for example, were public finance people, broadly construed. I have in mind people such as Knut Wicksell and Erik Lindahl as the foundational movers and, in the more recent incarnation, scholars like Mancur Olson, and of course James Buchanan and a large assembly of Buchanan students.¹ It is on this influential Buchanan stream that I shall primarily focus here.

If much of public choice arose out of public finance, it is no less clear that public choice emerged quite explicitly *in reaction to* standard public finance. The source of the opposition at stake here lay in what public choice scholars identified as the ideologically biased assumptions about political processes that orthodox public finance embodied and supported. Perhaps that ideological bias was unintended and largely implicit; but public choice theory saw its mission to be that of exposing the (implicit?) bias and offering a more 'neutral' approach. As public choice critics saw it, orthodox public finance was committed to a so-called 'benevolent despot' model of politics. This model was (or better, 'is', because it is still alive and flourishing) characterized by two features. First, democratic electoral (and/or other political) constraints were treated as non-operative – or certainly not viewed as important enough to merit inclusion in the model of policy determination. That is the 'despotic' aspect. Second, the agents who determined policy – and those who advised them – were taken to be motivated solely by a desire to promote the public interest (with the 'public interest' here understood in the broadly consequentialist terms that orthodox public finance inherited from welfare economics). This is the 'benevolence' aspect. Public choice critics regarded both aspects as objectionable – on both descriptive and normative grounds.

It is not entirely clear whether public finance people themselves saw their enterprise in quite the same terms that public choice critics did. But for a long time the public choice exponents were in a sufficient minority that they could be written off as ideological cranks, or 'democracy bashers'² or economists who didn't know the limits of their own method.

To the extent that there was any kind of response to this critique at the time, it went more or less along the following lines. First, public finance is to be seen as a *tool* of politics, not as a method of political analysis. There is a proper division of labour both within the realm of ideas and within a democratic polity. Within the scholarly domain, it is for political scientists and philosophers to analyse the working of democratic politics, not for public finance experts. And within politics itself, the policy adviser's role is just to give the best policy advice she can. Politicians have to bear the responsibility for taking this advice or not. Whatever particular ends politicians have, they will presumably want to know the consequences of alternative policies, and this is broadly what public economics provides. Of course, public economists do make general background assumptions about the workings of democratic politics. In that general context, public finance scholars tend to share the general popular belief in the democratic process, and do their work within the context of a general faith that by and large democratic politics does work in the interests of the citizenry over the long haul. The idea that public finance endorses despotism – either explicitly or implicitly – is, on this reading, hopelessly misjudged and highly tendentious.

As to benevolence: well, any normative analysis is committed to normative premises. The particular premises adopted by public finance specialists are those that welfare economics uses to give substance to generalized consequentialist utilitarian norms of the kind inherited from David Hume and Adam Smith. To ask what policies would maximize the public interest so understood is not to assume benevolence of anyone. On this reading, it is just to do normative analysis.

Of course, public choice theorists had responses to these responses – some of them more thoughtful and nuanced than others. However, rather than pursue an imagined conversation any further, I just want to state that, basically, I think the public finance people are more or less right on the second issue, but wrong on the first.

The first issue is whether it is proper to finesse questions about political constraints in doing normative policy analysis. I do not think that it is. There shouldn't ultimately be any disagreement among economists over this claim. The economistic approach conceives of normative analysis as a kind of confrontation of the desirable with the feasible. The role of economics in this normative scheme consists in spelling out those feasibility constraints. Usually the focus is on those constraints as they operate in ordinary markets. In the case of public economics specifically, the focus is on the constraints implied by responses of ordinary market agents to tax rates or opportunities for tax evasion/avoidance or opportunities to free-ride in the provision of public goods. We know that mis-specification of those market agent responses leads to wrong policy choices. That's why it's important to get them right. This point can be generalized. Proper policy advice requires specification of *all* the important relevant constraints. Only if political constraints operated somehow independently from policy choice would it be possible to recommend on policy in ignorance of how the political process actually works. And it is difficult to see how any such independence proposition could hold, in general.

This is not to say that there is no comfort within public choice analysis for the kind of optimism about democracy that public finance seems to espouse.[3] It is just that no policy adviser worth her salt, at whatever level, can reasonably put her blind eye to the telescope and pretend that political questions are not her concern. If she is to play a game that has a normative purpose, she needs to have all the significant relevant constraints in play. Otherwise her policy recommendations simply won't have the effects she claims for them.

The second issue relates to the implications of normative analysis for questions of agent motivation. The complaint that public finance orthodoxy assumes policy makers to be benevolent and everyone else to be self-interested is, if correct, a telling one. The general requirement of motivational symmetry is one that has considerable presumptive force. And it is certainly true that public choice scholars differ from public finance ones in where they locate normative analysis – in what they take to be the appropriate 'lever' on which to work in achieving relevant improvements. For public finance, the relevant lever is policy. In public choice, the relevant lever is the more abstract rules of the political game. The reason why public choice exponents make this so-called 'constitutional' move is clear enough: they take politicians and voters to be equally motivated by self-interest. Once this assumption is made, policies are to be *explained* as outcomes of the political game; they are not available for direct normative choice. But the constitutional move itself does not dispose of the issue of motivational asymmetry. The public choice economist who does normative analysis is still purporting to be offering 'good advice'. But it is now the adviser on *rules* as distinct from the adviser on policy who is purporting to act in the public interest – or more generally as the adopted normative framework requires. Anyone who proffers normatively compelling advice purports to be acting according to normatively derived requirements. The bottom line here is that it is the model of *homo economicus* that is flawed. Anyone who does normative analysis ought to acknowledge that there are *some* persons who are normatively driven. And the principle of general motivational symmetry ought to rule out the possibility that that group of persons is restricted to the public finance or the public choice economist and a small group of her friends.[4]

3. OPTIMISM VERSUS SCEPTICISM ABOUT POLITICS

Buchanan in a nicely titled piece, 'Politics without romance', describes the motivation for public choice as being a desire to set against the theory of market failure characteristic of public finance[5] a corresponding theory of 'political failure'. One might have described the ambition more neutrally as being to open up to serious analytic scrutiny[6] assumptions about democratic political process that had hitherto been treated as sacred cows. But the basic purpose is the same. The second description is more neutral because it is not predisposed to identify instances of 'failure'; it is open-minded on whether the presumptions about the benign features of democratic political process will turn out to be justified or not. Unsurprisingly, the rational actor approach to political analysis is not univocal on this issue. The details of different models matter. So it is certainly possible to find, within public choice theory, models that permit a fair degree of optimism about democratic political process – and no less plausible models that are fairly pessimistic. I am intellectually ill disposed to going through the literature and pulling out the variants of models one will 'support' according to one's political prejudices. It seems to me that judgements among models ought to be made primarily on the grounds of their general empirical and conceptual fit. Nevertheless, I thoroughly approve of Don Wittman's agenda of emphasizing how much in orthodox public choice models is hospitable to relatively heroic views of democratic political process. However, I think that 'orthodox public choice models' largely mis-specify the possible dangers of democratic politics (on which a little more below).

The truth is that the 'median voter' family of models has generally rather nice normative implications. Within such models, the generalized principal-agent problem of politics is seen to be solved by creating incentives for electoral candidates to offer policies in the interests of voters (rather than their own interests). Further, the median outcome serves to resolve aggregation problems in a way that comes close to achieving an 'optimal compromise' between competing interests in most plausible cases. Although, strictly, majoritarian voting procedures generate a stable median result only in the case of unidimensional policy space with single-peaked preferences, there are multidimensional versions of the median result of various kinds. These include: models in which voters vote probabilistically, so that interests map only stochastically into voting behaviour; and models in which institutional arrangements structure independent decisions on each dimension separately. There are, in short, circumstances – and arguably not too implausible ones – in which electoral competition operates somewhat like an 'invisible hand', both aggregating the interests of different voters in an appropriate way and bending the interests of the 'suppliers' of public policies to give citizen-voters what they want. Precisely how plausible the relevant conditions for such invisible hand processes are, of course, remains a contested issue in public choice circles.

The normative attractiveness of all these models depends – as do almost all invisible hand mechanisms – on the assumption that agents' actions reliably mirror their interests. Public choice theory, in offering an account of voter behaviour, has tended to take that notion for granted: interest-based voting has seemed to be the only assumption consistent with general axioms of rationality. In fact, it is in my view quite a heroic assumption – and is certainly not logically required by rationality axioms. The relevant argument is laid out in my book with Loren Lomasky (Brennan and Lomasky, 1993) and does not need detailed defence here. The basic idea is that individual action in the electoral context is asymptotically inconsequential: if I make a mistake in casting my ballot and vote for the 'wrong' candidate, it almost certainly won't make any difference to the electoral outcome. This fact has been widely recognized in public choice circles since Downs (1957) in the context of so-called 'rational ignorance'. But the 'rational ignorance' picture is itself not quite right. According to that picture, voters will not have an incentive to be adequately informed about the implications for their interests of different candidates, but *will* vote according to their interests as (dimly) perceived. On the expressive account, voting is more like cheering than choosing: cheering expresses a preference, but the preference expressed need logically bear no relation at all to the cheerer's *interests*. The act of cheering is presumably rational; but this fact says nothing at all about the content of what is cheered for. Voting is analogous.

On this reading, voters are more likely to vote for 'truth, justice and the American way'[7] than for an extra dollar of individual benefit for themselves. And electoral competition consists much more in mobilizing symbolic and affective values than in distributing individual benefits. What this means is that the conduct of politics is a more overtly 'normative' exercise than ordinary public choice theory allows. Electoral politics is not best thought of as an 'invisible hand' process. It might, however, be thought of as a '*visible*' one. Voting is characterized by a 'veil of insignificance',[8] which, though not by any means identical with John Rawls's veil of ignorance, has the same property of backgrounding individual interest. Of course, 'expressive' voting opens the door to all sorts of influences that the more standard *homo economicus* account does not normally accommodate – candidates' appearance, or their charm, or their sexual proclivities. It also allows, though, for aspects like fairness and efficiency and being in the broad national interest – aspects of policy that public economics has always treated as directly relevant. To put the point another way, expressive voting allows us to explain why there might be a political demand for public finance policy advisers, as well as for political spin merchants, speech writers and television personalities.

In short, the expressive account allows room within the description of political process for the direct entry of the normative apparatus – and specifically the direct normative assessment of alternative policies – on which public finance has always focused. I do not mean to imply by this that the public interest is all that counts in the democratic electoral process. That would be much too heroic a view. There is still plenty of room within the expressive account for particular kinds of political pathology: large numbers of voters can perfectly rationally vote for outcomes they would never actually *choose* if they were individually decisive. There is here the prospect of a 'voters' dilemma' not unlike the familiar prisoners' dilemma of market failure fame. Nevertheless, a picture of democratic politics in which political parties choose policy platforms to promote the public interest *explicitly because it promotes the public interest* is not a hopelessly implausible picture. And it is a picture certainly no less consistent with the axioms of rational behaviour than is the picture of political process as a desperate scramble of rival individual interests.

Markets and politics are different in this respect. In markets, where agents' individual choices are decisive, the revealed preference logic applies. In politics, where each individual's choice is almost certainly non-decisive, the revealed preference logic is inapplicable. At the very least, this fact raises questions about the status of the preferences voters 'reveal' at the ballot box that no proper normative analysis can just ignore.

4.   INTERIM SUMMARY

The following is a brief summary of the points made so far.

- Public choice theory is right to insist that proper policy analysis requires an account of political process.
- The account of political process thereby offered ought to take seriously the incentives that are embedded in the institutional structure.
- Public choice is wrong to conceive of large-scale democratic politics as a battle of individual interests, on a par with market processes. Voters cannot be expected to vote routinely for policies that make them individually better off. They are no less likely to vote for policies that promote the general interest, or instantiate fairness or otherwise articulate commonly held values. This works against public choice orthodoxy and in favour of orthodox public economics.
- In particular, the application of normative criteria directly at the level of policy is perfectly consistent with a rational actor account of political processes.

A further proposition that could be added is that 'merit goods' (appropriately understood) are a more important category in politics, and more important relative to public goods, than either public choice theory or orthodox public economics allows.[9]

With this as backround, let us turn to the political economy of regulation.

5.   REGULATION AS A POLICY INSTRUMENT

My interest in regulation arises from four ps: a perception; a prediction; a proposition; and a prejudice.

1.   The *perception* is that over the last three decades or so in most Western democracies, fiscal dollars have become increasingly scarce. That is, the

political shadow price of taxes has increased. (Perhaps I should add here that I reckon this increasing scarcity to be mainly an 'expressive' rather than a 'real' matter. In other words, I do not think that it is to be explained in terms of underlying changes in the real economy – at least not exclusively.)

2. The *prediction* is that this shadow price will continue to increase, mainly for real reasons, mostly connected with increased globalization and the rise of e-commerce. It will be harder to raise revenue politically in the future than it has been in the past.

3. The *proposition* is that this fact means that there will be an increased demand for 'public-revenue-saving' policy technology – and specifically there will be increased pressure to substitute regulation for budgetary operations in all those cases where budgetary options are revenue-using.

4. The *prejudice* is that any such substitution would be a bad thing. This *is* a 'prejudice' because it is not a claim that I have fully reasoned out. It is a prejudice that I suspect most public finance scholars share – though it is in the nature of 'prejudices' that one can never be sure how widespread they are. My reason for thinking this prejudice may be widespread lies in commonly articulated arguments against so-called 'tax expenditures', which have some of the same character as the arguments I shall rehearse.

Neither the perception nor the prediction is central to my argument here. Whether either (or both) is (are) wrong is a matter of interest to me, but is of second-order importance for the argument. My basic concern is to interrogate the *prejudice* – and that exercise could be of some interest even if the issue is not as pressing as I believe it to be.

I should emphasize the restricted scope of the inquiry here. I am not going to attempt to catalogue the general properties of regulatory, as against budgetary, instruments *tout court*. I am focusing, rather, on the marginal substitution of a regulation for a Pigouvian subsidy, in some case where expansion of the provision of some good X is sought. I want to direct attention to the pros and cons of such a marginal substitution, holding constant what can plausibly be *held* constant within the structure of the 'general political equilibrium' model I have in mind.[10] I focus on the subsidy case because I am interested in the effects of an increased political supply price of public revenue. The fiscal technology is a 'revenue-using' one.

6.   A BASIC CLAIM

The analysis takes as its point of departure a claim that a given increase in the output of some commodity X can be secured either by subsidy or by regulation. This claim I take to be uncontroversial. The general point that subsidy and regulation are alternative technologies for securing the same policy objective is familiar to those who make international comparisons of public sector size. The point is often acknowledged that measuring the 'size' of the public sector in terms that make much sense requires one to investigate the *regulations* in place. In some countries, for example, workplace protection is secured through a publicly funded scheme, whereas in others there are regulations that require employers to insure workers privately. The difference this makes in terms of measures of 'size of government' can be quite considerable, whereas the difference in the level of workplace protection may be negligible. What goes for workplace insurance applies no less to a variety of other policy areas: pollution abatement; social welfare delivery; industry protection; education; even defence.[11] Of course, expenditure/GDP or tax/GDP measures are still routinely used as indicators of effective 'government size', whether in comparative or time series exercises – but a little reflection indicates that such measures are extremely dubious in either context.

In any event, the point of departure here is the observation that the aggregate output effects of a Pigouvian subsidy can be simulated by a regulation that specifies the equivalent output level. The question at issue then is what the difference between the two policy 'technologies' amounts to. Of course, the details of the regulation have to be specified. We have to know whether the regulation is imposed on the producer or the consumer side of the market in order to know who gains and who loses from the regulation. And those details will also affect how the aggregate response to the regulation is distributed across individual actors.[12]

My chief interest here, however, lies not in these details but in the more systematic, revenue effects of the two technologies. The Pigouvian subsidy uses up revenue; the regulation does not. There are three implications of this difference. The first relates to standard excess-burden/efficiency arguments. The second relates to incidence arguments. The third is a 'cost of enforcement' argument. These are now considered in turn.

6.1 Excess Burden Considerations

The fact that the subsidy option involves additional revenue counts against it. Suppose the revenue source is a proportional income tax. Then the use of the subsidy involves increasing the marginal excess burden under the income tax – and as we know these marginal excess burdens can be quite considerable even where total excess burdens are relatively small. The regulation option involves no corresponding excess burden – no change in the marginal relative price between work and leisure of the kind that the subsidy involves. In the subsidy case, if I decide to work longer hours I increase public revenue and create thereby an external benefit to all other taxpayer/beneficiaries. In the regulation case, if I work harder, I keep the entire increment for myself.[13] If this line of reasoning is valid, then the implication is that public revenue *is* a scarce resource not only politically but also in welfare-relevant terms. Other things being equal, achieving policy ends with less call on the fisc is a good thing *ceteris paribus*. So Pigouvian subsidies are presumptively superior to direct public provision and regulation superior to Pigouvian subsidies.

Under a standard median voter model of the political process, the superior efficiency of revenue-saving policy technologies counts as a reason (possibly a major one) why revenue-saving is politically preferred. Under the expressive account, the efficiency considerations are just an incidental consequence of a 'taxes bad: spending good' kind of voter nostrum. As I have indicated, my conception of rational actor democratic politics is disposed towards the latter line.

6.2   Incidence Considerations

Under regulation, consumers or producers of the regulated commodity must be made worse off. Suppose that the regulation is imposed on the consumer side of the market – say, consumers are legally compelled to consume more health services (or take out more health insurance) than they would otherwise do. And each is made worse off in relation to two parameters: the increase in consumption that the law imposes on the individual in question; and her elasticity of demand for health services (inversely).[14] Under the subsidy, consumers are made better off – with the gain being a direct function of post-subsidy consumption level. Producers (more accurately specific factors in the health provision industry) are made better off by the regulation – to exactly the same extent that they would be under a Pigouvian subsidy with equal aggregate output effects. Clearly, taxpayers are made worse off under the subsidy arrangement.

Denote the three relevant groups as P, C and T. Then P is indifferent between regulation and subsidy; C prefers subsidy; T prefers regulation. The standard incidence story is a matter of comparing the distributional effects of a transfer from T to C. By hypothesis, the T option involves distributing the cost in proportion to income. Accordingly, the redistributive impact is simply a matter of whether the C group is richer or poorer than average and how X consumption is distributed among the C group. This latter aspect is, as we have noted, not just a distributional question: it may, for example, in the maximin case isolated above, be a desirable feature of a policy that it focuses response on the *lowest* consumers of health insurance. A regulation that requires a certain minimum level of cover will only affect those whose cover in the absence of regulation falls below that minimum – presumably, most of whom will be lower-income persons. On the other hand, the Pigouvian subsidy will primarily cause an increase in the cover levels of those above the minimum – which by hypothesis provides no external benefit at all. All consumers prefer the Pigouvian subsidy even if the regulation is such that large numbers of consumers (conceivably the vast majority) are not affected by the regulation.

6.3 Enforcement Costs

A Pigouvian subsidy involves voluntary action on the part of the C constituency; regulation does not. This suggests that enforcement costs may be higher under the regulation option. I say 'may be' here because subsidies can also create incentives for defrauding the fisc and require an enforcement apparatus. But if individuals are going to be forced by law to do something that they would not otherwise do, there does seem to be a first-round enforcement aspect that is absent in the Pigouvian case. Perhaps this cost will be offset somewhat by lower enforcement costs of the tax system as a whole. The subsidy option increases general tax rates; and incentives to evade taxes are a positive function of the tax rate. But the tax enforcement apparatus must be in place anyway,[15] and the incremental enforcement cost attributable to the subsidy must be of second-order magnitude.

So there may be some presumption in favour of the subsidy on enforcement grounds.[16] It is difficult to generalize here without a much more detailed specification of the regulation and the subsidy alternative.

6.4 Information Costs

There is a question that arises in the regulation/tax comparison about how much information each instrument requires about the public-good demand that generates the underlying normative case for intervention in the X market. Consider the simple case in which only aggregate X consumption is relevant. Then it seems clear that the Pigouvian tax requires the policy maker to have information about the 'external' demand curve for X – the demand curve for X as a 'public good'. The policy maker needs no information about the supply of X or the purely private demands. To specify an optimal quantity requires, however, all information about both public and private demands and supply conditions. The regulation option is in that sense more informationally demanding.

In the more complex situation where we need to allow for best shot, weakest link and similar cases, we will need to specify the nature of the externality/public good in a more fine-grained way. But the same point remains. If we can operate the behavioural modifications through the medium of prices, we need less information than if we insist on working those modifications directly. The relevant difference is that between estimating the true demand curve (including external benefits) and estimating both the true demand and supply curves.

6.5 Bottom Line

From a standard public economics point of view, then, the issues that seem relevant in an assessment of regulation as against subsidy are these:

- Regulation is more efficient on the 'tax' side of the ledger, because it avoids an additional excess burden in the total revenue-raising system.
- Regulation may be more efficient on the 'expenditure' side because it provides greater degrees of freedom in focusing behavioural adjustment on those individuals whose performance generates external benefits.
- Regulation seems likely to involve higher enforcement costs.
- Regulation is presumptively more informationally demanding.

Whether the first two considerations – both pro regulation – are sufficient to outweigh the latter two, both con regulation – seems an open question. Certainly, however, no clear case against regulation seems to emerge within the standard public economics framework. In other words, no general pro-budget prejudice emerges from the examination, given that one restricts attention to the more or less standard repertoire of normative considerations that orthodox public economics adopts. Can public choice considerations add something significant here?

7. THE PUBLIC CHOICE STORY

The standard public choice approach takes as its point of departure the patterns of gains and losses across the relevant groups affected by the regulation/subsidy substitution. The more or less standard incidence analysis employed in public economics becomes the basis not for a normative assessment of the exercise but for a political/explanatory one. Counting up gainers and losers and calculating the political influence of the respective groups is, however, only part of the story. Whereas in the public economics account, we can ignore the feedback effects of the substitution on levels of policy pursuit, in the political model these effects become central. In other words, public finance focuses on the set of behavioural adjustments *within* the set of marketable private goods, the public choice approach must attend also to the private/public margin. In the case in hand, how much X expansion we get depends on the instruments used to achieve that expansion.

In the public economics analysis, we can for example background the effects of the substitution on the group(s) who benefit from the expansion of X – from the public good that the policy provides. In the public choice case, that group enters analysis explicitly. We have to derive the new political equilibrium, of which the level of X expansion is a critical parameter. A neat example of this general point is the treatment by Buchanan and Tullock (1975) of pollution regulation. The question they pose is why regulation rather than Pigouvian taxation is the more typical means of pursuing environmental goals. Why don't we see more Pigouvian taxes in the Pigouvian exemplary laundry/factory case? The answer they proffer is that both the environmentalists and the industry prefer regulation over taxes: the latter because they effectively receive the taxes not collected as extra profit; and the former because this fact means that powerful industrial interests will be supportive of more extensive regulation. The regulation enables the industry to charge a price above the competitive level. In the Buchanan and Tullock example, taxpayers as an interest group are taken to be totally quiescent. If taxpayers were powerful, then an analogous coalition between environmental interests and general taxpayers would emerge in favour of the Pigouvian tax; and the political equilibrium Pigouvian tax rate would be higher (and the level of pollution lower) than if regulation had been used.

In the subsidy example I am envisaging, we need to consider the effects of a regulation–subsidy substitution on five groups in all – general taxpayers (T); consumers of X (C); producers of X (P); beneficiaries of the public good that X expansion provides (E); and the interests of political agents who are charged with the determination of 'X-policy' (B).

Take a simple case of education: compare a regulation of the maximum compulsory school-leaving age with subsidy of education services. Those in favour of the regulation option over the tax option will be producers of education services and general taxpayers; while those against will be consumers of education. Consumers of education in general will prefer the Pigouvian subsidy, even though the regulation as such will actually leave only a subset of those consumers worse off (namely those who would otherwise leave school before the minimum age). Supposing beneficiaries to be more or less independent of those groups, then they will side with that policy arrangement that generates more of the public good. So if producers and general taxpayers are relatively powerful – and more so than education consumers – then beneficiaries will prefer the regulation because it will give them more X than they would get under the subsidy alternative. And I conjecture that the relevant political agents will follow the beneficiaries here. That is, I think that bureaucrats can plausibly be presumed to prefer more X than less. They do so not so much because more X activity means larger bureau budgets (actually in this case it does not) but because bureaucrats in education tend to self-select in the belief that education is a 'good thing'. In other words, I side with those (like Migue and Belanger, 1974) who attribute to bureaucrats an 'own demand' for bureaucratic product that is independent of effects on bureaucrats' incomes.

If the beneficiary group and the set of general taxpayers is virtually coterminous, this fact will establish a general normative presumption in favour of the tax option. Political processes are likely to work better when those who benefit also pay the cost. This is what might be called the 'Wicksellian presumption', and the logic of public choice analysis clearly supports it. But it is not clear how such an arrangement would become politically feasible. If the choice of policy instrument is taken through the same general policy process as the choice of the tax rate (or extent of the regulation), then regulation seems likely to triumph. Obversely, of course, if general taxpayer interests were weakly represented, the tax option would be politically preferred. And if the group that demanded X expansion also happened to be the group that the regulation harmed, then the regulation would become the more efficient policy instrument.

What seems clear, however, is that the strength of the political forces in favour of the policy will be greater the more the policy serves to redistribute from politically weak to politically strong groups. And such redistribution is larger precisely when the politically inefficient instrument is chosen. If there is a general presumption here, it is that the general taxpayer group and the general beneficiary group are likely to be broader than the X consumer and X producer groups. The claim that political process works better in general when beneficiaries pay for what they get is then a general argument in favour of the 'fiscal option' – that is, Pigouvian subsidy financed out of general taxation. My anxiety here is that as tax resources become increasingly scarce (for whatever reason), the likelihood is that there will be greater reliance on regulation – and correspondingly less matching of those who benefit with those who pay.

The foregoing story is very much interest-based. It moves more or less directly from the distribution of gains and losses to the attribution of political support. I do not want to deny that there is *something* in this account, but I think it is a partial story. The folk aphorism 'spending good; taxes bad' is perhaps a more accurate description of voter attitudes; there is no necessary suspension of rationality on the part of voters in taking this view. For this reason, I do not think that the application of the old Wicksellian presumption is either necessary or sufficient to secure more efficient political outcomes. Of course, under the expressive account of politics, we could hardly conclude that the Wicksellian presumption was a *bad* idea. Opinions of 'interest' can play an important role in politics. It is just that it does not have the status of panacea.

8. THE SUPPLY SIDE

There is, however, an additional point that seems to me to considerably strengthen the presumption against regulation and in favour of fiscal arrangements. Imagine that you are the Minister for Education sitting around the cabinet table as the budget is being drawn up. You have a scheme to which you and your Department are heavily committed. You and your policy advisers have worked long and hard to formulate the details of this policy initiative and you have a good supply of justificatory arguments at hand to persuade your cabinet colleagues. However, you know that you will have a hard time of it: opposite you is the Minister for Defence, the Minister for Health and the Minister for the Environment, all with their own pet schemes. And in the budgetary context, with the general electoral attitude to tax increases, you know that if your scheme gets approval, theirs will fail. Likewise, that if one of theirs gets approval, yours will almost certainly not. Ergo, you are natural adversaries. The 'opportunity cost' of any proposal being approved is someone else's forgone. And all the players know that.

So your arguments had better be good. And your policy advisers had better have spent a few months of serious work scrutinizing the proposals of your colleagues and finding the holes. Perhaps in the process you will come to the conclusion that your policy initiative is not as good as some other, and so decide not to proceed. But your ego is at stake. And you have come to think, over the last few years, if indeed you did not think so before, that education is a high priority.

So the battle commences. The setting is such that there will be fierce competition for the best-argued, most compelling case. This is a game in which there can be only one winner.

Now suppose that (at the eleventh hour) your chief policy adviser passes you a note saying: 'We can get this project approved at no revenue cost. Try the regulation option.' All of a sudden the competition disappears. Now, the opportunity cost of your project is *not* someone else's forgone. You can have your project and they can have theirs as well. Indeed, if they *all* have policy proposals that involve regulation rather than spending, then the policy platform can in principle accommodate them all. There may be some element of competition over time to debate, or the capacity of the legal drafters to formulate the legislation. Tax revenues are not the only scarce resource. Nevertheless, the shift from fiscal to regulatory technology removes one important constraint – probably the most important one. And it is a constraint that plays a significant role in disciplining policy action. It is the mechanism that most supports effective competition among the policy enthusiasts around the cabinet table and their respective supportive policy advisers. Budgetary process raises the stake in the argumentative arena.

Institutionally speaking, regulation is a means of finessing that intrinsically competitive argumentative structure. If the success of the Defence project has no implications one way or the other for the likely success of my project, I have a very substantially diminished incentive to scrutinize it. If it sounds satisfactory, then why not?

In short, then, a rule that says that wherever possible policy ends should be pursued through budgetary processes supports a more rigorous process of internal evaluation and justification than would occur if no such rule were in place. A significant shift to regulatory technology would substantially diminish the quality of our policy-evaluative institutions.

A couple of comments about the line of argument may be in order. First, it is worthwhile noting that it is an argument that sits more naturally with an expressive than a standard interest-based version of political process. It does so because under an instrumental/interest-based account the patterns of political support are essentially a function of who gains and loses, and the effective political power (for example distribution across electorates) of the various groups. If there are net electoral gains to different policies under the tax alternative, then there is no reason to refrain from pursuing them. The size of the budget should just emerge from the aggregation of those policies that have positive electoral payoffs. The idea of an aggregate budget that is difficult to increase seems to flow more naturally from a setting in which the virtues of expenditure proposals and the political opprobrium of additional taxes are substantially independent – which is a characteristic feature of expressive voter settings.

Second, although we might make a strong normative case for budgetary over regulatory technology, it is not obvious what forces make that case politically relevant. There will always be pressure within governments to pursue policies through regulatory means, *ceteris paribus*, on exactly the lines indicated. A policy adviser who can invent ways of securing policy objectives at negligible fiscal cost will be a valuable asset – and if my predictions are right, an increasingly valuable one. What forces within politics might one mobilize in support of the budgetary option? Here, the strict Niskanen model of budget maximization is a conceivable friend. There do seem to be systematic reasons why bureaucrats might prefer a larger budget over a smaller one. One does not have to hold that budgets are the only thing that bureaucrats care about to hold that they might care about them to some extent – and essentially for Niskanen-like self-interest reasons. A larger aggregate budget probably does mean a larger source of perqs and more scope for discretionary expenditure for bureau managers. A little self-interest on the part of political agents and policy advisers may not be all bad.

And of course, there is always the hope that principled arguments of a 'public interest' kind in favour of budgetary over regulatory technology of the type that I have offered here may strike some chord in the body politic. As the expressive voting account indicates, that is not a hopelessly pious hope.

9. THE BOTTOM LINE

In brief, then, I believe that there is an argument in favour of budgetary over regulatory policy technology as a matter of general presumption. I do not think that that argument can be very plausibly sustained using the resources of ordinary public economics: some appeal to institutional analysis of a more broad-ranging kind is necessary – specifically of a kind that is characteristic of 'public choice' scholarship.

However, I part company with public choice orthodoxy on the issue (indeed, a fairly crucial issue) of how to model voter motivations. The view of political process as an unrelieved scramble for interests is, in my view, basically misconceived. This has the incidental implication that there is more scope within electoral politics for direct normative analysis at the level of policy than public choice orthodoxy allows.

Accordingly, although public choice orthodoxy offers a presumption in favour of the use of budgetary means – essentially along Wicksellian lines – that argument is not enough in itself. Choosing policy instruments that match beneficiary groups with 'paying' groups is neither necessary nor sufficient to ensure tolerably working political processes. Besides, the logic of the normative argument carries with it the implication that correcting the problem is likely to be extremely difficult politically.

Nevertheless, there does seem to be a strong institutional case for budgetary instruments – based on the way in which policy determination through budget processes supports serious (competitive) deliberation. And the desire of bureaucrats for larger budgets – which is a familiar theme in public choice models – may give us some reason to think that, over at least some range, the budgetary technology might just conceivably prevail.

NOTES

1. Of whom, just for the record, I am not one – at least in any formal sense.
2. The term 'democracy bashers' was coined by Mark Kelman (1988) in a boots-and-all critique of public choice theory.
3. I shall take up the issue of what these resources might be briefly in Section 3 below.
4. I have argued this position at length in a collaboration with Alan Hamlin and will not pursue it further here. See Brennan and Hamlin (2000).
5. Especially its 1960s and early 1970s variant.
6. The word 'serious' here is to be understood as invoking the analytic repertoire and assumptions about human nature drawn from mainstream economics.
7. As Superman articulates his values in the 1990s film.

8. The phrase is originally Hartmut Kliemt's.
9. For relevant argument, see my paper with Lomasky in *Finanzarchiv* (1983) and the final chapter of Brennan and Lomasky (1993).
10. This concern distances the current discussion from 'natural monopoly' context in which regulation is increasingly discussed in economics circles.
11. As the extensive literature on the differences between a conscript army and a professional one testifies.
12. The Pigouvian subsidy distributes the individual increases in X_i so that the aggregate increase in X is secured at the least aggregate cost. But that may or may not be a desirable feature. Whether it is so or not depends on whether the relevant 'externality' is a matter of total X alone, or whether the external benefit is influenced by the distribution of X across individuals. In many familiar cases, the distribution matters. We care, for example, whether all the immunization shots are consumed by the one person or equally across all persons. And in the education case, a regulation that requires all to attend school until age 16 may generate external benefits greater than a simple subsidy for schooling. There is much more to be said about the nature of the 'public good' involved in these various cases. The point here is just to register that the greater flexibility of the regulation option in how the behavioural adjustments are distributed across agents can be an asset.
13. Of course, the price of X is higher in the regulation case, and that may seem to give me an incentive to reduce work effort in the same way as a rise in the price of all the (other) goods I buy. But it is the effect on tax revenue of a marginal work effort increase/decrease that is crucial here - or so it seems to me.
14. That is, higher elasticity implies smaller loss.
15. Recall that the issue at stake is the replacement of a subsidy by regulation *at the margin*.
16. I am grateful to Dhammika Dharmapala for this suggestion.

REFERENCES

Brennan, Geoffrey (1999), 'Public Finance and Public Choice', *Finanzarchiv*, **56**, 1-19.
Brennan, Geoffrey and Alan Hamlin (2000), *Democratic Devices and Desires*, Cambridge: Cambridge University Press.
Brennan, Geoffrey and Loren Lomasky (1983), 'Institutional Aspects of Merit Goods Analysis', *Finanzarchive*, **41** (4).
Brennan, Geoffrey and Loren Lomasky (1993), *Democracy and Decision*, New York: Cambridge University Press.
Buchanan, James (1975), 'Public Finance and Public Choice', *National Tax Journal* 28 December, 383-94.
Buchanan, James (1979), 'Public Choice and Public Finance', in his *What Should Economists Do?*, Indianapolis: Liberty Fund, pp. 183-97.
Buchanan, James and Gordon Tullock (1975), 'Polluters' Profits and Political Response', *American Economic Review*, **65** (March), 139-47.
Downs, Anthony (1957), *An Economic Theory of Democracy*, New York: Harper and Row.
Kelman, Mark (1988), 'On Democracy-Bashing', *Virginia Law Review*, **72**, 199-273.
Migue, Jean-Luc and G. Belanger (1974), 'Toward a General Theory of Managerial Discretion', *Public Choice*, **12** (Spring), 27-47.

3. Public and welfare economics under monopolistic and competitive governments

Albert Breton*

Public and welfare economics still have to come to terms with democracy and democratic governments.[1] To put the matter differently, the economists who labor in these two fields have to recognize that the policies that are conducive to greater welfare may be different depending on whether the apparatus of state is in the hands of 'the people' or in those of a benevolent despot.

As things now stand, governments are (tacitly) assumed to be monopolies – not, to be sure, rent-maximizing monopolies, but social-welfare-maximizing bodies and therefore benevolent agencies. It makes no difference therefore whether governments are made up of elected representatives, hereditary monarchs, party secretaries, or military juntas, as long as they behave as they should! Public and welfare economics scholars do not, in most cases, believe that *in practice* governments maximize social welfare functions, though some could lead an inattentive reader to the impression that they do. The general view is that governments *should* maximize such functions.

As a foundation for a normative public and/or welfare economics, the assumption that governments should maximize social welfare functions comes dangerously close to denying any virtue to democracy – virtues that distinguish this form of political organization from the governments-as-monopolies variety, whether benevolent or not. Indeed, doctrines that would instruct 'the people' as to what can make them better off in matters such as the pattern of resource allocation, the private versus the public organization of supply, the properties of the tax structure, and the configuration of market and other prices should, on the basis of elementary logic, disallow all electoral contests as wasteful of valuable resources.[2]

In other words, it is a travesty of democracy to assume that its purpose is to insure the election of representatives who would do what is best for the people who have elected them by seeking from public and welfare economists the

*I wish to thank Silvana Dalmazzone, Dennis Mueller, and participants at the Linz Conference for comments on an earlier draft of the chapter. The usual disclaimer applies.

decalogue of public finance and welfare economics commandments they should implement. The same authoritarian approach to democracy is to be found in the dominant economic models of federalism – a form of political organization, one would have thought, that should have been immune to that conception of politics. Indeed, in the conventional treatment of the subject, public and welfare economics students have been able, on the basis of criteria that do not embody or reflect the preferences or the opinion of citizens, to assign powers (functions, responsibilities, or competences) to different tiers of government – assignments that are deemed to be optimal and presumed to maximize social welfare.[3]

In the literature of public economics, the fountainhead of that view of federalism is surely Wallace Oates's (1972) treatment of the matter. The assignment of welfare economics' tripartite classification of all public sector functions into allocation, redistribution and stabilization derived from that basic contribution uncannily meets the criteria of 'classical federalism' as they are found in another first-rate work, that of Kenneth Wheare (1963). In that literature and in the one that it has begotten, governments are trusted to pursue the common good (social welfare) to the point that an optimal assignment of powers denies any productivity to concurrency (with or without paramountcy), to invasive strategies, to actual and potential duplication, and so on – all standard features of the real world that, one imagines, that literature would simply expunge.

Competitive electoral contests are a necessary, but not a sufficient, condition for democracy. In other words, electoral contests cannot alone motivate representatives to make self-interested decisions that lead, through mechanisms that mimic the operation of an invisible hand, to the common good or maximum social welfare. Sufficiency is guaranteed by what is often called 'checks and balances' or 'checks and counter checks', which I call competition or competitive behavior in the remainder of this paper.[4] Competition in governmental systems, as in markets, pertains to their internal organization and structure and, also as in markets, can be perfect or imperfect. There are many real-world problems of great interest that appear to require an assumption of imperfectly competitive governments.[5] The main concern of this chapter is not, however, with problems of competition, but with the consequences for public economics of the assumption that governments are benevolent monopolists. To make things as simple as possible I will, as a consequence, proceed on the assumption that governmental systems are perfectly competitive.

In the next section I briefly describe the organization of democratic governmental systems. In Section 2, I provide an overview of a few of the problems that the traditional framework of governments as benevolent monopolists seems incapable of explaining, among them the assignment of powers in federal states, and redistribution. Then, in Section 3, I look at two theoretical public finance problems whose solutions vary considerably depending on whether governments are assumed to be benevolent monopolists or genuinely democratic, that is at once popularly elected and internally competitive. The theoretical problems relate to the presumed relationship between revenues and expenditures and to the measurement of excess burden. In Section 4, I propose a hypothesis to explain why students of public choice have given so much importance to realities that, it would seem, can only be derivative secondary dimensions of politics – things like rent-seeking, corruption and logrolling. The hypothesis finds its source in the benevolent monopoly assumption of public economics. Section 5 concludes the chapter.

1.   COMPETITIVE GOVERNMENTS

The notion that democratic governments are nothing more than the assembly of representatives who have been elected in popular electoral contests must be jettisoned. Instead, governments must be conceived as structures or organizations generally made up of a large number of centers of power, some of which are elected while others are not. I suppose that each and all of these centers of power maximize expected consent (which for elected centers of power, can be assumed to be proportional to expected votes). In other words, each center of power is assumed to act in such a way as to maximize the probability that citizen *j* will grant it her consent. That probability (which can take any value between zero and one) in turn is a function of what all centers of power do to increase or reduce *j*'s welfare (or utility).[6]

To understand that functional relationship, it is sufficient to recognize that in the production and delivery of goods and services (including regulations and redistribution), subsets of centers of power must coordinate their activities. Centers of power are therefore 'forced' to interact with each other, first as producers of goods and services, and second, through the effect of supplies on the welfare of citizens. It is because of this second effect that centers of power are induced to compete with each other – that their interaction as producers and suppliers becomes a competitive interaction.

Three objections – all of them empirical – have been raised against the hypothesis briefly adumbrated in the preceding paragraph. So far, the objections are in the nature of assertions about facts or of impressions regarding the latter, rather than solidly documented empirical propositions. First, it is alleged that citizens do not have enough information to identify the contribution of individual centers of power to their own welfare, nor do they have sufficient incentive to acquire that information. On the matter of incentives, I accept as indisputable Donald Wittman's (1995) view that if citizens do not have the incentive to acquire information, centers of power have the incentive to diffuse it widely when it is beneficial to them and when it is detrimental to their competitors. On the question of the information available to citizens regarding the performance of individual centers of power, not much on a priori grounds can be said. It is important to keep in mind, however, that it is possible for intra-governmental competition to be vigorous even if only a few citizens are informed. The only empirical study I am aware of on this matter is that of Arthur Schram and Frans van Winden (1989), which supports the proposition that citizens do identify the individual contribution of each center of power to aggregate output.

A second objection, very closely related to the first, denies that centers of power have 'constituencies' – especially non-elected centers of power. In other words, the question is asked whether the ministries, departments and agencies in compound governments that are responsible for the provision of such services as the police and the military, for granting funds to academics, scientists and artists, for formulating and implementing policies in matters related to education, health, the environment, agriculture, justice and foreign affairs, have constituencies. To ask the question is to provide the answer. The empirical literature on interest and pressure groups makes that abundantly clear (see, among many contributions, Bennett and DiLorenzo, 1985; Pross, 1986; Young, 1991), as does a careful look at a detailed organizational chart of any modern democratic government.

Finally, there is the objection raised most forcefully by Dennis Mueller (1997) in his review of my 1996 book. In that review, Mueller contends that the judicial branches of government, at least in the constitutionally based democracies, are basically independent and, consequently, do not maximize expected consent. This view raises two questions, both empirical in nature. The first has to do with the evolution of the law through jurisprudential opinions. Consider how the opinions in supreme and other courts have been changing on questions such as divorce, birth control, abortion, homosexuality, marriage, child abuse, sexual harassment, and the host of other subjects that are at the forefront of social concerns at the onset of this new millennium. Why do judges change their minds? Is it because they keep abreast of debates and developments in ethics, deontology and moral philosophy? Possibly, but I think it more likely that they do so because they do not want to lose the consent of the people.[7] How do judges (and others) ascertain that consent? That is a difficult question to answer because expected consent – the objective function that is being maximized – is a mixture of public opinion (measured through polls and appraised through contacts and connections), of outlook and ideology, and of the maximizers' capacity to influence beliefs and preferences.

The second question has to do with the politics of judicial branches. Mueller, in his review of my book, took it as axiomatic that supreme courts were above engaging in political competition. The role of the US Supreme Court and of the Florida Supreme Court in the outcome of the November 2000 presidential election in the USA should put that idea to rest forever. The courts (supreme or other), like all other centers of power that make up compound governments, have constituencies. It is possible that Mueller thought that the constituency of the US Supreme Court was the whole nation. We now know this is not the case.[8]

2. DESCRIPTIVE OR POSITIVE FAILURES

There are many real-world problems that the ruling public economics paradigm cannot explain. I look at three of these though, space permitting, it would be easy to extend the list. I consider first the problem of the assignment of powers in decentralized governmental systems; I then look at the treatment of redistribution in public economics and in real-world democracies; finally I dwell very briefly on interest or pressure groups.

In the conventional economic approach to federalism – often labeled fiscal federalism – there is no explicitly identified agency (persons, organizations, or mechanisms) that would implement the assignments or reassignments which are derived on the basis of 'fundamental principles'. It is tacitly assumed, one must surmise, that assignments and changes in them are executed by benevolent monopolists incarnated in central governments.

It is true that in the fiscal federalist story, there are levels of jurisdiction – very often, only two – each inhabited by governments. Each of these, however, is a benevolent monopolist that never overruns the powers it has been assigned. Because the policies implemented under each power either do not spill over into other jurisdictions, or if they do, because the spillovers are assumed to be costlessly (more or less) fully internalized, the status of the benevolent despots is never disturbed.[9] Consequently, monopolists do not interact. Each governs in its own realm, oblivious to what goes on elsewhere. The difference between a centralized unitary state – the world of public economics before the chapters on federalism – and a federal state is that in the first there is only one benevolent monopolist, whereas in the second there are many – the oxymoron notwithstanding.

All in all, the fiscal federalism story is, as a consequence, a fairly uneventful one, and this for two closely related reasons. The first is that the story is a *normative* one derived from a strictly nominalist ethics, that is one with no foundation in a positive theory of individual and institutional behavior.[10] It is a story that gives instructions to history on the way it should write itself while disregarding all the interesting and important historical facts. The second reason for the rather staid character of the story is that it has only the remotest relation to real-world problems – those that beg for the attention of individuals whose minds have not been professionally trained to overlook them. Questions such as the following are not asked and therefore not answered. Why are assignments of powers almost always asymmetrical – the content of powers is different from one junior jurisdiction to the next, as when the design and implementation of agricultural, environmental and other policies vary from province to province or from region to region? Why is it that in the earlier years of European integration, the notion of 'subsidiarity' was used to promote centralization and after the Treaty of Maastricht (which became effective on 1 November, 1993) to foster decentralization?[11] Why is decentralization used when the evidence points to the capacity of central governments to design and implement policies in a non-uniform way over their territory? Why do equalization grants exist in some decentralized governmental systems and not in others? Why is there so much coordination machinery and activity in some decentralized federal states and not in others?

These and other questions like them are difficult – impossible? – to answer in a frame of reference which assumes that governments are social-welfare-maximizing monopolistic agencies. However, they have simple and almost obvious answers in a framework in which governments compete with each other and are internally competitive. It would be a waste of time and space to provide these answers here.

The inability of the benevolent monopolist model to deal with the assignment problem pales in significance when compared to its incapacity to address the questions that are posed by the real-world problems of wealth, income and goods redistribution. In the public and welfare economics tradition, as I need not insist, there is a rampart – a sort of Berlin Wall – between matters pertaining to allocation and those related to redistribution. Even the structure of textbooks and curricula is respectful of the Wall. The implicit positive model of redistribution is never articulated; it is a hard one to understand. In it, citizens, who are assumed to be focused on their own interest and to act in such a way as to make that interest a maximum, choose from among their midst a number of individuals who, upon being elected, stop being concerned with their own interest. These elected individuals then choose a redistribution program and proceed to implement it. They do, however, remember their days as commoners. They know, for example, that if as politicians in the city of Toronto they attempt to do any redistribution by, let us say, requiring downtown office buildings to make available, within their structures, low-rent apartments so that the core city will not, at night, be empty of people – except for gangsters and other crooks – poorer Canadians (and even foreigners) from everywhere will flock to Toronto, inducing some better-off Torontonians to move to (say) Edmonton where no such program is in place.

But the job of the elected redistributors is more complicated than the above suggests. Redistribution should be separate from allocation. It should be respectful of the Wall. It would have been better, for example, if the British government had transferred funds directly to the needy instead of providing them with orange juice, milk and school meals, as doing so distorted the allocation of resources – created positive excess burdens.

Why then does Toronto require low-rent apartments in downtown office buildings while many other Canadian cities do not? Why did the British government implement an orange juice and milk program for some twenty-five years following World War II? Why did it subsidize mid-day meals in schools? Why, in other words, is there so much redistribution in kind – redistribution that distorts resource allocation and creates excess burdens? Why do all governments, whatever their jurisdictional location, engage in redistribution? Does it help to say that benevolent monopolists, to maximize social welfare, are providing their citizens with 'merit goods'? To put it differently, does labeling interventions in the allocation of resources through the provision of goods identified as meritorious help us understand the real world of politics as it unfolds before our eyes? Again, the answer to the above questions is obvious once it is recognized that governments are internally competitive and compete with each other. The idea of merit goods itself becomes otiose.

But I will be asked, is the conflation of the Musgravian (1959) allocation and redistribution branches efficient? The answer to this question is at once easy and difficult. If one uses the canons of public and welfare economics, the answer is a simple no – it is not efficient but wasteful of scarce resources. That is obvious. However, if one makes use of normative canons based on a positive theory of democracy – a democracy founded on competitive elections *and* internal competition between constituent centers of power – the answer is more complicated. I, for one, would start by looking at the organization of competition inside governments and at the structure of property rights undergirding that organization. I would ask whether either or both the organization of competition and the structure of property rights can be improved. I would only then turn my attention to the electoral rules in place, and ask whether they are congruent with the existing organization of competition. Starting with electoral rules – or limiting oneself to these rules, as is often the case – is like placing the trailer in front of the tractor, simply because the way competition organizes itself often compensates for deficiencies in the electoral rules (see Breton and Galeotti, 1985). If the two building-blocks of the organization of competition and of electoral rules are 'optimal' in some relevant sense, I would say that what these democratic governments were doing was efficient. To put the matter differently, in democracies redistribution is willed by the people whose preferences in the matter change with circumstances – hence the variations in redistribution over time which are easy to document. If democracies are tolerably well functioning, what is implemented has to be tolerably efficient.

Interest or pressure groups – lobbies – have no place or role in conventional public and welfare economics. It can, however, be argued (see Breton, 1996) that they are essential to an efficient functioning of democracies. Lobbies move information from citizens to governmental centers of power and from these to citizens. Information about preferences is difficult to obtain because citizens have an interest in bluffing and in adopting other deceitful stratagems. Lobbies are organizations that (eventually) have a past and a future and are, as a consequence, less likely to bluff – they are more reliable. The game of politics on the other side of the ledger is one of compromise on the part of the centers of power engaged in crafting a policy. Seldom, if ever, does a center of power obtain exactly what it wants by way of policy. It is important to centers of power that citizens know why they are getting less than what they wanted. Lobbies convey information to citizens about the nature and the rationale of compromises. The main problem with lobbies is that there exist in all societies citizens who belong to no lobby. As a consequence their preferences have no institutional way of being registered – these citizens are not empowered (on this problem see Breton and Breton, 1997).

3.   ANALYTICAL OR THEORETICAL FAILURES

From the point of view of what used to be called the pure theory of public economics, the monopoly model of the public finances also fails in a number of ways. I give two examples. First and most basic is the apparent impossibility in this model of building a bridge between the expenditure side of the budget and its revenue side, except for a purely accounting bridge. Total expenditure has to be equal to total revenue plus changes (positive or negative) in outstanding indebtedness. If one looks at the budgetary processes of real-world democratic governments, the existence of links of all sorts is apparent in these processes. These links or connections (which I called 'Wicksellian connections' in Breton, 1996) are real and not particularly difficult to understand in a frame of reference in which governments are internally competitive. I have offered models of budgetary processes in congressional and parliamentary governments in that same book.

Given the connections – the institutional links between line expenditure items and their tax prices – the concepts of the burden and excess burden of taxation have to be jettisoned. Indeed, in the conventional model there is a burden and, in particular, an excess burden attached to taxes because they are assumed to be levied as a general means of finance, not to pay for a particular good or service. Taxation is conceived of as a gross amount or global sum one transfers to a merchant for the delivery of a basket of goods, and not a price paid for the purchase of a particular good (or service) in that basket from which one derives utility equal, at the margin, to that price. Even in conventional theory, benefit taxes or user fees generate no excess burden.

Recognizing that a connection between line expenditure items and tax prices exists does not mean that one must espouse the view that excess burdens are zero. They can be, and, in the real world of experience, usually are, positive. They arise from a mismatch between the volume and/or quality of goods and services supplied by governmental centers of power at given tax prices. The mismatch may be a consequence of the fact that certain goods and/or services are public goods *stricto sensu* and are supplied to populations whose individual members have different preferences. The mismatch may also be a consequence of the high cost to governmental centers of power of acquiring information about the preferences of their constituents, even when the latter are willing to reveal their true preferences. Finally, the mismatch can be a consequence of the implementation of taxation policies based on the principles of taxation derived from the model of the benevolent monopolist. The implementation of 'neutral' tax regimes – regimes in which taxes strike all goods and services at the same *ad valorem* rate, and in the conventional model, generate no excess burden of *taxation* – creates excess burdens of *public supply* that are, in all likelihood, enormous because they systematically break the (Wicksellian) connection between public expenditure items and their tax prices. To put the matter differently, if preferences for publicly provided goods and services differ among individuals in a jurisdiction, charging them the same tax prices will inflict on them utility losses or excess burdens. In genuine democracies, engineered tax neutrality is inefficient and, for that reason, one should expect efforts at legislating such tax-neutral structures always to fail – as happened in Canada with the 'goods and services tax'.

In Breton (1996), I have tried to show that the more vigorous the competition – the more vibrant the democracy – the smaller will be the excess burden attached to the governmental provision of goods and services (including regulations and redistribution). One implication of this proposition is that if real-world governments did in fact behave as monopolists – benevolent or not – they would run roughshod over expenditure–tax price connections and would, in the process, generate a large excess burden of public supply. Another implication of the same proposition is that in democracies monopoly governments – assuming these governments to be stable, in violation of a conception of true democracy – would be smaller than competitive governments, simply because the excess burden of public supply would be less in the latter than in the former.

4.   A HYPOTHESIS CONCERNING PUBLIC CHOICE

Notwithstanding the sustained efforts of scholars such as James Buchanan (1967, 1968), William Niskanen (1971) and others,[12] public choice is still without a generally accepted theory of government.[13] Instead, the discipline has focused on subjects such as rent-seeking, the mischievous influence of interest and pressure groups, corruption, the deviousness of bureaucrats, and other matters like these which are, without doubt, of great importance, but are secondary and derivative of something much more basic. One finds rent-seeking, industrial spying, corruption (for example, through direct tax evasion; or tax evasion through transfer pricing; or insider trading, and so on), and devious bureaucrats in corporate enterprises and in the marketplace, but microeconomics would be a very lame theory to analyze the behavior of firms and of markets if it had nothing more to offer than a set of models of these various realities.

I would like to suggest that one of the reasons for this state of affairs derives from the conception of government embodied in the benevolent monopoly model of conventional public and welfare economics. If one is brought up in a world which conceives of governments as agencies inhabited by selfless individuals bent on maximizing social welfare, one is bound, when confronted with real-world governments, to notice that the maximization of social welfare is not dominant. First, one is sure to observe that politicians and bureaucrats, like most other human beings, are very much preoccupied with their own welfare which, incidentally, may include a particular ideology. The pursuit of own welfare by agency actors points to waste and corruption. One will also observe the presence of interest or pressure groups – lobbies. These do not exist in conventional public and welfare economics in which social welfare is maximized. One easily concludes that the presence of lobbies signals rent-seeking and deviations from the common good. That lobbies may be essential components of democratic governments and thus play an important role in their functioning is unthinkable.

To put the matter differently, for someone brought up on the gruel of conventional public and welfare economics, the model of democratic government that is absorbed with the gruel is so otherworldly that when it has to confront real-world governments, every move, every action, every decision of public agents that one observes is a deviation from the gruel-inspired construction. The deviations then become the material on which one seeks to erect a theory. However, the deviations are only deviations in respect of a construction that is fundamentally flawed from the word go.

In attempting to answer the thematic question posed by the organizers of this Conference as to whether public choice (political economy) and public economics (public finance) need each other, the answer must be a resounding yes. However, that need can only be met and satisfied if scholars in the two disciplines strive to create a true positive theory of government formulated within the methodology of neo-classical economics – a theory from which testable propositions can be derived. Then a really useful non-nominalist normative theory would be possible.

5. CONCLUSION

From the point of view of descriptive or positive analysis as well as from that of their status as internally consistent theoretical constructions, public and welfare economics are in need of an empirically relevant theory of democracy and of democratic government. I have, in the preceding pages, pointed to positive and analytical failures that I ascribe to the absence of a theory of government. I have, in other words, pointed to the inability of public and welfare economics to deal with real-world phenomena such as the assignment and, especially, the reassignment of powers in federal states, redistribution, and the pervasiveness of interest and pressure groups. I have also given examples of theoretical failures born of the way public expenditures and revenues are assumed to be related to each other in the basic public economics construction. Finally, I have suggested that the failures of public and welfare economics provide us with a reasonable hypothesis for why public choice has focused much of its attention on what are in effect derivative elements of a theory of government.

NOTES

1. We must, I believe, admit that the attempts of Abba Lerner (1944) and of William Baumol (1952) to formulate a theory of government largely based on the welfare economics paradigm were failures.
2. Walter Hettich and Stanley Winer's pathbreaking research on the determinants of tax structures, which they have so well brought together and extended in their recent volume (Hettich and Winer, 1999), is an eloquent demonstration that existing tax structures cannot be understood by reference to principles derived from public and welfare economics.
3. Breton and Scott (1978), Breton (1996), and recently Winer (2000), in a most insightful historical analysis, have emphasized the importance of reassignments in the workings of federal states. Conventional public economics is largely silent on the matter. And for cause: once an optimum is found, it is there!
4. A basic reference for understanding checks and balances is Panagopoulos (1985).
5. See Breton (1998) and Breton (2001).
6. The probabilistic model I use rests on a number of assumptions which are sometimes violated in the world of experience. The alternative to that model - the deterministic voting model from which the widely used median voter theorem is derived - also rests on assumptions which are sometimes disregarded in the real world. My own view is that the assumptions of the second model are considerably more restrictive than those of the first. That, of course, is ultimately an empirical matter. I add that the backdoor reinstatement of

the ethical observer or social planner in the guise of a median voter is a sleight of hand which I find disingenuous.

7.	The idea that supreme courts are concerned with 'legitimacy' – consent in my language – and therefore with public opinion is forcefully made in Sullivan (1998, p. 16).
8.	The view that the Supreme Court in the USA at least has constituencies can also be found in Landes and Posner (1975).
9.	In Breton (1965), spillovers are internalized by the implementation of Pigouvian grants by the central administration; in Oates (1972), by increasing the size of jurisdictions. Weldon (1966) correctly argued that if a central government can devise the required vector of grants that would internalize the spillovers, federalism is not needed – it has no *raison d'être*. Breton's remedy is no solution. Once inter-state mobility (not only fiscal mobility, but any sort of mobility including that associated with the movement of tourists) is recognized, spillovers are everywhere and significant. Oates's solution would also make federalism unnecessary.
10.	Oates (1999) makes the point time and time again that the fiscal federalism story is a normative or prescriptive story.
11.	Many writers (for example, Berman, 1994; Inman and Rubinfeld, 1998; Oates, 1999) place the origin of the notion of subsidiarity in Pope Pius XI's Encyclical *Quadragesimo Anno* (1931). That is inaccurate. The idea goes back at least to the Franciscan monk Johannes Eberlin (1521) and has a long and complicated history. On this see Kühnhardt (1992) and Breton et al. (1998).
12.	I tried my hand at the problem in Breton (1974) and with Ronald Wintrobe in Breton and Wintrobe (1982).
13.	Theories of voting are not theories of government.

REFERENCES

Baumol, William J. (1952/1969), *Welfare Economics and the Theory of the State*, 2nd edn with a new introduction, 'Welfare and the State Revisited', Cambridge, MA: Harvard University Press.

Bennett, James and Thomas J. DiLorenzo (1985), *Destroying Democracy. How Government Funds Partisan Politics*, Washington: Cato Institute.

Berman, George A. (1994), 'Taking Subsidiarity Seriously: Federalism in the European Community and in the United States', *Columbia Law Review*, **94**(2), March, 331–456.

Breton, Albert (1965), 'A Theory of Government Grants', *Canadian Journal of Economics and Political Science*, **31**(2), May, 175–87.

Breton, Albert (1974), *The Economic Theory of Representative Government*, Chicago: Aldine.

Breton, Albert (1996), *Competitive Governments. An Economic Theory of Politics and Public Finance*, New York: Cambridge University Press.

Breton, Albert (1998), 'Public Sector Efficiency Under Incipient Globalization', *Revista di Diritto Finanziario e Scienza delle Finanze*, **57**(4,I), 442–57.

Breton, Albert (2001), 'Some Political Consequences of Economic Globalization', mimeo.

Breton, Albert and Margot Breton (1997), 'Democracy and Empowerment', in Albert Breton, Gianluigi Galeotti, Pierre Salmon and Ronald Wintrobe (eds), *Understanding Democracy. Economic and Political Perspectives*, New York: Cambridge University Press, pp. 176–95.

Breton, Albert and Gianluigi Galeotti (1985), 'Is Proportional Representation Always the Best Rule?', *Public Finance*, **40**(1), 1–16.

Breton, Albert and Anthony Scott (1978), *The Economic Constitution of Federal States*, Toronto: University of Toronto Press.

Breton, Albert and Ronald Wintrobe (1982), *The Logic of Bureaucratic Conduct. An Economic Analysis of Competition, Exchange, and Efficiency in Private and Public Organizations*, New York: Cambridge University Press.

Breton, Albert, Alberto Cassone and Angela Fraschini (1998), 'Decentralization and Subsidiarity: Toward a Theoretical Reconciliation', *University of Pennsylvania Journal of International Economic Law*, **19**(1), Spring, 21–51.

Buchanan, James M. (1967), *Public Finance in Democratic Process. Fiscal Institutions and Individual Choice*, Chapel Hill: University of North Carolina Press.

Buchanan, James M. (1968), *The Demand and Supply of Public Goods*, Chicago: Rand McNally.

Hettich, Walter and Stanley L. Winer (1999), *Democratic Choice and Taxation: A Theoretical and Empirical Analysis*, New York: Cambridge University Press.

Inman, Robert P. and Daniel L. Rubinfeld (1998), 'Subsidiarity and the European Union', in Peter Newman (ed.), *The New Palgrave Dictionary of Economics and the Law*, London: Macmillan, Vol. 3, pp. 545–51.

Kühnhardt, Ludger (1992), 'Federalism and Subsidiarity', *Telos*, **25**(1), Spring, 77–86.

Landes, William M. and Richard A. Posner (1975), 'The Independent Judiciary in an Interest-Group Perspective', *Journal of Law and Economics*, **18**(3), December, 875–901.

Lerner, Abba P. (1944), *The Economics of Control. Principles of Welfare Economics*, New York: Macmillan.

Mueller, Dennis (1997), 'Review' of Breton (1996), *Canadian Journal of Economics*, **30**(4a), November, 997–1002.

Musgrave, Richard A. (1959), *The Theory of Public Finance. A Study in Public Economy*, New York: McGraw-Hill.

Niskanen, Jr William A. (1971), *Bureaucracy and Representative Government*, Chicago: Aldine-Atherton.

Oates, Wallace E. (1972), *Fiscal Federalism*, New York: Harcourt Brace Jovanovich.

Oates, Wallace E. (1999), 'An Essay on Fiscal Federalism', *Journal of Economic Literature*, **37**(3), September, 1120–49.

Panagopoulos, Epaminondas P. (1985), *Essays on the History and Meaning of Checks and Balances*, Lanham, MD: University Press of America.

Pius XI (1931/1981), *Quadragesimo Anno*, in Claudia Carlen (ed.), *The Papal Encyclicals*, Wilmington, NC: McGrath.

Pross, A. Paul (1986), *Group Politics and Public Policy*, Toronto: Oxford University Press.

Schram, Arthur and Frans van Winden (1989), 'Revealed Preferences for Public Goods: Applying a Model of Voter Behavior', *Public Choice*, **60**(3), March, 259–82.

Sullivan, Kathleen M. (1998), 'Behind the Crimson Curtain', *New York Review of Books*, **45**(15), 15–18.

Weldon, Jack C. (1966), 'Public Goods (and Federalism), *Canadian Journal of Economics and Political Science*, **32**(2), May, 230–38.

Wheare, Kenneth C. (1963), *Federal Government*, 4th edn, London: Oxford University Press.

Winer, Stanley L. (2000), 'On the Reassignment of Fiscal Powers in a Federal State', in Gianluigi Galeotti, Pierre Salmon and Ronald Wintrobe (eds), *Competition and*

Structure. The Political Economy of Collective Decisions: Essays in Honor of Albert Breton, New York: Cambridge University Press, 150–73.

Wittman, Donald A. (1995), *The Myth of Democratic Failure: Why Political Institutions Are Efficient*, Chicago: University of Chicago Press.

Young, Robert A. (1991), 'Tectonic Policies and Political Competition', in Albert Breton, Gianluigi Galeotti, Pierre Salmon, and Ronald Wintrobe (eds), *The Competitive State. Villa Colombella Papers on Competitive Politics*, Dordrecht: Kluwer, pp. 129–45.

PART II

Should Collective Choice Play a Role in the
Standard of Reference Used in Normative
Public Finance?

4. The role of public choice considerations in normative public economics

Robin Boadway[*]

INTRODUCTION AND OVERVIEW

The topic of this chapter is a daunting one – to contemplate to what extent public choice or political economy considerations ought to be taken into account in normative public economic analysis. In particular, should the prescriptions obtained from normative analysis be constrained by considerations of political feasibility? The issue is of fundamental importance for the formulation and execution of economic policy, which is necessarily a prescriptive exercise with normative content. My view is that, with some exceptions, political feasibility considerations should generally not constrain policy analysis and advice, at least by non-partisan economists. My purpose is to explain why I hold that view. I hope that readers will find the position to be provocative and one that stimulates debate even if it is not found to be persuasive.

The term 'normative approach' is a very general one and can be used for many purposes. It is useful to distinguish two broad ones at the outset. Normative analysis can be used for *evaluative* or for *prescriptive* purposes. In the former case, one is evaluating the normative properties of actual or potential outcomes, outcomes that may well be the consequence of collective choice processes. In the second case, one is actually prescribing or recommending courses of action as an input to collective choice process. This chapter is primarily directed to the prescriptive use of normative public economic analysis. It is in this case that the role of political economy constraints is the most relevant. Of course, the normative content of public economic analysis is basically the same whether the purpose is evaluative or prescriptive. Thus, much of our discussion will apply to either. But it seems inherently less controversial to ignore political economy considerations in

*Nicolas Marceau, Gordon Myers and Motohiro Sato have provided many helpful comments on earlier versions of this chapter. They do not necessarily share all the views put forward.

evaluating outcomes than in prescribing policy. What might be controversial is the evaluative exercise itself. There are economists who completely eschew normative analysis, and who view the scientific role of economics to be purely positive. This is a difficult position to maintain in practice, since it would imply that even seemingly innocuous statements about the benefits of free markets could not be advocated. Thus, we take it as given at the outset that normative analysis has a legitimate, and indeed necessary, role to play in the economic policy process. The issue is whether and how political feasibility should play a part.

The chapter proceeds as follows. To put matters in context, it is useful to begin with an overview of the key ingredients and methodology of the normative approach. In fact, they are not as far from the concerns of public choice as is sometimes depicted. Next, we summarize some problems facing the normative approach. Then we turn to the question of what and when public choice considerations ought to condition normative analysis. This will involve both matters of principle – why public choice considerations should not be treated as a constraint on normative analysis – and matters of practicality – why public choice considerations are not in a position to be used as constraints. The latter involves essentially a brief critique of public choice or political economy as it has developed to date.

It should be stressed at the outset that, although this chapter is focused mainly on the normative approach, nothing in it should be taken to suggest that the normative approach has a monopoly on being the correct one. Normative and positive approaches to collective decision making and the analysis of economic policy issues are complementary. Neither one rules out, or is more legitimate than, the other. The only concern is with defending at least one approach to normative analysis, one that explicitly ignores political feasibility constraints in prescriptive analysis. This involves thinking about when and how the descriptive should influence the prescriptive. Indeed, the issue could fruitfully be put the other way as well: when and how should normative principles be used to judge positive outcomes?

PRINCIPLES OF NORMATIVE PUBLIC ECONOMICS

The ultimate purpose of much normative public sector analysis is prescriptive: what are good policies or good reforms? Normative analysis can serve a policy evaluation purpose and an advisory purpose, and can have a real impact on actual collective decision making. It is therefore important to be clear about what it involves.

There are three ingredients that go into normative analysis. The first is a presumption about *how a decentralized market economy functions*, and its formalization in demand and supply functions, profit functions, and indirect utility functions. This ingredient is essentially a positive one, at least in so far as indirect utility functions simply reflect revealed preference and not social weights. Impediments to the functioning of markets may be important, such as monopoly, unions, free-riding, market imperfections due to uncertainty and information, and coordination failures. Moreover, non-rational behavior may be relevant. But, in general, there seems to be broad consensus in the profession about how markets operate and when they fail, although refinements are continually being discovered, as exemplified in the enormous literature on the so-called New Institutional Economics recently surveyed in the *Journal of Economic Literature* by Oliver Williamson (2000). This might be contrasted with the case of political markets, where much less consensus exists with respect to their functioning. This may simply reflect the earlier stage of development of their study.

The second ingredient used in normative analysis is the set of *constraints* facing the analyst. These can be classified into three types. The first are the constraints imposed by the availability of existing *technology*. These will already be reflected in the excess demand functions mentioned above that describe the functioning of the market economy. The second type of constraint involves *resource balance*. These are captured in the market-clearing conditions that apply in equilibrium, taking due account of any endogeneity of resource supplies over time. The third type of constraint involves *information*. As mentioned, there may be imperfect information in the private sector, which will be reflected in market outcomes. But the government may be ill informed in many ways as well, and this can limit the range of policy prescriptions that can be implemented. It has imperfect information about household preferences (and thus market responses) especially where these vary across households, about household abilities, about non-market activities, and about the extent of illegal or underground behavior. These are important constraints on policy prescription, and can lead to quite different policies than in a first-best world of full information. Thus the set of feasible points along the economy's relevant utility possibilities frontier (UPF) can differ considerably among the first-best, the second-best when only incomes are observable, and the third-best when even incomes can be misreported to evade taxes. Indeed, much modern normative public economics is driven by characterizing second-best or *n*th-best policies in a world constrained by imperfect information of various sorts, and as an extension, by searching for ways to reduce informational constraints by monitoring, penalizing illegal behavior, and so on. My purpose in this chapter is to consider whether political economy constraints should play a similar role to informational constraints: should policy advice be constrained to be politically feasible as well as informationally feasible?

Third, and most controversially, normative analysis and policy prescription require *objectives*, and these *necessarily* involve at least minimal value judgements. Some value judgements commonly used in prescriptive analysis are relatively non-controversial for standard purposes (and many even creep into the public choice literature). Examples include those that underlie conventional social welfare functions (SWFs): (a) individualism (that household preferences ought to be respected); (b) anonymity (that all households be given equal weight in the objective function regardless of their identification); (c) symmetry (that the SWF be symmetric in utilities); (d) the Pareto principle (that the SWF be increasing in individual utilities). Taken together, these result in the notion of *welfarism*, which forms the basis for Bergson–Samuelson SWFs. These value judgements alone are sufficient for giving normative significance to economically efficient outcomes (points along the UPF), and some useful prescriptive properties of policies require only that. For example, the so-called 'production efficiency theorem' of Diamond and Mirrlees (1971) relies only on them, as do shadow prices for project evaluation in a small open economy.

However, in general, we cannot get very far with policy prescriptions that are based on efficiency alone, especially in a second-best world where the Second Theorem of Welfare Economics fails. That is, we simply cannot separate efficiency from equity considerations, and pursue the Musgrave (1959) strategy of providing advice on efficient policies so as to get to the UPF, while leaving it to some other unspecified process for choosing the appropriate point along the UPF. More important, many policies are explicitly redistributive in nature, to an extent that we economists are not always willing to acknowledge. In fact, it can be argued that governments are not primarily involved in exploiting gains from trade arising from free-riding and market failure. Instead, like it or not, government is primarily an institution for redistribution. This redistribution occurs in many dimensions, including through equalizing outcomes, equalizing opportunities, and providing social insurance. For prescriptive purposes, we need a means of evaluating these policies, and that inevitably involves making interpersonal welfare comparisons, if only implicitly.

Interpersonal Welfare Comparisons

More generally, as the welfare economics literature has made clear, interpersonal comparisons are mandatory for policy prescriptions of all sorts, not just those with explicit redistributive intent. In a second-best setting, all policies – even those with efficiency objectives – have gainers and losers, and it is impossible to avoid taking account of that somehow. There have been many attempts to get around that problem and to focus on the efficiency effects of policies to avoid interpersonal comparisons of welfare, but all have been bound to fail. Appealing to the various compensation tests, such as those proposed by Kaldor (1939), Hicks (1940), Scitovsky (1941) or Samuelson (1950), does not work, even if one accepts the demanding value judgement involved in the hypothetical compensation principle. Adopting the Harberger (1971) dictum that 'a dollar is a dollar' – or a 'euro is a euro' – implies a rather peculiar implicit SWF that is additive and linear in money metric utility, which is unlikely to generate much ethical consensus. The more appealing Musgrave (1959) approach of leaving redistribution to the so-called distributive branch of government fails demonstrably in a second-best world, essentially because the failure of the Second Theorem means the distributive branch cannot do its job. In effect, the distribution and allocation functions of government are inextricably intertwined. Thus, explicit interpersonal comparisons are necessary, and public choice is not likely to be particularly helpful in avoiding that. Indeed, part of what normative economists do is to inform the political process with respect to interpersonal welfare judgements and their consequences for policy.

The argument that interpersonal comparisons of welfare cannot in principle be avoided is a rather important one, and one that we often honor in the breach. Major policy prescriptions like free trade, tax reform, competition policy, unemployment insurance and so on are typically proposed by economists on the basis of efficiency arguments. As a matter of principle, such advice is potentially incomplete if it does not take account of the redistributive impacts that these policies necessarily have. That is not to say that as a matter of expediency those in government ought to use distributive weights as a matter of course. But those of us in the academic business of normative policy prescription and evaluation cannot assume that the concept of efficiency is a sufficient concept for normative analysis. Put another way, in a second-best world, given the failures of the First- and Second-Best Theorems of Welfare Economics, market prices do not have the normative content that is often attributed to them. They do not reflect shadow values as in a first-best world.

In fact, the sort of interpersonal judgements that are involved in standard normative analysis are often not that controversial, and might enjoy a fair amount of consensus. At least, they do among practitioners of normative analysis. In the context of welfaristic objectives (of which more will be said below), many of the most important qualitative policy prescriptions found in the normative literature – those emanating from the optimal income tax literature – require only a non-negative aversion to inequality. This assumption alone, which one expects would command fairly widespread support, narrows down the range of outcomes on the second-best UPF considerably: all those between the utilitarian outcome and the Rawls (1971) outcome would be included. Although this seems like a wide range, the qualitative features of the solutions are quite similar, and distinct from those in the other range of the second-best UPF. Moreover, the degree of aversion to inequality can be readily parameterized, and policy proposals can be posed in such a way that allows decision makers to see the implications of different degrees of aversion to inequality.

PROBLEMS FOR NORMATIVE PUBLIC ECONOMICS

Normative analysis, like positive analysis and public choice, is obviously developing constantly. It is in a constant process of evolution as new problems come to light, and new interpretations are found. Let me highlight what at this stage of development seem to me to be some of the main conceptual problems facing normative public economics.

The Need for Value Judgements

As mentioned, prescriptive analysis cannot be done without value judgement: almost all policy evaluation requires interpersonal welfare comparisons implicitly or explicitly. There is no natural or scientific way to choose among value judgements, and we know from public choice theory that societal consensus will almost certainly be difficult to achieve. Progress will be made in ways of formulating interpersonal welfare comparisons, developing new insights from them, and studying their implications for policy. Indeed, that is one dimension of normative policy analysis. It is apparent that the analyst must choose his/her own value judgements, presumably reasonable ones, make them explicit, argue for them, and be accountable for them. In the end, the decision maker must have a normative basis for choosing among options.

Non-welfaristic Objectives

Normative public economics continually strives to clarify value judgements and discover new ones. In recent years, there has been growing emphasis on non-welfaristic objectives. These include notions such as equality of opportunity and capability, fairness and poverty alleviation. This poses challenges in its own right, not just in the value judgement associated with the objective itself and the fact that a different dimension of interpersonal comparisons is necessary, but also because welfaristic and non-welfaristic objectives are typically in conflict, as the social choice literature has convincingly shown. Resolving this conflict itself involves a value judgement. None the less, such conflicts among objectives must be resolved: it is not enough for policy purposes simply to show the impossibility of satisfying two conflicting objectives, as is often the focus in the social choice literature. Normative analysts are in a good position both to pose the ethical issues involved, and to suggest ways to the political process of resolving them. What should be noted is the role that normative analysis plays *vis-à-vis* the political process. It poses, discovers and clarifies objectives as well as ways of achieving them and in so doing informs collective decision making.

Differences in Preferences

If the economy consists of households that have identical preferences (as in the standard optimal income tax world), non-negative aversion to inequality provides a natural and reasonably acceptable interpersonal value judgement to adopt. However, if preferences differ, things are much more difficult. There is no natural way to compare persons with, say, different tastes for leisure. Nor is it clear what political economy can contribute to that. Different parts of the literature have adopted different assumptions. For example, some economists hold that differences in preferences should not count in policy analysis, and households should be compensated only for differences in their ability to generate incomes. Others hold that the decision maker must explicitly compare the welfare of those with high and low tastes for leisure, even if they have the same income-earning ability. But perhaps the greatest contribution of the literature is to analyze systematically the ethical issues involved and the consequences of adopting alternative ethical stances. Adopting a particular ethical perspective in one's research is necessary, given that some value judgement must be made in order to offer policy prescriptions. Given that, it is obviously important to be forthright about one's ethical choices.

Irrational Behavior

Various forms of 'irrational behavior' emphasized recently in the behavioral economics literature pose an even greater challenge for normative economics. Examples include addiction, myopia, hyperbolic discounting, misjudging odds, and simply irrational decision making because of mental illness or age. Addressing these issues would seem to challenge the fundamental norm of individuality by having the state adopt paternalistic policies.

Intergenerational Issues

Taking account of the interests of future generations is also a challenge, quite apart from the fact that the future is unpredictable. There is presumably a tendency for political processes (as well as many economic analyses) to put relatively high weight on the utility of the current generations (including their altruistic urges). The normative analyst would feel free to adopt alternative ethical principles with respect to the well-being of future generations.

Time-inconsistency

One of the biggest challenges to normative welfare economics comes from the fact that in a second-best intertemporal setting, second-best policies of well-intentioned, benevolent and 'rational' governments can be time-inconsistent. Unless governments are somehow able to commit to pre-announced second-best optimal policies, the best they can do is to implement time-consistent ones, which are necessarily welfare-inferior to second-best ones. The consequences of this can be devastating for the quality of outcomes. For example, in some circumstances, well-meaning time-consistent government intervention can actually be Pareto-inferior to *laissez-faire*. Taking time-inconsistency into account leads to some reasonably strong prescriptive advice. For example, mandatory pensions, investment and savings subsidies, education policies, and various forms of social insurance can have as part of their rationale the undoing of the consequences of time-consistent government policies. It seems clear that this type of constraint is one that normative analysts should – and do – take into account.

Does this amount to accepting political economy considerations as a constraint? After all, time-inconsistency is a result of governmental political choice that renders second-best optimal policies infeasible. Although it is partly a matter of semantics, I would argue that time-inconsistency considerations do not represent public choice constraints in the usual sense of ruling out options that are not politically feasible. The genesis of time-inconsistency is the timing of the implementation of decisions and the inability of governments to commit in advance. The problem applies even when governments are fully benevolent and rational, and do not rule out any option, including second-best policies.

However, the constraint imposed by time-inconsistent government behavior provides us with a natural lead-in to the main concern of this chapter, which is: when should normative public economics take account of public choice considerations?

POLITICAL FEASIBILITY AS A CONSTRAINT ON NORMATIVE ANALYSIS?

Political economy analysis is very much the fashion nowadays. It might seem natural to many economists that political feasibility should play an important role in normative policy analysis. After all, if optimal policies are not feasible, what is the point of recommending them? Moreover, recommendations that do not pass the political feasibility test run the risk of being discounted, and not being taken seriously. It seems clear that such reasoning does color much policy advice. I can certainly think of many instances in Canada when political feasibility has been allowed to overrule what could be considered on normative grounds good policy advice. Examples that come to mind are the reform of business taxes (where proponents have striven to ensure that the number of losers is minimized), reforming health care (where it is taken as a matter of faith that any attempt to introduce pricing into the system will cause the edifice of public health insurance to fall down), or targeting of universal social programs (where it is assumed that the middle classes will not agree to lose their entitlements). Reinforcing this is the fact that there have been instances in the past where good policy advice was simply not acted on by the political system (proposals for a guaranteed annual income, or for introducing some actuarial principles into unemployment insurance). At the same time, there have been some instances in which good policy advice persuaded governments to undertake reforms that many might have considered to be politically infeasible. A good example of this is free trade, which, until a high-profile advisory commission advocated it, was considered to be politically impossible. Another example was the introduction of a federal value-added tax, despite its political unpopularity. Thus, from a purely empirical point of view, it does not seem clear that political feasibility is anywhere near a binding constraint. (It should be acknowledged that the political party that introduced both free trade and the value-added tax was summarily dismissed from office shortly thereafter, and lost virtually all its seats.) In some instances, the political feasibility argument may be used as the scapegoat for choices being driven by decision makers' preferences.

The position I would like to argue is that, in general, political feasibility should not be taken into account in pursuing normative prescriptive policy analysis. First I give two main reasons for holding that position – one a matter of pure principle and the other of practicality – and then I discuss some exceptions to the rule.

Prescriptive Analysis Informs Public Choice, not Vice Versa

The first reason for ignoring political feasibility constraints in normative public economics is based simply on the notion that the ultimate purpose of normative analysis is to inform the policy process in its task of choosing among options, and perhaps to persuade it of a preferred alternative. As a matter of principle, it seems inconsistent to rule out on a priori grounds options that are normatively superior simply on the basis of a perception that the policy process itself will choose not to adopt them. That seems incompatible with the notion of an economist as a professional social scientist.

To put the matter slightly differently, political feasibility constraints are qualitatively different from technology, resource and information constraints. Political feasibility does not reflect a set of circumstances that are deterministic or exogenous to the decision maker, but rather the consequences of the choice process itself, albeit a political choice process. The purpose of normative analysis is itself to assist in the taking of collective decisions, to persuade and inform policy makers, and to bring expert analysis to bear to clarify the ethical nature of the choices to be made, not to obfuscate them.

This point of view may seem radical since it contravenes the positivist strain of thinking that has been particularly prevalent in the Anglo-Saxon economics tradition. This strain holds that economics is analogous to a science, and that as such all propositions must be empirically verifiable. Unfortunately, a purely positive approach to economics is untenable from a policy point of view. As we stressed earlier, prescriptive policy advice – which is the *raison d'être* of normative public economics – cannot be purely positive. It necessarily involves some value judgements, including especially interpersonal comparisons of well-being. That is not to say that prescriptive analysis is not scientifically valid. On the contrary, it is entirely syllogistic in its nature. And, it is based on the same kind of analysis of private markets that is used in purely positive analysis.

I would further argue, somewhat more controversially, that to constrain prescriptive analysis by what is politically feasible is to bias it in favor of existing stakeholders (that is, property owners), and to make it more politically conservative than is necessary on ethical grounds. Existing property owners are, after all, the ones with the money, and therefore often the ones with the political power. It can be argued that this consequence of the positivist tradition, along with an ethical presumption in favor of the inviolability of property rights, has heavily influenced public choice theory. The result has been a serious philosophical rift between normative public economics and public choice, a rift that is fairly clearly reflected in the literature and no doubt motivates the need for symposia on the subject.

As evidence for this, one need look no further than Buchanan and Tullock's 1962 classic *Calculus of Consent*, which has undeniably been extremely influential. The core viewpoint of this book is that collective choice exists primarily to exploit the gains from trade that remain unexploited because of the free-rider problem. The possibility of interpersonal redistribution is treated as a potential 'cost' of the political process rather than as a social end in its own right. The ideal social choice procedure would be unanimity – which is as conservative as it gets – but transaction costs unfortunately preclude that. The optimal size of majority needed to take collective decisions is said to reflect the trade-off between these transactions costs and the costs associated with redistribution (that is, the fact that one may end up more or less arbitrarily on the wrong side of redistribution decisions).

This thinly veiled apology for the ultimate primacy of existing property rights is itself necessarily incomplete as an ethical norm against which to judge collective choice. For one thing, the market value of property rights (that is, prices) has no compelling ethical meaning: the wage one receives for one's labor is determined solely by the relevant excess demand function for the particular society one happens to find oneself in, not by any higher ethical evaluation. For another, there is no basis for determining how to share the presumably sizeable gains that are achieved by collective action, and even a perfectly functioning unanimous voting procedure *à la* Wicksell would be unable to prescribe one.

Finally, even from a positivist point of view, the Buchanan–Tullock approach to collective decision making is far from persuasive. It belies the fact that most of what government does is redistributive in nature and intent, so much so that the redistributive element seems to dominate the gains from trade element. Perhaps this strain of public choice analysis is not positivistic at all. A better, though perhaps unfair, interpretation is that it is every bit as normative as conventional normative public economics. Its intention is to persuade us of its own ethical position, which is that the sanctity of property rights is the ultimate ethical principle that should guide public policy, as vague as that principle might be.

In fact, it can be argued somewhat provocatively that public choice practitioners in the Buchanan–Tullock tradition do not feel constrained to take political feasibility into account in their analyses; nor do those conventional economic policy analysts who treat 'a euro as a euro' in the fictitious pursuit of efficient economic policies. There seems to be no compelling argument therefore to require normative public economics to take political feasibility into account, except perhaps as a hidden way of given extra weight to the most powerful stakeholders in the political system, that is, those with the property rights to protect.

What Political Feasibility Constraint?

The second argument for ignoring political feasibility constraints is a more practical one. We know too little about political processes to be able to constrain prescriptive analysis by what is feasible, especially since prescriptive analysis is itself intended to persuade and influence policy makers. There is a reasonable amount of consensus on the other constraints used in normative public economics, conceptually if not in detail. Economists agree with the general way in which markets operate, and with the resource constraints that policy makers face. Even here, though, our knowledge of the actual responsiveness of markets to exogenous changes in prices, incomes and policies is quite sparse. In addition, informational constraints are reasonably well understood, although the literature is in a constant state of evolution. The kinds of information constraints being applied are being refined regularly. This in itself is a problem for normative public economic analysis since the policy prescriptions can differ considerably under different assumptions about the government's information. That alone should make us cautious about the prescriptions that we advocate, but it should also make the process of research itself very worthwhile and rewarding.

Political constraints are, however, inherently more impractical than technological, resource and information constraints. Some of the reasons are given below.

Complexity and unpredictability
Outcomes of political processes are inherently complicated and unpredictable. They are the outcomes of many levels of decision making, most of which are not subject to the same kind of discipline as the profit motive in the private sector. Intangibles like leadership, the power of persuasion and the charisma of certain personalities can affect the outcome. There are certainly plenty of examples of changes in policy regimes that would have been very hard to predict. Had economists restricted their policy advice to those policies that were deemed to be politically feasible, they may well have ruled out superior options that might have been accepted, and have skewed others in order to make them politically palatable. It seems to me that given the complexity of political processes, it is not clear than any manageable political economy model can capture the intricacies and nuances of real-world political decision making.

Given this, it is not surprising that there is scarcely any literature that attempts to incorporate political constraints in any meaningful way into prescriptive analysis. Those contributions that do take political feasibility into account tend to use very simple public choice mechanisms, such as median voter models or Leviathan models. Interestingly, the most common examples of the use of political constraints involve their role in determining constitutional or political decision-making arrangements themselves. Thus political economy considerations are sometimes used as an argument for decentralizing government decision making or imposing constitutional constraints on government discretion. We return to this important issue below.

It might be objected that market processes are complicated as well, yet we accept them as constraints on public decision making. However, there is a fundamental difference between market processes and political ones, which makes the use of market constraints much easier to apply. Although market processes involve the interaction of the decisions of millions of private decision makers, market mechanisms serve as a coordinating device that allows us to characterize the outcomes in prices and excess demand functions. At least as a first approximation, this allows us to take into account the constraints imposed by markets in a reasonably satisfactory way, at least conceptually. No such decentralization result applies to political processes, even though we might adopt market terminology in the political marketplace.

Determinism and rationality

A further, related reason why political economy models are not suitable as constraints for prescriptive analysis is that they are typically deterministic and based on highly informed voters and political decision makers. Once the objectives of political decision makers are specified (for example vote maximization), and the technology for turning policies into outcomes postulated, simple game theory takes over and determines an outcome (assuming it is unique). One party or candidate is destined to win, and policies are fully specified. It seems there is no room for prescriptive choice and no room for political expertise or advice (such as an economist might give). These features of political models, which are a consequence of treating the political process as a form of political market analogous to an economic market, have the virtue of simplicity. However, it is not clear that they are realistic.

In models of the market economy, we might get away with assuming a high degree of rationality by decentralized decision makers because of the information that market prices convey. In public choice models, no such information-economizing device exists. The complexity of virtually all policy instruments makes outcomes inherently uncertain, and ensures that some citizens – the experts – are better informed than others. Political party platforms and ideologies are typically posed in terms of general policies or principles. Actual policies are the outcome of much more detailed analysis and advice, some of which comes from normative public economic analysis itself.

A further problem related to the deterministic nature of public choice equilibria is that outcomes in these public choice models are not only efficient (as in many models of party competition), but the allocations they choose on the UPF are simply dictated by the political mechanism. Far from acting as a constraint on normative analysis, the process dictates the outcome! There is no room whatsoever for prescription, which seems to me to be hardly a stylized feature that we want to use to characterize political economy models. It is not at all clear how to get out of this box of the political feasibility constraint wagging the prescriptive dog. Dropping the political feasibility constraint is one sure way to do so.

Cycling/instability

There is a further modeling difficulty that is endemic to virtually all public choice/political economy models, and that concerns the dictates imposed by the Arrow (1951) Impossibility Theorem. Even if one accepts the rationality, determinism and predictability features of these models, they fail to get around the problems of cycling and instability that constitute the most fundamental problem of collective decision making in democratic societies. This is particularly relevant given our observation that much of what governments do in the economic policy sphere is redistributive in nature.

To make the argument more concrete, consider the two main models currently used as models of public choice – party competition models and citizen candidate models.

Party competition models   These models draw on the insight of Downs that political parties exist to trade off the conflicting interests of the citizens, and many of the characterizing features of these models can indeed be found in Downs's definitive (1957) study *An Economic Theory of Democracy*. In Downs, political parties were decision makers whose objective was to maximize votes. More recent models, such as those by Dixit and Londregan (1998), have made the objective function of parties somewhat richer by allowing for an ideological component. In these models, there are two closely related ways in which a unique deterministic interior solution is obtained. In one version – the probabilistic voting variant – there is uncertainty about how voters will respond to policies because of some uncertainty inherent in voters' preferences. In the other version – the ideological attachment variant – voters of any observable class (for example income class) are distributed according to their exogenous ideological preferences for one party over the other. In either case, political parties cannot target policies (for example transfers) to individuals perfectly.

These models essentially avoid cycling by assumption. The assumed extent of uncertainty of voter responses or of the distribution of ideological preferences implies that the function relating expected votes to policies is strictly concave. For example, a party can always attract a few more votes from one group by increasing its transfer to them at the expense of losing a few votes to another group by reducing its transfer to them. The optimal policy is one that ensures that at the margin for all income groups, the incremental benefit in terms of votes from the last euro transferred is the same. Given that voting functions for all groups are concave, there will be a unique vote-maximizing platform for each party given the platform of the other party. This, in turn, implies that there will be a unique Nash equilibrium in party platforms.

The problem with this model, as Dan Usher (1994) has shown by example in a recent article in the *Canadian Journal of Economics*, is that voting functions are not likely to be concave in a world in which governments are engaging in redistribution (that is, in most party competition models in the literature, as well as in the real world). Concavity of voting functions requires that voter uncertainty or party attachment have to be strong enough that there will be at least some voters in a given income class who continue to vote for a party no matter how adverse their treatment by the party platform. It might be more realistic to assume that once the transfer offered by a party to a given group is low enough, no voters of that group will vote for the party. Once that point is reached, there is no cost to a vote-maximizing government of reducing the transfer to that group further in order to increase the transfer, and therefore number of votes, of other groups. Given that the vote distributions of all groups will be so truncated, the conditions required for an interior solution no longer apply, and vote cycling will be the norm. This problem will apply whether or not it is voter uncertainty or some unspecified party attachment that is at work. Unless voter distributions are very wide, there will be no unique interior voting equilibrium.

Introducing party ideology considerations into the model, as in Dixit and Londregan (1998) will mitigate this problem. Political parties trade off vote maximization with ideology in their objective functions, and this may preclude them from exploiting individual groups of voters enough to cause vote cycling. Such ideologies are essentially normative objectives, precisely like social welfare functions in Dixit and Londregan. Thus, political parties are seen as undertaking the kind of analysis we are eschewing – tempering normative analysis with political considerations, in this case the effect on votes. I suppose that implies that at least those normative analysts who advise political parties must necessarily take political consequences into account.

Citizen candidate models Party competition models assume that political parties can commit to pre-announced political platforms, even those that go against their self-interest or ideology, in order to get elected. Citizen candidate models, on the other hand, are premised by the notion that candidates for office cannot pre-commit. See Besley and Coate (1997) and Osborne and Slivinski (1996). Once they are elected, they are bound to do what is in their own self-interest, and voters know that. This not only tempers the kinds of policies that are eventually implemented; it also tempers the candidates who choose to run for office.

Citizen candidates might also avoid the cyclical majority problem, partly by drastically cutting down on the number of candidates and therefore on the competing policies. Indeed, the possibility of equilibrium (perhaps multiple) is an attractive feature of these models. However, there are a number of drawbacks to the models that make them ultimately unsuitable for use as a constraint on normative analysis. Three drawbacks are as follows:

1. The models are inherently implausible as descriptions of actual political decision making. There is no role for political parties and their platforms, which might otherwise be viewed as commitment devices. At best, citizen candidate models might be relevant for countries with weak party discipline, such as the USA.
2. Related to the first point, citizen candidate models are essentially models of elected dictatorship, since they are posed as models in which an individual politician seeks office and, once elected, carries out those policies that are in his best interest. They cannot represent the kind of representative democracy in which decisions get taken in legislatures.
3. Citizen candidate models do not really get around the problem of vote cycling. Even if individual candidates cannot commit to policies that are not in their self-interest, once they are elected on behalf of a particular constituency, they join a legislative body consisting of elected representatives from other constituencies. At the stage of decision making in legislatures, the same kinds of vote cycling can occur as in standard models of direct democracy.

The upshot is that these models would be quite unsuitable as a basis for formulating political feasibility constraints.

There are, of course, a number of other models in the literature that capture some features of actual public choice. A popular recent one is the so-called common agency model that is used to explain the doling out of favors to industry. Although there is no doubt some truth in them, it is hard to imagine them as determining the kinds of general policies, especially broad-based redistributive ones, that characterize much economic policy in industrialized economies. The same applies to models that use rent-seeking and lobbying as means of explaining the influence of special interests in public choice. Similarly, models of Leviathan public sectors maximizing their own interest are often used, sometimes constrained by political feasibility type considerations. To the extent that these kinds of models represented reality, there would be little point in using them as a constraint on normative analysis since they would predetermine the outcome. Indeed, normative analysis might actually serve as an intellectual discipline on the Leviathan tendencies that might otherwise exist in governments.

These criticisms of extant political economy models should not be taken as a criticism of the methodology of public choice. There is obvious social value in understanding how collective decisions are taken, and the fact that there are difficult problems that must be resolved makes the quest that much more important. Nor do we pretend to have an answer to these problems. In particular, the possibility of vote cycling continues to pose an extremely challenging intellectual problem. Clearly some societies have managed to obtain enough of a consensus to function in reasonably stable ways. How to square that with standard models of public choice remains an important item on the agenda. For our purposes, the inability of public choice models to address satisfactorily the vote cycling problem is simply one of the arguments for pursuing normative public economic analysis unfettered by political feasibility restrictions.

WHEN PUBLIC CHOICE CONSIDERATIONS CANNOT BE AVOIDED

Despite the compelling case for pursuing prescriptive analysis without constraining the prescriptions to be politically feasible, there are some circumstances in which public choice considerations cannot be avoided. We have already mentioned the case of time-inconsistency, which might be interpreted as a sort of political feasibility constraint, albeit one that does not arise from standard public choice considerations. There are, however, a number of other cases in which the behavior of government must be taken into account. Four examples of these are as follows. Three of them involve prescriptions that involve the mode of government decision making itself.

Prescribing Institutional Arrangements

In some instances, the choice among policies involves not only the substance of the policy itself, but also the institutional arrangements for delivering the policy. One important example of this concerns the decentralization of decision making in multi-level governments. This is the classic assignment problem in fiscal federalism. There are many arguments for decentralizing the provision of public services. Sub-national jurisdictions might be better able to cater to local preferences and needs, and might have better information about local cost conditions. They might also be better able to overcome agency problems in the management of public services. However, there are also some political economy considerations. Competition among jurisdictions is alleged to affect the cost of delivering public services, and to discipline the bureaucracy. It is also said to enhance innovation and to allow for the spreading of best practices through yardstick competition. It is even said to affect the amount of rent-seeking and corruption that might otherwise occur. Whether these arguments are compelling or not, it seems necessary to include them in any prescriptive analysis about decentralization. An implication of our agnosticism about the applicability of existing public choice models is that the outcome of the decentralization debate is bound to be inconclusive.

Similar issues apply with respect to the privatization debate. Much of the argument over privatization of key infrastructure industries turns on the (in)efficiency of the public sector relative to the private sector. More generally, the role of the private sector in the delivery of important public services like health and education relies to a considerable extent on performance of the public sector in delivering these services. The same might be said even for the collection of taxes and trade duties.

Interjurisdictional Fiscal Arrangements

Related to the above is the design of financial arrangements between levels of government, given the assignment of functions. In virtually all systems of multi-level government, there is a vertical fiscal imbalance, and the higher level exercises some influence over the lower level through the structure of transfers used to correct the imbalance. Although there are some purely economic arguments that would support such arrangements, political economy considerations cannot be avoided. Much of the case for a vertical fiscal imbalance and for central influence is based on notions of fiscal externalities caused by fiscal decisions of lower-level jurisdictions. These necessarily rely on models of the behavior of governments in which public choice considerations are invoked.

Constitutional Choice

Perhaps the archetypical example of prescriptive analysis where public choice considerations cannot be avoided is that of constitutional design. Of course, this is not a day-to-day decision, and it involves much more than economic analysis. The constitutions of many countries have various elements of economic prescription in them. Some of them impose constraints on the actions government can take. Examples might include protection of minorities, non-discrimination, equality rights, and the forbidding of lower-level government decisions that violate efficiency of the internal common market. There may even be provisions that require budget balance or impose constitutional limits on debt financing. Constitutions also provide for an assignment of functions in a multi-level government system, and perhaps also on the oversight that one level may have on another. Constitutions may even set out principles of economic policy, such as minimal standards of public services, or broad statements of economic and social rights. Although these are typically not binding in a court of law, they none the less presumably have considerable political and moral authority. In some cases, the constitution goes so far as to oblige governments to undertake some actions.

How one judges the economic content of constitutions presumably reflects one's views about the nature of collective decision making. Indeed, it would be virtually impossible to write a constitution without some preconceptions about how governments are likely to behave – whether they are benevolent or self-seeking in nature, whether they are likely to be well informed, whether electoral decision-making is stable or not, and so on.

Implementation Issues

So far we have construed public choice as being primarily concerned with the collective choice of public policies by governments. This may be too narrow an interpretation. As the literature makes clear, public choice might include not just the decisions taken by legislatures, but also their implementation by the bureaucracy. In fact, most economic policies are quite complicated. The efficiency of their implementation relies on the good management of those who are implementing the policies, and some assurance that the bureaucracy is acting in the public interest. In fact, there are plenty of opportunities for inefficiency in the public sector. There will be standard agency problems at various levels: between the legislative and executive branches; between various levels of management in the public sector; and so on. There will be informational problems. Those closer to the delivery point of public services or the collection point of taxes will be better informed about the relevant characteristics of the public they are serving than those to whom they are accountable. Professionals in the bureaucracy are likely to be much better informed about how to design policies to achieve the outcomes desired by the legislators. There will also be opportunities for rent-seeking, corruption and even extortion in the public sector.

These problems of public sector inefficiency ought to be taken into consideration when designing a policy. The optimal choice of a policy may well be affected by the extent to which the bureaucracy can be relied on to deliver the policy, especially if the quality of delivery depends on the effort of bureaucrats. These implementation issues may also lead normative analysts to propose alternative ways of delivering or administering public service programs, including improvements in the institutions themselves. This does not really violate the general principle that prescriptive analysis should proceed without treating political feasibility as a constraint. As a matter of semantics, we would distinguish between political feasibility – what policies legislatures would be willing to choose – and implementation feasibility – what the bureaucracy can be relied on to implement.

CONCLUDING REMARKS

We have taken the general position in this chapter that normative public economic analysis – which can be evaluative or prescriptive – should not take account of political feasibility constraints. We have argued for that on the basis of practicability, but more importantly on the basis of principle. This is especially true for purely evaluative normative analysis. At the same time, we have suggested that there are a number of exceptions involving situations in which prescriptive analysis applied at the policy-making stage cannot ignore public choice constraints. These involve cases where the policy decision taken at one level is contingent on public decisions taken at another level.

It might be useful as a schematic device to think that there are different layers of decision making involved in the formulation and implementation of any economic policy. (Motohiro Sato has suggested this scheme to me.) At the most general level, four layers or stages of sequential decision making can be distinguished:

1. *Constitutional stage*. At this stage, the rules governing government decision making for the future arc set out.
2. *Legislative stage*. Here, policies are enacted by collective decision making in legislatures. There can be more than one level of legislature at this stage.
3. *Implementation stage*. The policies enacted in the legislative stage are put into effect by the bureaucracy at the relevant level of government.
4. *Market response stage*. The private sector agents take their decisions, given the policies that have been implemented, and a market outcome results.

In a well-functioning world, participants at each stage take as given the outcomes of previous stages, and anticipate the outcomes of subsequent stages. There may be complications involved in so doing, such as imperfections of information, uncertainty, and lack of precision about the behavior of agents at other stages. None the less, we suppose that agents do the best they can with the information and knowledge at their disposal.

Positive analysis can fruitfully be applied at any stage. In a complementary fashion, normative analysis can come in at various places. Our concern has been mainly with prescriptive analysis applied at stage 2, the legislative stage. We have argued that a normative perspective taken at this stage should ignore political feasibility constraints *at the same stage*. However, it will take a positive perspective with respect to the implementation and market response stages. Things are more complicated if stage 2 itself contains more than one level of legislative decision making, say, a central and a local. In this case, normative analysis of central government decision making should take a positive perspective with respect to how local governments will respond. Indeed, part of the prescriptive analysis may involve inducing local governments to behave in a certain way. Normative analysis may certainly also be applied to the constitutional stage, in this case taking a positive viewpoint with respect to subsequent stages. This is likely to be a challenging task, given uncertainty about how the subsequent stages will play themselves out.

A couple of final caveats should be mentioned. As mentioned earlier, none of our arguments should be taken to imply that either normative or positive analysis is better than the other. Both are obviously legitimate lines of inquiry that have demonstrably led to many insights into the economy and the society more generally. Indeed, pursuing normative analysis with political feasibility constraints in place is itself also a useful line of research. My main point is that it is not desirable to require normative analysis to take account of political feasibility constraints.

Also, none of our discussion is meant to have any implications for the level of abstraction at which either normative or public choice analysis is carried out. In particular, it is not imperative for normative policy models to be realistic for them to be scientifically useful. Highly abstract models, such as those we use in optimal tax theory, have provided considerable insight into the policy problem, even though they do not yield policies that are applicable in the real world.

REFERENCES

Arrow, K.J. (1951), *Social Choice and Individual Values*, New Haven: Yale University Press.

Besley, T. and S. Coate (1997), 'An Economic Model of Representative Democracy', *Quarterly Journal of Economics*, **112**, 85–114.

Buchanan, J.M. and G. Tullock (1962), *The Calculus of Consent*, Ann Arbor: The University of Michigan Press.

Diamond, P.A. and J.A. Mirrlees (1971), 'Optimal Taxation and Public Production: I – Production Efficiency', *American Economic Review*, **61**, 8–27.

Dixit, A.K. and J. Londregan (1998), 'Ideology, Tactics, and Efficiency in Redistributive Politics', *Quarterly Journal of Economics*, **113**, 497–529.

Downs, A. (1957), *An Economic Theory of Democracy*, New York: Harper and Row.

Harberger, A.C. (1971), 'Three Basic Postulates for Applied Welfare Economics: An Interpretive Essay', *Journal of Economic Literature*, **9**, 785–97.

Hicks, J.R. (1940), 'The Valuation of Social Income', *Economica*, **7**, 105–24.

Kaldor, N. (1939), 'Welfare Propositions and Interpersonal Comparisons of Utility', *Economic Journal*, **59**, 549–52.

Musgrave, R.A. (1959), *The Theory of Public Finance*, New York: McGraw-Hill.

Osborne, M.J. and A. Slivinski (1996), 'A Model of Political Competition with Citizen-Candidates', *Quarterly Journal of Economics*, **111**, 65–96.

Rawls, J. (1971), *A Theory of Justice*, Cambridge, MA: Harvard University Press.

Samuelson, P.A. (1950), 'Evaluation of Real National Income', *Oxford Economic Papers*, **2**, 1–29.

Scitovsky, T. (1941), 'A Note on Welfare Propositions in Economics', *Review of Economic Studies*, **9**, 77–88.

Usher, D. (1994), 'The Significance of the Probabilistic Voting Theorem', *Canadian Journal of Economics*, **27**, 433–45.

Williamson, O.E. (2000), 'The New Institutional Economics: Taking Stock, Looking Ahead', *Journal of Economic Literature*, **38**, 595–613.

5. Better than what? Policy analysis, collective choice and the standard of reference

Walter Hettich[*]

1. INTRODUCTION

A major reason for the success of microeconomic analysis is the well-balanced theoretical structure that underlies it. There are relatively few essential elements that support the intellectual enterprise, and their complementary nature allows for a cohesive examination of economic reality, even though the level of abstraction is rather high at times.

As I see it, there are four essential elements: a start from simple behavioral assumptions; a focus on allocation mechanisms; modeling using general and partial equilibrium; and the ability to examine questions from both a positive and a normative point of view.

Most economists are familiar with the use of the four theoretical elements in the study of private markets. For reasons related mostly to the historical development of the field, the same comprehensive approach is less common in the examination of public policy. The chapter argues that we should employ the same perspective in both areas, and that application of a broad approach to the public economy has specific implications for how we ask normative questions in studies dealing with the public sector.

The chapter begins by reviewing the use of the four essential elements in the analysis of competitive private markets. It then shows how the same comprehensive framework can be applied to research on the public sector when collective choice is a basic component of the analysis. To make things more concrete, the discussion is illustrated with reference to the theory of taxation and to the shortcomings that arise from adopting a more limited approach in this context. Next, the chapter proposes a new standard of reference and examines issues of measurement in welfare analysis. The discussion ends with a few concluding remarks.

* Some of the ideas presented in this chapter were first developed in joint research with Stanley L. Winer.

2.   THE STRUCTURE OF ECONOMIC ANALYSIS IN THE PRIVATE SECTOR

Figure 5.1 displays the logical structure of economic analysis as it has been developed for competitive markets. We start from behavioral assumptions, usually an axiomatic description of what is meant by rational behavior. Stated more informally, individuals are assumed to maximize their own utility, subject to a set of specified constraints that arise from the nature of scarcity and from existing institutions. Although formal analysis usually does not spell out the set of assumed institutions, it is implied that an orderly system of property rights exists, and that there are mechanisms for enforcing such rights.

Individuals transact in a multiplicity of markets. Economists are interested in the outcomes of such transactions, particularly in the prices that result and the quantities that are produced and exchanged in equilibrium. Thus existence and stability of equilibrium are fundamental to the analysis, and the proof that stable outcomes will arise has been one of the most important steps in creating a secure basis for microeconomics.

Equilibrium analysis can be conducted from both a positive and a normative point of view. In each case, we may vary the degree of generality for the system that is examined. Partial equilibrium analysis focuses on one, or at most two, markets, while general equilibrium analysis refers to a system of linked consumer and factor markets. In positive inquiry, we focus on observed outcomes, either in one market, or in a complete system of markets, while in normative analysis, we examine the optimality properties of market outcomes in one or more markets.

Positive analysis generally leads to the making of predictions and to hypothesis testing with the use of econometric methods, as indicated in a box on the lower left-hand side of Figure 5.1. Normative analysis, on the other hand, results in so-called welfare analysis. Here we inquire into market failure, that is deviations from optimality, and in the reasons for such failure. In addition, economists have developed a set of concepts and measures that allow us to quantify the losses caused by such deviations in dollar terms.

The box at the bottom of Figure 5.1 refers to an interesting tool developed by economists in recent decades, namely computational general equilibrium analysis. This approach allows us to ask both positive and normative questions in a more inclusive and more complex setting than is usually the case. Although such computational models depend to some extent on parameter estimates determined separately in other studies, they make it possible to simulate the effects of changes in institutional arrangements and in policies while taking account of the pervasive linkages that exist among markets, thus adding in a significant way to the understanding of how markets succeed or fail (Ballard et al., 1985).

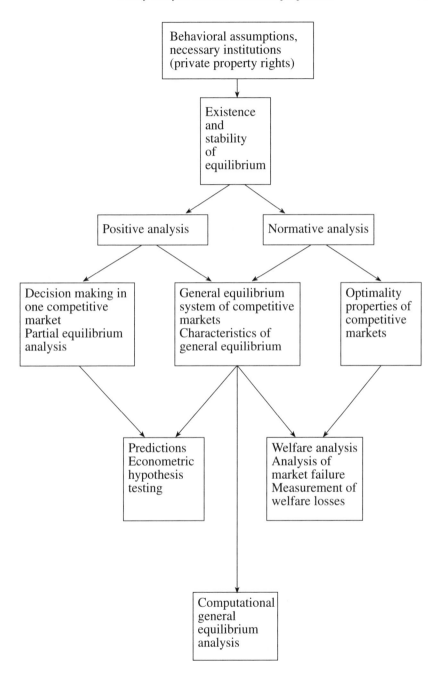

Figure 5.1   Comprehensive analysis of competitive markets

3.   A MORE GENERAL CONTEXT FOR THE ANALYSIS OF PUBLIC POLICY

Figure 5.1 provides an outline of the approach that has made economic analysis such a successful enterprise. Although it applies to the study of private markets, it also highlights the elements that play a significant role in the examination of public policy. A comparison of analytical steps will make the similarities apparent.

Much like the study of the private sector, the examination of the public sector also starts from basic assumptions concerning individual behavior and underlying institutions. This is most clearly seen in the tradition called the public choice approach. It treats the actors in the public sector as decision makers that maximize their own utility, subject to given constraints. Instead of consumers, producers and owners of factors of production, we now have voters, politicians or bureaucrats. A similar parallel exists with regard to institutions – the analysis generally assumes a given constitution that defines voting rights and the voting mechanisms available to the society.

In the public sector, voting mechanisms serve the function of allocating resources, much as markets do in the private economy. Thus it is crucial to study the outcomes produced by voting of various kinds. Since equilibrium analysis remains the main tool, the questions of existence and stability again arise. Furthermore, the distinction between approaching questions from a positive or a normative point of view continues to be relevant.

In the same manner that we can study particular markets in the private sector, we can focus on the determination of single policy choices in the public arena (partial equilibrium analysis). Or we can adopt a more general approach, and study policy structures, where related policies are examined as a connected whole. Finally, hypothesis testing, welfare analysis and computational general equilibrium models continue to be the main tools available to the researcher who wants to carry out applied work.

Although the logical parallels between private and public sector analysis seem clear, writers in the literature on the public sector have often limited themselves to a more restricted approach than is suggested by Figure 5.1. An examination of one of the oldest fields within public economics, namely the theory of taxation, will show the problems that arise from adopting a more restricted approach, and the opportunities for further development of research that open up when a comprehensive view is accepted.

4.   LIMITATIONS OF NORMATIVE TAX ANALYSIS

The study of taxation has a long and distinguished history in economics. This is not surprising since taxation is a requirement for the functioning of any state or government that needs resources to carry out public projects. Although taxation in its modern form may depend on the extensive systems of record keeping now common in most nations, it existed in different guises in most earlier societies, being mentioned in some of the oldest written documents discovered by archeologists.

Taxation is one of the subjects in economics where a strong normative tradition has flourished. This is certainly true for the economic literature in English, but it also holds for writings in other languages, such as Italian and German. Since taxation is imposed on citizens, and since it often defines their relation to the state, notions of justice in tax treatment have always been an important element in discussions of fiscal policy.

In recent decades, three different normative traditions have played a significant role in professional and public discussions of tax policy. We may characterize them as equitable taxation (ET), the constitutional approach, sometimes called fiscal exchange (FE), and optimal taxation (OT). Although each tradition has added significant elements to our understanding of fiscal issues, I shall concentrate on their shortcomings rather than on their contributions. The discussion is not meant to present a full evaluation of the three approaches, but rather to review them in the context of Figure 5.1, a necessary step for the later arguments concerning a new normative standard for tax analysis.[1]

Figure 5.1 shows that in the study of private markets positive and normative analysis are part of the same consistent framework, both deriving from the same underlying foundation. When we turn to tax analysis, this unity is lacking. The criticism applies to all three normative approaches, although the shortcoming takes a different form in each of the analytical traditions.

Equitable taxation derives primarily from the work of Henry Simons (1938, 1950), who was influenced in turn by earlier German writers, such as Schanz and Haig. Simons made a deliberate decision to eschew utility theory as a basis for his normative discussion of taxation. He put his focus on the development of a broad base for the income tax, and on the problems associated with its implementation. He believed that definition of an income tax base consistent with accounting principles would allow the government to impose taxes in relation to ability to pay and to satisfy the principle of horizontal equity (Hettich, 1979).

Although Simons's ideas had a profound impact on policy discussions for several decades, his decision to sever normative tax analysis from utility theory eventually exacted a high price. This is indicated by the comment of a later writer who quipped 'equal treatment of equals may be in Aristotle, but it is not in economics'. Because it was not derived from the same behavioral assumptions as other parts of economics, ET could not be integrated systematically with an analysis of the efficiency consequences of taxation, a central criticism made by those who developed the OT tradition.

Consideration of Figure 5.1 allows us to see a second shortcoming that may be even more fundamental. Simons did not provide a collective choice mechanism, that is an analogue to private markets for resource allocation in the public sector. As a result, it remains unclear whether a comprehensive tax base could ever exist as a stable equilibrium outcome. To Simons's credit, his writings indicate that he was aware of one aspect of the political process that is relevant to economic analysis. He believed that public policy decisions often interfered in private markets to the detriment of individual economic choices, and he offered the comprehensive tax base as a policy rule that would limit such interference in the future. However, he failed to consider in what manner and in what circumstances rational individuals would adopt such a rule.

Unlike ET, the constitutional or fiscal exchange approach puts its focus on the political aspects of taxation. Well-known contributors to this tradition include Geoffrey Brennan, James Buchanan and Bruno Frey (1979). In their seminal books, Brennan and Buchanan (1980, 1985) emphasize the danger of public power and the need to limit its misuse in taxation.

Brennan and Buchanan propose a tax constitution that would limit the government's power to tax. Their analysis follows logically from the assumption that every government acts as Leviathan, trying to maximize the amount of resources that it takes from the private sector. Constitutional restrictions on the power to tax would check such behavior. Brennan and Buchanan analyze the nature of particular limits and the design of tax bases as part of such a constitution.

Like ET, FE fails to integrate its analysis fully with the rest of economic theory. Although the approach specifies behavioral assumptions that underlie governmental decisions, it does not provide a broadly consistent decision structure. As regards the Leviathan model itself, it is not clear who in society belongs to the 'government', what controls entry and exit into the governing elite, and under what circumstances such an elite would exist as a stable group. Similar questions must also be raised with regard to the conventions that would be responsible for drawing up the constitutional document. It remains unclear whether the choice of delegates and the decisions in such conventions could ever be removed effectively from the ongoing political process that the constitution is designed to reign in.

The lack of integration with the broader design of economic theory limits the possible contributions of these traditions. We may recall from the review of Figure 5.1 that a normative discussion for private markets may include the analysis of optimality in a general and partial equilibrium context, as well as the evaluation and measurement of market failure in a general and partial setting. In addition, normative work can be expanded further with the use of computational general equilibrium models. Because of their starting points, neither ET nor FE are suited for applied normative analysis of this type.

The last of the three traditions, optimal taxation, fares better in this regard.[2] It is specifically linked to welfare economics, as generally carried out for private markets, and is connected to a rich literature of applied welfare analysis. The major criticism of OT relates to the top of Figure 5.1. The approach assumes existence of a planner who maximizes a social welfare function that is given exogenously. It thus reminds the reader of the plays from antiquity where a god descends in a chariot at the end to provide a much-needed solution for the troubles of contending factions. The planner as *deus ex machina* (or *dea ex machina*) seemingly avoids the necessity for a discussion of decision making on the ground, but does so at the expense of realism. We have argued that voting mechanisms (or other mechanisms that aggregate preferences in a political context) are analogous to markets in determining resource allocation in the public economy. It is difficult, at least for me, to accept an analysis that proceeds as if such mechanisms were irrelevant to an understanding of public policy.

5. THE SCANDINAVIAN TRADITION AND THE ANALYSIS OF VOTING CHOICES

Although they play no role in recent normative tax theories, such as ET and OT, voting mechanisms have a central place in the writings of several Scandinavian writers on public finance. More than a century ago, Knut Wicksell (1896) recognized the analogue between political and economic institutions in his discussion of resource allocation in the public sector. In addition, he saw the need to search for a normative standard by which such resource use could be judged. Eric Lindahl (1919, 1959) extended the analysis in a most interesting direction by providing a formal mechanism for the joint determination of tax shares and public goods consumption. A clear understanding of the role of political factors is also found in the writings of later Scandinavian writers, such as Leif Johansen (1963, 1965).

The contributions of the Scandinavian economists are of great importance since they represent an attempt to create a new, more broadly defined foundation for public sector analysis. Their work suggests the possibility of approaching public resource allocation with the same level of generality that we find in theoretical work on private markets. It indicates furthermore that behavioral assumptions similar to those used in the study of private markets can be employed in the analysis of public decision making, and that the need for a basic political framework must be recognized. In addition, Lindahl's model shows that formal equilibrium concepts can be applied in a setting where collective choice is a necessity. Viewed in terms of Figure 5.1, the Scandinavian contributions for the first time deal with the subject matter of the top two boxes in the figure in a theoretically substantive manner.

The formal analysis of collective choice mechanisms made great strides in the second half of the twentieth century. Mathematical investigation of different types of voting models elucidated conditions for existence and stability of equilibria. Voting processes were related to economic questions in pioneering work by authors such as Anthony Downs (1957), James Buchanan and Gordon Tullock (1962). Public choice was established as a separate and flourishing field within economics. (For an excellent survey of work in this field, see Dennis Mueller, 1989.)

Wicksell's work provided a starting point for many of the later contributions on collective choice concerned with the public sector. In particular, his proposal of unanimity or near-unanimity as a standard for collective decision making led to extensive discussions concerning the normative basis for judging outcomes of political mechanisms. Although he was not concerned with the concept of Pareto optimality, later writers noted that unanimous choices would satisfy the Pareto criterion so commonly used in normative analysis of the private sector. However, Wicksell did not propose a formal voting mechanism that could be analyzed in a technical manner regarding stability and existence of equilibrium, and for which outcomes could be linked to specific observed public policies. Nor did later writers starting from his work take the additional theoretical steps needed for a complete analysis of this nature.

Despite the many valuable contributions to the study of collective choice during the past 50 years, the initial promise in the work of the Scandinavian writers was not fully realized. The generality of approach characterizing the study of private markets (outlined in Figure 5.1) was not achieved in the study of the public economy. Normative analysis remained separated from work taking a positive approach because of different starting assumptions, as illustrated in the extensive (and theoretically sophisticated) literature on OT. Contributions by writers interested in normative collective choice, on the other hand, did not develop methods for the analysis of specific policies and provide quantitative means for measuring the impact of policy failure, as defined in their framework. This left the field of welfare economics to those who started from the social planner model and who showed little interest in relating their conclusions to the logic of collective choice.

Although these statements may appear as overly critical to some, they are not meant to question the value of work that has been carried out in the past five decades. Rather, they represent an invitation to take stock of what has been achieved, and to see clearly what must still be accomplished. The next section discusses some of the remaining challenges in more detail, again using the theory of taxation as an illustration.

6. THE NORMATIVE STANDARD OF REFERENCE IN A COMPREHENSIVE APPROACH TO TAXATION

Taxation is well suited for the discussion of implementing a comprehensive approach, both because of the range of literature devoted to this area of public economics, and because positive as well as normative questions are of major importance in this area. We shall use Figure 5.2 as a guide to the discussion, in the same manner that we based the previous analysis on Figure 5.1.

To implement a comprehensive approach, it is essential to choose a particular voting mechanism that governs decisions on resource allocation. In past work, carried out jointly with Stanley Winer (1988, 1999; Winer and Hettich, 1998), I have used probabilistic voting as the underlying framework. I believe that this model has several advantages over other approaches, but the following examination could, in principle, start from any well-formulated model of collective decision making.[3]

Analysis based on probabilistic voting presumes the existence of a constitutional framework that allows two or more parties to compete freely in the political arena.[4] Parties offer policy platforms to voters, but they are uncertain of the degree of support that they will receive from any particular voter or group of voters, although they know the relevant probability density functions. In view of this, they formulate policies so as to maximize the total expected support in the next election. Taxpayer-voters make their choices based on expected net benefits from the public sector. In their calculations, public goods provide positive utility, while taxes (including the welfare losses associated with them) result in a reduction in utility. While the decision mechanism and the behavioral assumptions are thus clearly specified, probabilistic voting does not attempt to explain the specific institutional arrangements that surround the functioning of the political system. This can be seen as a desirable property – it allows greater theoretical generality – but it also has the drawback of making the link to existing institutions more difficult.

We can see a major advantage of the model by turning to the second box from the top in Figure 5.2. The technical literature on probabilistic voting provides a discussion and proof of the existence and stability of equilibrium in such a framework. If we assume a two-party system, we deal with a Nash equilibrium with well-known properties. Furthermore, it is possible to link positive and normative analysis in a systematic way. Because of the properties of the model, it is possible to describe the equilibrium platform by optimizing a function that is a particular weighted sum of taxpayer utilities, a proposition

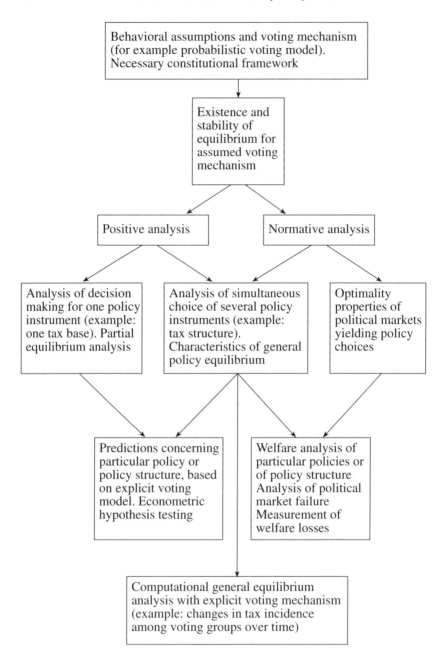

Figure 5.2   Comprehensive analysis of policy choices in the public sector

first proved by Coughlin and Nitzan (1981). For convenience, Stanley Winer and I have referred to this property as the Representation Theorem in our previous work, a term that I shall continue to use in this discussion (Hettich and Winer, 1999, ch. 4).

Probabilistic voting can be used as a framework from which to derive empirical hypotheses about the nature of tax systems, both as regards particular features of such systems, and as regards the nature of the fiscal system as a whole. Thus we have partial equilibrium analysis, as well as an equilibrium analysis of a more general nature, applying to the simultaneous determination of various interrelated parts, such as tax bases, rate structures and special tax provisions. Empirical research may focus, for example, on why different political entities, such as states or provinces, exercise very different reliance on the income tax, or on other well-known tax instruments, or on why whole tax systems evolve in a particular manner over time.[5]

It is an important advantage of the probabilistic framework that it can also be employed to study the right-hand side of Figure 5.2. Analysis using the Representation Theorem makes clear that equilibrium platforms will be Pareto optimal.[6] This can be seen intuitively as well: in a situation where it is possible to make some voters better off, without making anyone else worse off, it will be feasible to propose a new policy platform that will attract greater total expected support. As a result, equilibrium must describe a policy set where all such potential gains have been eliminated, thus representing a Pareto optimum.

While the Representation Theorem preserves the symmetry of approach between normative and positive analysis found in the comprehensive analysis of private competitive markets, it also puts the focus squarely on the nature of collective decision making. It is political competition that leads to a Nash equilibrium in political party platforms of the type characterized by the theorem. In turn, Pareto optimality or efficiency is attained in such a Nash equilibrium if we have freely operating competition between or among parties.

The traditional approach to formulating an optimal allocation of resources in the private sector that is then used as a standard of reference in normative analysis relies on preferences, technology and endowments to characterize the allocation, without making specific reference to any institutional mechanism. However, the resulting definition is only of interest because of the first theorem of welfare economics that links the allocation to competitive equilibrium. A standard of reference having no link to a posssible way of achieving it would be of little relevance for policy analysis.

In doing policy analysis in the public sector, we also need a standard of reference *and* a related mechanism for achieving it. It is thus necessary for the analyst as part of his or her work to identify a mechanism that serves this purpose. Furthermore, the mechanism or process should have some philosophical support. Note that a similar requirement is satisfied for private markets. An optimal allocation of resources in the private context is also attained if we have perfect price discrimination in all markets. However, few economists concerned with policy would be interested in such a standard if perfect price discrimination were the only way of implementing it.

As indicated earlier, normative analysis for the private sector is concerned primarily with deviations from an optimal allocation of resources. A focus on deviations must also play a primary role in the normative analysis of the public sector. However, we must now focus on failures at the political level which would prevent the collective mechanism from producing an optimal allocation. Viewed from this perspective, it is not appropriate to define failure in terms of a theoretical framework that does not include the relevant mechanism as an integral part, as is done, for example, in a model relying on a social planner.

The discussion suggests three conclusions: (a) that we should focus on the study of equilibria having some demonstrable relation to a political process with desirable characteristics (such as, for example, universal franchise); (b) that we should investigate problems in the operation of the relevant political process (that is, investigate political market failure); and (c) that we should identify specific ways in which political market failure influences policy, leading to inefficiency in relation to the postulated standard.

The implications for applied welfare analysis are extensive and quite radical. If we continue to use taxation as our example, the argument implies that *we must focus on failures in the collective choice mechanism and trace the link between such failures and specific tax policies.* There is relatively little work in the present literature on fiscal systems that deals with this task.[7] Progress in this area of research requires us to characterize tax policies or tax structures that arise from the efficient operation of specific well-defined voting systems, and to identify changes in policy outcomes caused by impediments to the efficient functioning of these systems. For example, if probabilistic voting is the theoretical basis for the analysis, the challenge is to determine how non-competitive behavior between or among parties in this framework will affect equilibrium tax policies or tax structure. Furthermore, such an analysis should be sufficiently detailed to have a meaningful counterpart in observed fiscal systems.

Most welfare analysis related to taxation uses a traditional standard of reference, such as an allocation with lump sum taxes, and pays little or no attention to how such a standard may differ from a politically optimal reference situation. The question 'different from what?' thus assumes genuine importance, both in the identification of so-called policy failure, and in the measurement of observed deviations from policy optima.

7. MEASUREMENT ISSUES AND THE STANDARD OF REFERENCE

The most common standard of reference in current normative analyses of taxation is a fiscal system where all revenues are raised by lump sum taxes. In such a system, there are no distortions at the margin, since voter-taxpayers cannot adjust their behavior in response to lump sum levies. Resource allocation with lump sum taxes is then compared to allocation under the current tax system, and welfare losses are inferred from the deviations that are observed when the comparison is made. Since losses in consumer and producer surplus can be expressed in dollars, this procedure can be used to give numerical estimates of the efficiency losses from taxation.

If we rely on probabilistic voting (or any other voting model) as our allocation mechanism, we must question a standard based on lump sum levies.[8] Such taxes have proven most unpopular politically and are not a likely equilibrium outcome of a competitive political system. Furthermore, taxpayers will be able to make some economic adjustments if lump sum taxes become a predictable and repeated occurrence.

A Pareto-optimal equilibrium tax system in a world with probabilistic voting will in all likelihood employ a variety of taxes, most of which give taxpayers some room for tax avoidance. For this reason, the reference system will contain some welfare losses as now measured. The true efficiency costs are the welfare costs in excess of the 'necessary' losses, that is, in excess of the welfare losses that would occur in a politically competitive world.

One may also note that a party that maximizes expected votes will design fiscal policy so as to equalize the political costs of the last dollar raised across tax sources. Marginal political costs, as perceived by political parties, will include three components. They are the utility loss to the voter associated with giving up the marginal dollar, the welfare loss to the voter connected with the marginal dollar, and a weight reflecting the voter's political response to having the marginal dollar taxed away. Because of the last component, we cannot infer that marginal efficiency losses, as traditionally measured, would be equalized across tax sources in a politically optimal tax system. At present, such equality is often made the cornerstone of policy recommendations for efficiency improvements in the tax system.

The discussion shows that normative analysis based on a standard of reference that includes collective choice as an essential element raises several theoretical challenges. It becomes essential to consider the nature of a politically optimal tax system and the composition of the budget as drawn from different tax sources in equilibrium. In addition, it is necessary to find ways of measuring deviations from the new standard in dollar terms. At present, the literature offers only limited guidance on how to proceed in this area of study.

I believe that we can make a good start on these issues by examining the likely biases inherent in the welfare measures currently used in tax analysis, when they are evaluated in the light of a comprehensive approach to taxation, such as outlined in Figure 5.2. Such work can be carried out in conjunction with studies trying to understand how political market failure leads to specific changes in tax policies. There seems to be room both for descriptive or historical studies and for more theoretical development on these issues.

8.   CONCLUSION

The chapter argues that a comprehensive approach to the study of public sector policies is possible. Such an approach parallels the successful framework used in microeconomic analysis of private markets. In a comprehensive framework, positive and normative analysis both derive from the same behavioral assumptions and use the same voting framework to serve as the underlying mechanism for public resource allocation.

A comprehensive approach that includes collective choice as an essential element requires a new formulation of the standard of reference in normative analysis. While choice of certain collective decision models, such as probabilistic voting, allows for the continued use of Pareto optimality as the governing principle, the concept must now be applied at the political level, rather than at the level of private markets.

A challenging task ahead is to develop an analysis of political market failure that parallels the extensive work on economic market failure. It is crucial to identify particular examples of such failure and to link them to specific changes in policy outcomes. In addition, ways must be found to quantify the costs of political market failure and to compare the efficiency costs of different policies that are politically non-optimal.

While I have used taxation to examine the various points made in the chapter in more detail, the argument is not linked to a specific area of public policy analysis. The same is true with regard to the choice of model. Because of my previous work, I have repeatedly turned to probabilistic voting when illustrating a framework that allows for a comprehensive approach. The proposed research agenda is broader, however; it does not depend on the use of a particular model. Rather, it will help us to see the choice of a particular framework from a wider perspective than has been applied in public sector studies so far.

NOTES

1. A more detailed review of the three traditions is presented in Hettich and Winer (1999), ch. 5.
2. A classic exposition of OT is found in Atkinson and Stiglitz (1980). For a recent text book treatment of public economics, see Myles (1995).
3. For a different analysis that deals with normative questions related to taxation in a collective choice framework, see Inman and Fitts (1990). Their work falls into the structure-induced equilibrium tradition. A brief review of this approach can be found in Hettich and Winer (1999), ch. 2.
4. Probabilistic voting is reviewed in Coughlin (1992) and Enelow and Hinich (1984, 1990). See also Persson and Tabellini (2000).
5. Probabilistic voting can also be incorporated into a computational general equilibrium analysis. See Hettich and Winer (1999), ch. 7 and Winer and Rutherford (1993).
6. See Hettich and Winer (1999), chs 4 and 6 for a more extensive discussion of this point.
7. For illustrative examples, see Hettich and Winer (1999), ch. 6.
8. A more detailed critique is found in Hettich and Winer (1999), ch. 6 and in Hettich and Winer (2002), where lump sum taxation is analyzed together with other widely applied normative rules of taxation.

REFERENCES

Atkinson, A. and J. Stiglitz (1980), *Lectures on Public Economics*, New York: McGraw-Hill.
Ballard, C.L., J.B. Shoven and J. Whalley (1985), 'General Equilibrium Computations of the Marginal Welfare Costs of Taxes in the United States', *American Economic Review*, **75**, March, 128-38.
Brennan, Geoffrey and James Buchanan (1980), *The Power to Tax: Analytical Foundations of a Fiscal Constitution*, New York: Cambridge University Press.
Brennan, Geoffrey and James Buchanan (1985), *The Reason of Rules*, New York: Cambridge University Press.
Buchanan, James and Gordon Tullock (1962), *The Calculus of Consent*, Ann Arbor: The University of Michigan Press.
Coughlin, Peter (1992), *Probabilistic Voting Theory*, New York: Cambridge University Press.
Coughlin, Peter and Shmuel Nitzan (1981), 'Electoral Outcomes with Probabilistic Voting and Nash Social Welfare Maxima', *Journal of Public Economics*, **15**, 113-21.
Downs, Anthony (1957), *An Economic Theory of Democracy*, New York: Harper and Row.
Enelow, J. and M. Hinich (1984), *The Spatial Theory of Voting*, Cambridge: Cambridge University Press.
Enelow, J. and M. Hinich (1990), *Advances in the Spatial Theory of Voting*, Cambridge: Cambridge University Press.
Frey, Bruno S. (1979), 'Economic Policy by Constitutional Contract', *Kyklos* **32**, 307-19.
Hettich, Walter (1979), 'Henry Simons on Taxation and the Economic System', *National Tax Journal*, **32** (4), March, 1-9.
Hettich, Walter and Stanley L. Winer (1988), 'Economic and Political Foundations of Tax Structure', *American Economic Review*, **78**, September, 701-13.

Hettich, Walter and Stanley L. Winer (1999), *Democratic Choice and Taxation: A Theoretical and Empirical Analysis*, Cambridge: Cambridge University Press.

Hettich, Walter and Stanley L. Winer (2002), 'Rules, Politics and the Normative Analysis of Taxation', in R. Wagner and J. Backhaus (eds), *Handbook of Public Finance*, Kluwer Academic, forthcoming.

Inman, Robert P. and Michael A. Fitts (1990), 'Political Institutions and Fiscal Policy: Evidence from the U.S. Historical Record', *Journal of Law, Economics and Organization,* **6**, Special Issue, pp. 79-132.

Johansen, Leif (1963), 'Some Notes on the Lindahl Theory of Determination of Public Expenditures,' *International Economic Review*, **4**, 346-58.

Johansen, Leif (1965), *Public Economics*, Amsterdam: North-Holland.

Lindahl, E. (1919), *Die Gerechtigkeit der Besteuerung*. Reprinted as 'Just Taxation: A Positive Solution', in R.A. Musgrave and A. Peacock (eds), *Classics in the Theory of Public Finance*, London: Macmillan, 1958.

Lindahl, E. (1959), 'Om Skatteprinciper och Skattepolitik,' in *Ekonomi Politik Samhalle*, Festschrift for Bertil Ohlins, Stockholm. Translated by T.L. Johnston as 'Tax Principles and Tax Policy', in A. Peacock, R. Turvey, W. Stolper and H. Liesner (eds), *International Economic Papers*, No 10. London: Macmillan, pp. 7-23.

Mueller, Dennis (1989), *Public Choice II*, New York: Cambridge University Press.

Myles, Gareth D. (1995), *Public Econmics*, Cambridge: Cambridge University Press.

Persson, Torsten and Guido Tabellini (2000), *Political Economics: Explaining Economic Policy*, Cambridge, MA.: MIT Press.

Simons, Henry C. (1938), *Personal Income Taxation: The Definition of Income as a Problem of Fiscal Policy*, Chicago: University of Chicago Press.

Simons, Henry C. (1950), *Federal Tax Reform*, Chicago: University of Chicago Press.

Wicksell, Knut (1896), 'A New Principle of Just Taxation', in Richard Musgrave and Alan Peacock (eds), *Classics in the Theory of Public Finance*, New York: Macmillan, 1958.

Winer, Stanley L. and Walter Hettich (1998), 'What is Missed if we Leave out Collective Choice in the Analysis of Taxation', *National Tax Journal,* **51** (2), 373-89.

Winer, Stanley L. and Thomas Rutherford (1993), 'Coercive Redistribution and the Franchise: A Preliminary Investigation Using Computational General Equilibrium Modeling', in A. Breton et al. (eds), *Preferences and the Demand for Public Goods*, Dordrecht: Kluwer.

COMMENT ON HETTICH

Robin Boadway

The agenda proposed in this chapter is a worthy one – to construct a scheme for analyzing policy choices that parallels the one used in the analysis of private markets. This involves treating choices and outcomes in the political sphere analogously, and with similar rigor, to the way in which resource allocation decisions are taken and reconciled in the private sector. The political marketplace would be treated as playing a similar coordinating role as private markets. Political decision makers acting according to well-specified objectives (for example, to be elected and/or to implement their most preferred policies) and with appropriate resource constraints interact to determine outcomes. The policy outcomes could then be analyzed from both positive and normative perspectives, as is the case with outcomes of private markets. Positive analysis would involve studying the characteristics of equilibrium policy outcomes. Normative analysis would evaluate such outcomes from an efficiency point of view. Welfare losses from political market failure could be studied and quantified. Insisting that policy outcomes reflect both political and market processes would add some much-needed realism to the study of economic policies. Walter Hettich, along with his co-author Stanley Winer, has already made much progress in showing us how such a methodology can be operationalized for a particular sort of political equilibrium model – probabilistic voting.

This is an ambitious research task, though one that is not that far removed from mainstream public choice analysis. It is also one that would complement and inform a well-established strand of public finance research – that which models the effects of real-world policies and proposed policies using such techniques as econometric-based empirical analysis, applied general equilibrium analysis and simulation analysis. Such studies are typically institution- and politics-free and do not restrict their attention to those that can be achieved as political equilibria. What makes the task especially difficult is the fact that, unlike with market mechanisms, there is really no consensus about which model or models correctly represent political processes.

This absence of a consensus model can, in principle, be overcome. However, there are also some conceptual problems that in my view preclude the suggested approach from subsuming normative economic policy analysis entirely. These problems form the basis for continuing to pursue a branch of normative policy analysis that is not constrained by political feasibility. Let me mention what seem to me to be stumbling blocks whose existence requires a multi-faceted research agenda that leaves room for a purely normative approach as well as one based on political equilibrium.

The main such problem concerns the very nature of normative or welfare analysis. Hettich, in concert with much of the mainstream public choice literature, equates welfare analysis with the analysis of the efficiency consequences of equilibria. Thus, in his Figure 5.1, normative analysis is interpreted as the analysis of market failure and the measurement of welfare loss. This is carried over to the analogous scheme suggested for political equilibria in Figure 5.2, where political market failure may occur, leading to welfare loss.

There are a number of difficulties with equating normative analysis to the study of market failure (the failure of the First Theorem of Welfare Economics). The first is that attempts to measure efficiency loss are fraught with difficulties. Put simply, there is no unambiguous measure of welfare or deadweight loss in a multi-consumer economy. More than that, there is no way of evaluating economic policies from a purely efficiency point of view. Such policies necessarily affect different persons differently, and there is no way to aggregate such effects across households without making at least implicit interpersonal comparisons of welfare. Attempts to avoid such comparisons by, say, treating a euro as worth the same to everyone involve an implicit scheme of interpersonal welfare comparisons that many would find unsatisfactory.

This is compounded by the fact that much of what governments do is explicitly redistributive. Unlike what is emphasized in much of the public choice literature, government is not solely an institution for exploiting gains from trade and internalizing free-riding. It is an institution for redistribution in all its dimensions. The ideal of unanimity as a collective decision-making procedure, which is based on the notion of Pareto improvement, is therefore misplaced. Unanimity cannot adjudicate outcomes satisfactorily even when the distribution of gains from trade is at stake, let alone when policies are redistributive in themselves. To insist on unanimity as a benchmark is to adopt a very conservative set of values, one that again corresponds to an implicit set of interpersonal welfare judgements that many would find satisfactory.

Given the importance of redistribution as an objective of policy, it seems to me that the function of normative analysis involves a much broader set of inquiries than evaluating outcomes of political equilibria with a view to determining the magnitude of welfare losses relative to some benchmark. I would emphasize two ways in which normative analysis might go beyond what Hettich has recommended.

First, the evaluation of political outcomes is certainly a legitimate normative inquiry. However, to be complete, that evaluation must involve more than studying welfare losses. It must involve analyzing how political outcomes stack up against somewhat broader ethical criteria than just efficiency ideals. Obviously this is very difficult to do since by their nature ethical criteria involve value judgements. But that does not preclude economists from adopting alternative value judgements and evaluating resource allocations from those perspectives. In doing so, they need not feel constrained to restricting attention to value judgements that might be thought to be politically palatable.

Second, normative analysis is more than evaluation: it can also be prescription. Again, prescription necessarily involves value judgement, including interpersonal comparisons of welfare. Indeed, as the welfare economics literature has made clear, it cannot avoid it. I see no compelling reason why the ethical values that are implicit in prescriptive analysis must be conditioned to be those that are deemed to be politically feasible. For what is politically feasible depends not upon some predetermined set of voter attitudes, but upon ethical positions that the electorate might be persuaded to adopt. The normative analyst certainly has some role in that process.

So, while I commend Hettich for setting out a relevant and worthwhile research agenda, I think that no research agenda can be monolithic (and I am sure Hettich did not intend to imply that). Purely normative lines of inquiry unconstrained by considerations of political feasibility are as justified from a scientific point of view as those that put political equilibrium at the center. Exploring the full consequences of adopting an ethical perspective is all the more important when the well-being of human beings is at stake.

COMMENT ON BOADWAY

Walter Hettich

There is a fundamental difference in the way that Boadway and I look at the contribution of collective choice analysis in our chapters. He tries to give it a limited role and to confine it, at least as regards normative questions, to those areas where public choice constraints cannot be avoided. I see the collective choice approach as an opportunity to broaden and generalize the economics of the public sector, and I try to show in my chapter that this opportunity has not yet been fully seized.

Public choice analysis still plays a somewhat ambiguous role in public finance. In most textbooks on the public sector, it is assigned a separate chapter, often near the beginning, where public goods are discussed. Yet the main ideas are rarely integrated into the remaining parts of the exposition. It is highly unusual to find a text that relates collective choice to the discussion of taxation, for example, a subject that generally takes up much of the second half of the book.

To make its full contribution, collective choice analysis must break out of the arbitrary walls that seem to confine it in the minds of many. I try to set out a research program that shows the broad potential of work in the collective choice tradition for public finance. In particular, I point out that it is possible to develop a normative approach that parallels the one that has been used with such success in the study of private markets. This will require careful attention to the working of political markets and to the consequences for economic policy of market failure in the political arena.

Those of us working in the collective choice tradition must share some responsibility for the tentative way in which our research has been adopted by public finance scholars. We have largely avoided asking certain basic questions that more orthodox analysis has examined with care, and in a manner that has proven useful to decision makers. This is particularly true with regard to the normative and quantitative evaluation of specific policies. It is here that I try to encourage my colleagues to adopt a bolder approach.

I believe that public finance can benefit considerably by integrating collective choice concerns more deeply into its fabric, even apart from the specific normative issues that are the focus of my chapter. I would like to give just one example in this connection. Traditional analysis has made the possibility of time-inconsistency, an idea briefly mentioned by Boadway in his chapter, into a major theoretical problem. Yet this surely represents an incomplete understanding of the working of political markets, where a great variety of formal and informal contractual agreements affects the behavior of participants, and where trust relationships continue to retain their meaning after any election has occurred. It is unrealistic to assume the existence of institutions where capital owners cannot protect themselves from expropriation in the future and where they will not invest in political resources to insure themselves against such an eventuality. Political activities to achieve this end are simply another cost that must be borne by society in order to have a working democratic system.

I also believe that traditional analysis puts too much emphasis on what may appear as a lack of consensus concerning the formal modeling of political markets. Disagreements of this nature are common in many areas of economics. In general, progress is made by adopting a suitable model and by fully exploring all important problems from the perspective of this particular framework. Consensus can only develop after such work has been carried out.

I have adopted such a course in my joint work with Stanley Winer, mentioned in my chapter, by relying on probabilistic voting as the main approach, while relating our work to results from other modeling traditions. It is only because of the consistent application of probabilistic voting to all important problems concerning taxation that I realized the possibility of a more general approach to the study of the public sector, where collective choice is integrated into all aspects of positive and normative analysis. I also found that probabilistic voting is a surprisingly robust framework for the study of democratic societies, most of which show a reasonably stable pattern of political participation.

While the theoretical possibility of instability mentioned by Boadway remains even with this model, it does not appear to apply to the political circumstances existing during recent periods in most democratic countries. In the end, all institutions, including economic markets, will break down if society undergoes serious convulsions. Yet I believe that more is to be gained by using our models to explain the fairly stable world that we observe than to focus our energies on unusual corner solutions.

Of course, researchers in the field of collective choice can also learn from established welfare analysis. Boadway's careful and systematic review of problems that may arise is most helpful in this regard, and I cannot do justice to all the points that he raises in his chapter in the limited space of this reply. We should thank him for taking on the task of skeptical observer and for using his extensive experience and knowledge concerning normative economics to illuminate possible problems and conceptual difficulties.

Boadway's emphasis on distributional questions is certainly well taken in this regard. I put the focus on efficiency in my chapter, since I believe that it is particularly concerning this topic that more work from a collective choice perspective is needed. I continue to feel that a deeper understanding of how imperfections in political markets affect efficiency is of paramount importance, and that such an understanding is crucial to the broader acceptance of collective choice analysis by those primarily interested in policy. Given Robin's thoughtful comments, I would now add the analysis of the distributional consequences of such imperfections to the list. And I fully agree that it is of major importance to investigate the distributional implications of existing policies, and to examine the philosophical assumptions concerning distribution that underlie our institutions.

In the end, research is a highly individual enterprise. We are most successful in dealing with those problems that engage and energize us. I try to show in my chapter that significant problems remain to be solved and that the return on intellectual work dealing with normative questions can be high if we approach them from a collective choice perspective. While I hope that there are others who will agree and join in this work, my chapter is not meant to disparage research that follows a different course. I fully agree with Boadway's remarks, made in his most generous 'Comment' on my chapter (see below), that research is a pluralistic enterprise, and that different perspectives all have valuable contributions to make.

COMMENT ON BOADWAY

William A. Niskanen

Robin Boadway's perspective that 'political feasibility considerations should generally not constrain policy analysis and advice' is a counsel of despair for two reasons.

First, for any set of political values, the optimal policy is often dependent on the probable behavior of the government that would implement the policy. The case for a mandatory pension, for example, is very dependent on whether the government would finance a safety net pension for those for whom their own pension is not perceived to be socially adequate. The case for increased spending for education is very dependent on whether the additional funds would be available to both public and private schools. The case for a flat tax is very dependent on whether the government is an autocracy or a constitutional democracy. The case for increased spending for defense is very dependent on how the spending is likely to be allocated and how the additional forces are likely to be used. And so forth. As a practicing policy analyst for 44 years, I cannot imagine making a policy recommendation without taking into account the characteristics and probable behavior of the government whose decision I was trying to influence.

Second, at a minimum, indifference to political feasibility will severely reduce the scope of policy analysis for which there is any audience, at least in the short run. For the same reason, indifference to the market response to a proposed policy is likely to limit the political demand for policy analysis. In some cases, of course, policies that were once regarded as infeasible or ineffective have since been implemented and are perceived to be successful; flexible exchange rates, economic deregulation, and welfare reform come to mind. In other cases, policies that were once regarded as infeasible or ineffective are now subject to serious debate; school choice and social security privatization come to mind. So policy analysts should not be deterred by current perceptions of political feasibility and should focus on important policy issues with professionalism, principle, and, above all, patience. But there remains a broad scope of potential welfare-increasing policy changes for which attention to the politically feasible is necessary to command a policy audience.

Boadway may have the luxury of focusing on the very long run for which current perceptions of the politically feasible are less important. Most of us who make a living as policy analysts do not have that luxury, and the quality of public policies would probably be lower if we did.

COMMENT ON BOADWAY

Geoffrey Brennan

In his chapter, Robin Boadway defends the traditional practice of public finance by insisting that it is perfectly legitimate for economists to make policy recommendations – or do policy analysis – in total abstraction from 'political factors'. By 'perfectly legitimate' here, he means that public finance people don't need to apologize for what they are doing. And they don't, in Boadway's view, because basically there is no case to answer.

There are three kinds of considerations to which Boadway appeals in making his case. One is a 'division of intellectual labour' argument. The second is an appeal to the legitimacy of advocacy. The third is that political considerations are too 'unpredictable' to justify taking them into account.

These arguments are fine as far as they go. But there are difficulties in their reach. For the latter two arguments do not go far enough. That is, they do not do the work that Boadway needs them to do, or seems to think they do. But the first goes much too far. I want to take these arguments briefly seriatim.

No economist worth his salt can deny the force of the notion of an intellectual division of labour. So one might well say that public finance specialists are right to concentrate on tax incidence or on chasing down externalities, and leave the details of political implementation to others. And that is perhaps Boadway's position. But note two things. First, this view carries with it an implication of *necessary* incompleteness in all of the individual specialisms. Public finance experts cannot *by definition* tell us what the best tax system would be, because they have only focused on some of the relevant factors. The factors that they have ignored have been left to public choice experts or political scientists or politicians or other kinds of experts (philosophers, perhaps). There can be no denial of the legitimacy of those other activities. On the contrary, they are all necessary. And none of them is in itself complete.

Now, this would be a very cosy message for the relations between public choice and public finance. Each could just get on with doing its own thing, trusting to the expertise of the other. But on this reading no serious conflicts could ever emerge. We have simply removed all conflicts by assumption. I am reminded in this connection of the words of the Prophet Jeremiah: 'he hath healed the wound of my people lightly, saying peace! Peace! when there is no peace!' For the regime of perpetual peace is not an accurate picture of the relations between public finance and public choice – or indeed between any of the disciplines in the social sciences. There are, it seems to me, serious differences about the importance of different factors that the 'intellectual division of labour' picture just obliterates.

Imagine, for example, a public finance treatment of, say, the effect of the income tax on the distribution of income that simply ignored the possibility (reality) of avoidance and evasion. We could always say that this ignoring simply reflected the division of intellectual labour. But that would obscure the fact that we think that an analysis that makes hopelessly implausible assumptions is not much good – that it is 'wrong' in some simple, professionally relevant sense. Put another way, there is a genuine issue about where the relevant 'divisions' in the division of intellectual labour should fall. I am doubtful whether any strong case can be made for drawing those lines neatly along the divide between public choice and public finance. But in any event, this is not a case that Boadway has made.

The second possible line is that of advocacy. Again, no one denies that advocacy may be proper. Or, if some extreme 'positivists' do deny it, I am certainly not of their number. But more needs to be said here. First, note that the advocacy line is at odds with the 'intellectual division of labour' line. You can't plausibly be a vigorous advocate of half a recommendation. It would be a strange piece of advocacy that said: 'This is the best income tax if we abstract from evasion and avoidance – about which I neither know nor care anything!' There may be a more subtle (and deep) point to be made here about what constraints can properly count in normative judgement. But the economist's general presumption surely has to be that in principle *all* constraints are relevant. To make policy recommendations when only in possession of half the relevant facts is, on the face of it, morally reprehensible. Just as a consumer in a store will make mistakes if he miscalculates relative prices, so a policy maker will make mistakes if she does not take into account all the relevant constraints. And as the theory of the second-best reminds us, adding an additional constraint can radically alter the appearance of the ideal. Public finance economists are not disqualified from the advocacy role. That is surely not the point. The point is whether that which is advocated is likely to have the claimed ethical consequences: it is in denying such claims that the public choice critique aims to bite. References to the propriety of advocacy are just beside the point.

Finally, we come to the point about the uncertainty of political factors. This is a point worth taking seriously; but I am puzzled as to why it would be identified as grounds for *ignoring* political constraints. Surely the analytically proper course is to model the political constraints as stochastic – say (if this is what Boadway has in mind), that politicians have a utility function that has a randomly determined benevolence factor, or that various different electoral constraints apply with relevant probabilities. Once it is accepted that political factors *matter*, then uncertainty about their role could only be grounds for ignoring them under very special circumstances. Further, if we know a lot about the 'pure' public finance effects and very little about the political aspects, doesn't a relative scarcity principle suggest that we ought to be focusing our attention on the matters we know less about? That would be an argument for public finance people to attend *more* to public choice issues rather than less.

Perhaps though – as I suspect – the reference to 'uncertainty of political factors' is code for a different claim – namely, 'I hear what you public choice people say about political processes, but I just don't believe it!' This seems to me to be an entirely proper response *in principle*. But note that it is a substantive claim precisely on the territory of political theorizing that public choice asserts is important. It is to say that public finance orthodoxy does embody presumptions about political process and that these presumptions are indeed different from those that seem to be derived by most public choice theorists. (I say 'most' here because there are some, like Don Wittman, who draw more heroic conclusions from public choice analysis and others, like myself, who argue for a more explicitly moralized version of public choice models.) I like this kind of response because it helps to clarify what the battle lines are. It makes it clear where the disagreements might lie – and therefore how they might be resolved.

But if this *is* Boadway's view, or his judgement as to the views of the public finance community, it would help if this were stated explicitly. Then we could engage the issue, rather than talking at cross purposes.

REJOINDER TO NISKANEN AND BRENNAN

Robin Boadway

William Niskanen's comments are very useful since they highlight the importance of a diversity of approaches to policy analysis. The general point of my chapter was to argue that those of us who study normative policy analysis need not feel intellectually or ethically bound to treat political feasibility as a constraint in considering policy alternatives, in part because political feasibility is itself an elusive and malleable concept. I explicitly acknowledge that one cannot avoid issues of government behavior when it comes to implementation (see my section entitled 'Implementation Issues'). And I have no methodological objection to approaches to policy analyses that do attempt to take political feasibility into account. But to argue that it is unimaginable to make a policy recommendation that does not take account of government behavior, and that indifference to political feasibility reduces the scope for policy analysis of current interest, overstates the case. Niskanen's many years of experience may put him at an advantage when it comes to judging what policies might or might not be politically feasible. However, I suspect that much of his policy analysis, and that of the institute with which he is affiliated, contains a large dose of policy advocacy. That is, rather than taking political feasibility as a constraint, it seeks to influence the political process and persuade governments to adopt a set of preferred policies. To my mind, that falls squarely into the category of normative analysis unconstrained by political feasibility, and carries with it the package of value judgements that the analyst prefers. That is certainly fair game, but it does not constitute a compelling case for taking political feasibility into account in normative policy analysis.

The only substantive disagreement that I have with his comments concerns the suggestion that I 'have the luxury to focus on the long run for which current perceptions of the politically feasible are less important'. In that, he is dead wrong.

Turning to Geoffrey Brennan's remarks, we are indeed, as he puts it, 'talking at cross purposes'. I do apologize to readers if my views are not explicit or clear enough. They were certainly not intended to be the way he has represented them. If indeed those were my views, he would be justified in trivializing them. Let me try to clarify matters by taking the three considerations he offers in reverse order.

The first concerns the unpredictability or 'uncertainty of political factors'. My point about the difficulty of formulating political feasibility constraints is not simply that political constraints are stochastic; nor is it that I just don't believe what 'public choice people say about political processes'. It is, I think, rather more profound than that. It is that political choice is not something that just happens exogenously, and outside of economic argument and pleading. On the contrary, economic analysis and the values that it inevitably contains help to influence political outcomes. That is the sense in which political feasibility is not a constraint like others. In other words, it is not just that I/we do not know what political feasibility constraint to use; it is that there is no such thing in the usual sense of the term constraint. For if there were, there would be limited value in normative analysis in the first place – everything would be determined by the political process. As a matter of principle, I do not see why I should be bound by political feasibility when what is feasible is precisely what I might seek to influence.

The second concerns the defense of advocacy. I simply do not understand the objection, which seems to be based on the notion that since all constraints are relevant, all must be taken into account. My point, to repeat, is that political feasibility constraints are not constraints like any other. I spent a good deal of my chapter pointing out why value judgements are unavoidable in policy advice, whether conditioned by perceived political feasibility or not. What is politically feasible depends upon what value judgements the electorate is willing to accept, and in my view that is not exogenous. Many of us who practice normative public economics unabashedly make explicit what value judgements underlie various policy recommendations. If the electorate is not persuaded, certain policies will not be adopted, but that does not justify our second-guessing the political process in advance. That is not to say that certain matters of process are not relevant, such as the realities of bureaucratic decision making, or evasion and avoidance, to use Brennan's example. I thought I was clear about those being relevant considerations that we ought to take into account. My charge in preparing this chapter was rather to address collective choice considerations, which in my view are much more malleable than public choice theory would generally admit.

The final consideration is the so-called 'division of intellectual labour' argument. This, in my view, is a rather bad caricature of my position, and is an argument that I did not use. The question is whether or not I should continue to ply my trade by, for example, analyzing optimal policies without being constrained by a preconception about whether what I recommend might be legislated. My position is that I should, and it is not based on a notion that I should leave to those with more expertise the analysis of whether it leads to electable platforms. My arguments were meant to be based on a matter of principle, that principle relying on the fact that political feasibility was of necessity an ill-defined concept. I simply would not know what political feasibility constraint to use at any given point of time, and nothing I have seen in the public choice literature to date has been able to help me. That does not preclude others from studying political processes to see what they can learn from them, or to try and determine how such processes can be manipulated.

In short, I do not see any contradiction between what normative public economists do and what public choice economists do. And I certainly do not think there needs to be any clarification of 'battle lines'. The search for knowledge is not analogous to a war.

PART III

What is a 'Failure' in a Non-market or
Policy Process?

6. Normative public finance without guilt: why normative public finance is positive public finance

Donald Wittman

1. INTRODUCTION

In the beginning, God created normative public finance and his prophet was Richard Musgrave. Musgrave's sacred text provided guidelines for a benevolent social-welfare maximizing-government. Then the Devil came in the guise of public choice. And his angels of destruction were James Buchanan, Gordon Tullock and William Niskanen. They claimed to provide a descriptive theory of government and it was very dark. Since then public choice has waged a war on normative public finance. Public choice offers an alternative vision of politics – special interest groups maximize their own welfare at the expense of the electorate.[1] This 'realistic view' of politics renders normative theory useless except as a standard by which to measure the failure of real politics.

No one wants to feel that his or her work is useless. So some in public finance embraced the devil of public choice and incorporated the role of special interests into their work, while others continued to do normative public finance, trying to ignore public choice but typically feeling guilty about it.

Today, normative public finance will be resurrected. Today, I will show that normative (prescriptive) public finance is positive (descriptive) public finance. That is, a realistic understanding of the democratic political process shows that special interest politics leads to welfare improvements just as self-interest leads to efficient outcomes in economic markets. In a nutshell, in democracies the prescriptive and the descriptive coincide.[2]

2. THE THEORY OF SPECIAL INTERESTS

There are many models of interest group politics, but the intuition behind most of these models is the same – politicians trade off good policy in return for campaign contributions from special interests. In turn, these contributions are used to pay for the advertising that persuades voters to vote for the candidate.

Now, the concept of special interest is not new to economics. After all, it is self-interest that drives the invisible hand in the private sector. So why has the public choice literature reached such contrary and dismal conclusions for the role of self-interest in democratic politics? My answer is that public choice theorists have conflated voter lack of information with irrationality. Once we realize that voters can be rational, albeit uninformed, then the dismal results of the public choice literature disappear. Indeed, when voters are aware of the model, campaign contributions by special interests (pressure groups) improve the welfare of the median voter.

To illustrate my argument, I will first review the standard public choice model of pressure group influence. I will focus on two very sophisticated examples – Baron (1994) and Grossman and Helpman (1996). In their models, there are two types of voters: (1) informed voters who know the positions of the candidates, and (2) uninformed voters who do not know the positions of the candidates or the position of the pressure group,[3] but who respond positively to advertising. Each candidate is only interested in winning. A pressure group donates money to a candidate. In turn, the candidate moves away from the median informed voter toward the position of the pressure group. In this way the candidate loses some of the informed voters' votes. However, the money is used for political advertising. The more advertising, the more uninformed voters vote for the candidate. Both the candidate and the pressure group are made better off if the loss of votes from the informed is more than made up by the increase in votes from the uninformed. Hence, if the most preferred position of the median uninformed voter is identical to the most preferred position of the median informed voter, the median voter is made worse off by the presence of a pressure group.

Note that the candidate and the pressure group are acting rationally (they both benefit from the pressure group donations), and so do the informed voters. But the uninformed voters do not act rationally. Instead, the uninformed voters behave according to a functional form (more advertising increases their likelihood of voting for the candidate). Furthermore, this functional form implicitly assumes that voters act contrary to their own interests. The argument proceeds as follows.

Suppose first that the median uninformed voter's most preferred position coincides with the median informed voter's most preferred position, and that this is known by the uninformed voters. Then the median uninformed voter knows that the candidate doing less advertising will be closer to his position than the candidate doing more advertising; so the median uninformed voter will vote for the candidate doing less advertising. And because the candidate doing more advertising has moved farther away from the median of the informed voters, the median informed voter will also vote for the candidate doing less advertising. This means that the candidate doing more advertising will lose the election. So neither candidate will accept campaign contributions from the pressure group in the first place.[4]

On the other hand, suppose that the uninformed voter is not at the median. Since the uninformed voter does not know whether the pressure group is on the left or the right, but knows that the candidate doing more advertising is farther away from the median voter, the uninformed voter will once again vote for the candidate doing less advertising since there is less risk with a similar mean. That is, from the uninformed voter's point of view, the candidate doing more advertising has the same expected position as the candidate doing less advertising, but the candidate doing more advertising is pulled farther away from the mean and therefore there is more risk associated with voting for the candidate doing more advertising. So, the uninformed will again vote for the candidate doing less advertising. And because the candidate doing the advertising is farther away from the median of the informed voters, a majority of the informed voters will again vote for the candidate doing less advertising. And therefore, vote-maximizing candidates will again not accept campaign contributions from the pressure group in the first place.

Thus campaign contributions cannot make the uninformed worse off. If voters are rational, and the model is otherwise correct, uninformed voters will realize that the advertising is harmful and vote for the candidate doing less advertising. So this is the problem with all models that claim that pressure group donations do harm. They require irrationality of voters, which is a big no-no for economists. It is ironic that those who have introduced rational behavior to politics have inadvertently assumed that uninformed voters are irrational.

From the opposite perspective, if uninformed voters are rational, then pressure group contributions and endorsements must improve their welfare. Otherwise, voters would not respond positively to such advertising and endorsements. To illustrate, assume the uninformed know that the pressure group is on the right. Then the uninformed can infer that the candidate doing the advertising has moved right. If the median uninformed voter is to the left of the median informed voter, a majority of the uninformed voters will respond negatively to such advertising. And thus the candidate would not agree to move right in the first place. However, if the median uninformed voter is to the right of the median informed voter (and certain other technicalities are satisfied – see Wittman, 2001a), then the candidate moving right and advertising will win the election with a position at the median of all voters rather than the median of the informed voters. Hence the pressure group endorsement aids the political process. The uninformed are able to make intelligent inferences from campaign advertising and endorsements and thereby become more informed.

There are other variations of the model, but they all lead to the same positive conclusion. In Wittman (2001b) voters know the candidates' positions but are uninformed about the relative quality of the candidates. In contrast, the pressure group has inside information about the candidates' relative quality. The pressure group may endorse the lower-quality candidate as the higher-quality candidate if the lower-quality candidate takes a position close enough to the pressure group's most preferred position. Nevertheless, in equilibrium the pressure group tells the truth. I show that pressure group endorsements regarding quality always improve the median voter's welfare, and under certain conditions such endorsements make *every* voter better off!

If uninformed voters know the model, then advertising by special interests will not lead the voters to vote against their own self-interest. In other words, once we understand how uninformed but rational voters behave, we realize that, in the real world, campaign contributions must on average improve welfare and that the predictions of positive theory coincide with the prescriptions of normative public finance.

From a more general perspective, efficient provision of public goods and other Pareto-improving choices help vote-maximizing politicians to garner more votes. Whatever the distribution of private goods, the equilibrium political outcome is efficient.

3.   OTHER ISSUES

Of course, one argument is not going to overturn 40 years of research. There are counter-arguments and counters to the counter-arguments. Here I will provide the reader with some additional intellectual machetes to cut through the intellectual tangle.[5]

1. *Rent-seeking uses up costly resources.* But it pays politicians to minimize such waste so that they can skim more for themselves or their constituents.
2. *It does not pay for the voters to be informed.* But it may pay political entrepreneurs to provide the requisite information. Voters do not know much about medicine either, but that does not mean that they do not get the correct advice from their doctors. Nor, for that matter, do most stockholders know anything about the company in which they hold stock, but that does not mean that the market for corporate control does not work.
3. *Voters receive biased information.* But voters can discount such biases or

only pay attention to information coming from those with similar preferences.

4. *The majority just rides roughshod over the minority.* But why would the majority be inefficient in this regard and not extract as much surplus as possible? Institutions of government such as legislatures reduce transaction costs thereby increasing the likelihood of efficient logrolling.

5. *The government has monopoly power.* But that ignores the competition for political office and the role of reputation in reducing opportunism by the political parties and their candidates.

6. *Bureaucrats have the 'real' power and use it to increase the size of the bureaucracy.* But why would elected officials cede so much power to the bureaucrats rather than appropriating the benefits for themselves and/or their constituents? Besides, bureaucrats may gain advancement by showing that they can cut costs.

7. *Legislators are only interested in their own districts and not in the cost imposed on other districts.* The result is inefficient pork barrel politics. But this ignores the role of political parties in creating positive-sum policy outcomes. Even in the absence of political parties, legislators would not collectively create policies that are negative-sum.

8. *Politicians equate the median voter's marginal cost to the median voter's marginal benefit rather than being efficient and equating the average marginal cost to average marginal benefit.* But real politicians don't behave this way; instead, they try to find winning coalitions that are Pareto-improving.

4. EMPIRICAL EVIDENCE

So far, I have concentrated on theoretical issues. What about the empirical evidence? In a nutshell, I am very skeptical about the research demonstrating government failure.

4.1 Non-random Selection of Case Studies and Evidence

Let me start with an account of my trip to the congress. I first drove through the city of Santa Cruz and then drove on to the state highway to the airport. I made the following observations: there were many traffic signals in the city of Santa Cruz but none on the state highway. Being an expert on public choice and on the topic of rent-seeking, I immediately came to the conclusion that traffic signal manufacturers were more skilled in extracting rents from city councils than from state legislatures. Perhaps if I had been better trained in public finance, I would have realized that normative theory is a much better explanation than the special interest theory, and that the actual as well as the optimal number of traffic signals is a function of the density of cross-traffic. Suppose that I did a more serious empirical study and showed this to be the case. Would it be published in a politics or economics journal and, if it were published, would anyone bother to read it? I suspect that the answer is no in both cases. As researchers, we are much more interested in the puzzle of political failure than of unproblematic political success, but that does not mean we should characterize the democratic process as one of failure. So as researchers we point to the existence of tariffs rather than to their relatively low levels, the existence of rent controls in some cities rather than the non-existence of rent controls in most cities, and the presence of political market failures rather than of political market successes. After all, no one is surprised that in the USA (or elsewhere, for that matter) a red traffic light signal means stop and a green signal means go, even though the colors could vary from one signal to another. That is, normative theory predicts uniformity in this case, but no one pays attention to this fact. So the first problem I have with the evidence in favor of rent-seeking and against normative public finance is that it is very selective and often of second-order importance.

4.2   Normative Theory Gives You Precision; Rent-seeking Does Not

A number of cost–benefit studies have shown government policies to be inefficient. Furthermore, many government policies are clearly so inefficient that no cost–benefit study is necessary. Examples include rent control, protective tariffs, and many farm subsidy programs. Does this evidence of inefficient policies undermine the efficient government hypothesis? My short answer is no, unless there is a competing hypothesis that is closer to the mark.

Governments may be inefficient because (1) their budgets are not the optimal size, (2) they do not produce the optimal mix of goods and services, (3) their production is not cost-effective, (4) the goods and services are provided to the 'wrong' people, (5) government regulations result in the private sector producing the wrong mix, (6) government regulations result in production that is not cost-effective, or (7) government regulations result in the wrong people receiving goods and services. I will amplify my short answer by referring to points 1 and 2. I start with 1, which is less interesting, but easier , to illustrate.

Suppose that the actual budget in country 1 is 38 percent of GDP and that the optimal budget is 18 percent of GDP. And to make the case against the efficiency hypothesis look even worse, suppose that similar observations are done across 50 countries, where the optimal budget is always 18 percent, but the actual budget varies between 36 percent and 40 percent. In this way, the null hypothesis that the budget size is optimal would be rejected.

Unfortunately, 'not efficient' is not much of a predictive theory. So let us consider some alternative theories.

Perhaps bureaucrats maximize the size of the government budget (in this case, bureaucrats are the powerful special interests). The maximum could be achieved by government ownership of the means of production so that all decisions were made by government bureaucrats. As a result, nearly 100 percent of GDP would be under the control of the government bureaucracy. While 38 percent is far from 16 percent, it is a lot farther from 100 percent. Therefore, we can reject the pure budget-maximizing model in favor of the efficiency model.

Next consider the more general rent-seeking model. Suppose that rent-seeking theory predicts that budgets are larger than optimal, but the theory does not say how much larger. The standard approach in the literature is to employ a one-tailed test. Given the above data, the hypothesis of rent-seeking would be confirmed. Unfortunately, this is the wrong way to go about choosing theories.

A theory that merely states that government expenditures are greater than optimal allows for government expenditures being anywhere between 18 percent and 100 percent. Given a uniform distribution of possibilities, this suggests that rent-seeking produces an average estimate of (100 + 18)/2 = 59. Since 59 percent is farther away from 38 percent than 18 percent is away from 38 percent, one would choose the efficiency hypothesis over the rent-seeking hypothesis. Now perhaps there are refinements of the rent-seeking hypothesis that predict a budget of 49 percent, in which case the rent-seeking hypothesis would dominate the efficiency hypothesis in predicting the size of the government. But this is not the way the research has been conducted. Instead, the one-tailed test has been the dominant approach of the literature.

In a nutshell, pointing to a 'failure' of the efficiency hypothesis is not sufficient grounds for rejection unless the alternative provides a more accurate prediction.

We next turn our attention to the distribution of government goods and services. Although articles on rent-seeking have concentrated more on this than the overall size of government, paradoxically, rent-seeking is on much weaker ground in this arena.

The normative theory of government predicts that the government will subsidize the production of public goods when the market is likely to fail in that endeavor. And by and large, the evidence conforms to the normative expectations. Governments subsidize vaccinations more than plastic surgeries, rather than vice versa. Governments subsidize a greater percentage of the cost of building streets than the cost of building cars, rather than vice versa. And the role of government relative to the private market is much greater in national defense than in consumption, rather than vice versa. None of these statements is very new or exciting to a public finance economist. But they are puzzling facts to those who believe in rent-seeking theory. Are those who build streets always more organized than those who build automobiles?

Once again, there are plenty of exceptions to the normative theory. But selectively choosing exceptions and then 'testing' them is not really good science. The sample needs to be random or at least reflect major items in the budget. And as already shown, in choosing theories, one must compare their point predictions (or somehow put them on equal terms). So showing that the defense budget is greater than optimal is not a reason to reject the efficiency hypothesis in favor of the rent-seeking hypothesis unless the actual level is closer to the prediction of the rent-seeking hypothesis than to the prediction of the efficiency hypothesis.

5.   WHAT DOES NORMATIVE PUBLIC FINANCE HAVE TO SAY FOR NON-DEMOCRATIC COUNTRIES?

I have argued that in democracies prescriptive public finance is descriptive public finance. A natural question to ask is whether the same holds true for dictatorships. Some of the same forces that encourage efficient outcomes in democracies also exist for dictatorships. A dictator always faces the threat of a *coup* and the rise of another dictator. That is, there is competition for the office. Even in the absence of competition, a dictator's desire to extort the maximum from his subjects would, other things being equal, make the dictator prefer an efficient economic system over an inefficient one. For example, the dictator would want to provide vaccinations for his subjects and other public goods that were not adequately provided by the private sector; in this way, there would be more surplus value for the dictator to extract. However, such forces are severely attenuated in a dictatorship. First the transaction costs of replacing a dictator are very high; this shields the dictator from competitive forces that eliminate inefficiency. Second, decentralizing economic control may undermine the dictator's political control. Very few dictators have chosen capitalism with its attendant property rights as the economic and legal system. Third, the system of dictatorship makes it difficult for the truth to prevail as those below the dictator do not want to lose their positions of power (see Wintrobe, 1998, for an illuminating analysis). Consequently, a dictator's lunatic ideas are less likely to be challenged. The evidence supports these arguments – North Korea versus South Korea; East Germany versus West Germany; and Mainland China versus Taiwan. In each of these cases, the more democratic, the more efficient and the more actual public finance looked like normative public finance.

6. CONCLUDING REMARKS

I have considered the case where a pressure group has extreme power: the pressure group is the only source of campaign funds; there are no other pressure groups to compete away any rents; and neither candidate is able credibly to transmit information on its position to the uninformed voters. The pressure group takes advantage of this power to improve its own welfare. Nevertheless, the by-product is improved welfare for a majority of voters.

I have provided a simple and intuitive micro-foundation model of the behavior of uninformed but rational voters. In the process, the almost universal disdain by academics and ordinary voters toward interest group campaign contributions and endorsements has been shown to be without a theoretical foundation. Indeed, special interests have been shown to help the democratic process. This result is not dependent on any special assumptions about pressure groups, but rather on the assumption that uninformed voters act rationally. Uninformed but rational voters are not going to respond positively to something (for example campaign advertising) that affects them adversely. From the opposite point of view, normative theory is positive theory in that special interests move the political equilibrium toward the welfare maximum.

Once we have the right perspective, the empirical evidence rejects the special interest theory in favor of the normative efficiency theory of public finance. To return to our biblical metaphor, the reality of democratic behavior is much closer to the garden of Eden depicted by normative public finance than the Sodom and Gomorrah depicted by some of the founders of public choice.

NOTES

1. Of course, special interest politics and public choice are not synonymous, except possibly for the 'Virginia' School. Here, however, I will use the terms interchangeably.
2. I will concentrate on efficiency; there is insufficient time to deal with issues of equity.
3. Initially, it is assumed that the uninformed only know that the pressure group's most preferred position is either to the extreme right or to the extreme left, each with probability one-half.
4. This argument and those following are modeled in greater detail in Wittman (2001a).
5. For other arguments and a detailed discussion see Wittman (1995).

REFERENCES

Baron, David P. (1994), 'Electoral Competition with Informed and Uninformed Voters', *American Political Science Review*, **88**, 33–47.
Grossman, Gene M. and Elhanan Helpman (1996), 'Electoral Competition and Special Interest Politics', *Review of Economic Studies*, **63**, 265–86.

Musgrave, Richard A. and Peggy B. Musgrave (1989), *Public Finance in Theory and Practice*, 5th edn, New York: McGraw-Hill.

Wintrobe, Ronald (1998), *The Political Economy of Dictatorship*, Cambridge: Cambridge University Press.

Wittman, Donald (1995), *The Myth of Democratic Failure: Why Political Institutions are Efficient*, Chicago: University of Chicago Press.

Wittman, Donald (2001a), 'Rational Voters and Political Advertising', University of California, Santa Cruz, Department of Economics Working paper no. 479, http://econ.ucsc.edu/faculty/wittman/rationalvoters.pdf

Wittman, Donald (2001b), 'Candidate Quality, Pressure Group Endorsements and Uninformed Voters', University of California, Santa Cruz, Department of Economics Working paper no. 478, http://econ.ucsc.edu/faculty/wittman/candquality.pdf

7. On the origin and identification of government failures

William A. Niskanen

1. INTRODUCTION

Government failures are rooted in the same set of conditions as market failures: biased or insufficient information, principal–agent problems, insecure or incomplete property rights, monopoly, externalities and so on. (My use of the term *government failures*, rather than *non-market failures*, is to make a distinction between the behavior of governments and that of the many types of institutions other than markets and governments.) The difference is that these conditions are pervasive and inherent in governments, whereas they are more often selective or temporary conditions in markets. Donald Wittman and others have made a valuable contribution by pointing out that the distinctive characteristics of democratic governments – such as elections, parties, pressure groups, legislatures, committees, vote trading, and so on – mitigate some of the problems that are rooted in these conditions, but they are a long way from convincing me and, at least, many other political economists that 'democratic markets promote wealth-maximizing outcomes [and] work as well as economic markets' (Wittman 1989).

What follows in this chapter summarizes my perspective on the conditions that lead to government failures, some evidence of the nature and magnitude of these failures, and the most important common problem of contemporary democratic governments. Some readers will recognize that my perspective on these issues has not changed much in the past several decades. (For a summary of my perspective many years ago, see Niskanen, 1976.)

2. CONDITIONS THAT LEAD TO GOVERNMENT FAILURES

2.1 Limited Information

The beginning of wisdom about democratic politics is that most voters have virtually no incentive to invest in information about candidate or policy choices. The value of such information is equal to the probability that a voter's decision will change the outcome times the difference in the net personal benefits of the leading alternatives, an expected value that is vanishingly small; moreover, the higher the probability of changing the outcome, the lower is the likely difference in the net benefits of that outcome. Most of the information on which voters make their decisions is a by-product of work, social relations, and entertainment – information that is likely to be both biased and insufficient for an informed vote. Groups that have a larger stake in the difference in political outcomes, of course, have more of an incentive to invest in information but to promote the distribution of only that information that serves their interest. Some of these conditions also affect market behavior except that the outcome of each transaction is determined by only one buyer and one seller, increasing the incentive to invest in information and the opportunity to learn from prior transactions and those by others.

2.2 Principal–Agent Relations

Most policy decisions in a democratic government are made by some *group* of representative agents, each of whom has the authority to address a *group* of policy issues and is elected by a *group* of voters. Very few voters, thus, are likely to be well represented on every policy issue, and the interests of many voters are likely to be poorly represented on many issues. One consequence of electing agents from single-member districts is a strong preference for district-specific net benefits; such 'pork' is the inherent price of government services that provide more general benefits. Another consequence is that our agents have almost no incentive to invest in oversight that might lead to more general benefits. Good law is a public good; that is why we have so little of it. In normative public finance, the primary role of government is to provide public goods, but 'politics without romance' provides such goods only at a substantial cost of the private goods that are necessary to motivate our agents.

A recent study of 17 US federal agencies and departments, for example, identified about $220 billion of questionable spending, about 12 percent of the total budget and a higher share of the consumption expenditures of these agencies (US General Accounting Office, 2001). Similar principal–agent problems in the market are much smaller because market participants use agents only for selective transactions, agents represent only one party in each transaction, and there is more competition among the agents.

2.3 Monopolies

Governments are generally monopoly suppliers of some services in a specific region. I am intrigued by the recent proposal by Bruno Frey for a system of Functional Overlapping Competitive Jurisdictions, or FOCJs, but this proposal needs both further study and a pronounceable acronym (Frey, 2001). For some services, one must either pay extra to a private supplier or move to another local government if one is dissatisfied with the services supplied in one's current jurisdiction. For other services, one must move to another province or state to find an alternate supplier. For yet other services, one must move to another nation to find an alternate supplier. And some regulations, such as on bank capital standards and the use of chlorofluorocarbons, are now enforced worldwide. Moreover, many governments have the power to prevent entry by a potential competitor. Such government monopolies have little potential to serve the diversity of demand within their jurisdiction and little incentive to be efficient. In contrast, monopoly power in the market is usually limited and temporary unless entry is limited by some government.

2.4 Externalities

In normative public finance, another important role of government is to correct for the external benefits and costs of private actions. The problem is that governments create pervasive and inherent externalities of a different kind. For many people the marginal value of some government activity is higher than the marginal cost to them, and these people would benefit from an expansion of this activity. For many people, the marginal value of some government activity is lower than the marginal cost to them, and these people would benefit from a reduction of this activity. Almost everyone would prefer either more or less of every activity of government. Given a diversity of demand for government activities, this would be the case even if the package of government activities were set at a level for which the net benefits were maximized. A government may be in a political equilibrium without clearing the market for any one activity, a consequence of charging the same tax price for all activities. Most market externalities, in contrast, are due to unclear or incomplete property rights, and the internalization of these market externalities is limited only by the cost of the available 'fencing' technology.

3.   SOME EVIDENCE OF GOVERNMENT FAILURE

Don Wittman is 'very skeptical about the research demonstrating government failure' (Wittman, 2001). In response, I will summarize some of the evidence that bears on this issue and let readers judge for themselves.

3.1 Economic Studies

A substantial number of studies have concluded that an increase in the relative size of government budgets reduces economic growth. (For a summary of these studies, see Holcombe, 2001.) Some of these studies are based on statistical analyses of the time series for a specific country. Edgar Peden (1991), for example, estimates that US economic growth would be maximized by total government expenditures of about 20 percent of GDP. Gerald Scully (1994), with spurious precision, estimates that the growth-maximizing level of total government spending in the USA is from 21.5 to 22.9 percent of GDP. My own recent study (Niskanen, forthcoming) estimates that government spending of 9 to 12 percent of GDP plus the expenditures for national defense and net interest payments would maximize US after-tax income. The most comprehensive recent study (by James Gwartney, Randall Holcombe and Robert Lawson, 1998), based on an analysis of combined time-series cross-country samples, concludes that the growth-maximizing level of government expenditures is less than 15 percent of GDP. Democratic governments clearly do not promote wealth-maximizing outcomes, except possibly for the members of the effective control group.

3.2 Voting and Migration Studies

A broadly popular increase in the government budget should increase the popular vote for the candidate of the incumbent party in the next election. My own studies of US presidential elections, however, estimate that a 10 percent increase in real per capita federal tax revenues since the prior election *reduces* the popular vote for the candidate of the incumbent party by 1.2 to 1.4 percent of the total major party vote (Niskanen, 1979 and 1992). A similar study by Sam Peltzman (1987) concludes that an increase in real per capita state tax revenues reduces the popular vote for the gubernatorial candidate of the incumbent party in the next election. The fiscal behavior of democratic governments, apparently, is not even consistent with vote maximizing.

A broadly popular fiscal program should also lead to net migration into the jurisdiction of that government. My own study of the net migration among the American states in the 1980s, however, estimates that a 10 percent higher level of state and local tax revenues per capita at the beginning of the decade *reduced* the net migration rate over the decade by 0.6 to 0.9 percent of the 1980 population (Niskanen, 1992). My preliminary estimates based on a sample of the states during the 1990s indicate that a relatively high level of state and local tax revenues per capita at the beginning of the decade reduced both the net migration rate and the growth of real personal income per capita over the decade.

Apparently, something is wrong with the fiscal rules that determine the level of government expenditures and tax revenues, at both the federal and the state levels. The economic growth, voting and migration studies suggest that government expenditures and tax revenues are higher than is consistent with either wealth maximization or vote maximization.

4. THE MAJOR COMMON PROBLEM OF CONTEMPORARY DEMOCRATIC GOVERNMENTS

For all the evidence of government failure, the alternative may be worse. The magnitude of the several types of government failures is appropriate to consider when the issue at stake is whether the government should undertake some activity, but the net benefits of the activity, given the feasible alternatives, may still be positive. A defense budget, a highway program, or a research budget, for example, may include substantial pork and may not be the optimal scale, but may still be better than any feasible alternative. Any social process, however, should be judged by whether one agrees to the *rules* of this process, not whether one benefits from a specific outcome of this process. Some of the outcomes of the market, I suggest, are also unlovely; since I endorse the market rule that any transaction requires the unanimous consent of those with the relevant rights, however, I accept these outcomes. In the end, democratic government should also be judged – not by whether some amount of pork is the price of those public goods that we value; whether government spending, taxes and regulation reduce the growth of the economy; whether we regard the distribution of the benefits and costs as 'fair' – but whether the rules that lead to these outcomes are broadly supported by the affected population.

The awkward truth is that we do not know the answer to this critical question, because most democratic governments now act as if they have the authority to define their own powers. The US federal budget in 1929, for example, was 2.6 percent of GDP, most of which was for the military and the deferred costs of prior wars. The federal budget is now over 18 percent of GDP, most of which is for programs for which there is no explicit constitutional authority. The massive expansion of federal spending, taxes and regulation in the USA in my lifetime has occurred without one amendment to the Constitution to authorize these additional powers. In effect, this expansion of federal authority represents a breach of contract, a change of the rules without our consent, a reduction of the clarity and security of property rights in the market and the authority of other levels of government.

The major common problem of contemporary democratic governments is that they now operate without effective constitutional limits on their powers. In the end, that is the most serious type of government failure. The first step toward correcting this failure must be to restore the *idea* of a constitution as a set of rules that the government itself may not change. The next step is to develop and promote rules to address this failure that would command a constitutional consensus. One step at a time.

REFERENCES

Frey, Bruno S. (2001), 'A Utopia? Government Without Territorial Monopoly', *The Independent Review*, **6** (1), 99–112.

Gwartney, James D., Randall G. Holcombe and Robert A. Lawson (1998), 'The Scope of Government and the Wealth of Nations', *Cato Journal*, **18**, 163–90.

Holcombe, Randall G. (2001), 'Public Choice and Economic Growth', in *The Elgar Companion to Public Choice*, Cheltenham, UK and Northampton, USA: Edward Elgar.

Niskanen, William A. (1976), 'Public Policy and the Political Process', in Svetozar Pejovich (ed.), *Governmental Controls and the Free Market*, College Station, TX: Texas A&M Press, pp. 73–93.

Niskanen, William (1979), 'Economic and Fiscal Effects on the Popular Vote for the President', in Douglas W. Rae and Theodore J. Eismeier (eds), *Public Policy and Public Choice*, Beverly Hills, CA: Sage Publications, pp. 93–120.

Niskanen, William (1992), 'The Case for a New Fiscal Constitution', *Journal of Economic Perspectives*, **6** (2), 13–24.

Niskanen, William (forthcoming), *On Regimes: Fiscal Choices and Economic Outcomes*.

Peden, Edgar A. (1991), 'Productivity in the United States and its Relationship to Government Activity: an Analysis of 57 Years, 1929–1986', *Public Choice*, **69**, 153–73.

Peltzman, Sam (1987), 'Economic Conditions and Gubernatorial Elections', *American Economic Review*, **77** (2), 293–7.

Scully, Gerald W. (1994), *What is the Optimal Size of Government in the United States?*, Dallas, TX: National Center for Policy Analysis.

US General Accounting Office (2001), *Government at the Brink: Urgent Federal Government Management Problems Facing the Bush Administration*.

Wittman, Donald (1989), 'Why Democracies Produce Efficient Results', *Journal of Political Economy*, **97**, 1395–424.

Wittman, Donald (2001), 'Normative public finance without guilt', paper prepared for the IIPF Congress, chapter 6 of this volume.

COMMENT ON NISKANEN

Donald Wittman

Because Niskanen and I come to such opposite conclusions about the nature of democratic politics, one might expect that I would find many things wrong with his chapter, 'On the origin and identification of government failure'. But, in fact, I agree with almost everything he says. The remainder of my comments will try to resolve this apparent contradiction.

1. Reasons for Government Failure

The first part of Niskanen's chapter is devoted to reasons for government failure. The reasons include limited information, principal–agent relations, monopoly and externalities.

With regard to limited information, Niskanen correctly points out that voters have little incentive to invest in information about candidates or government policies. He also points out that some groups may benefit from investment in information, but that these groups will only disseminate such information that serves the group's own interest.

Under the rubric of principal–agent problems, Niskanen highlights the strong preference of legislative districts for district-specific pork even when the benefit to the district is outweighed by the tax burden on the other districts.

He notes that governments are often monopoly suppliers of certain services to particular regions. He further notes that monopolists may choose the easy life rather than trying to be efficient.

Finally, Niskanen argues that even though government policy may lead to political equilibrium, individual preferences are unlikely to be in equilibrium – some individuals wanting more and others wanting less government intervention because their individual marginal costs and benefits are not equal.

Niskanen is right on all these points. But I would prefer to label these as challenges rather than failures. Let me illustrate by starting with the last point. Some policies are of necessity public goods or bads. Consider foreign policy. The USA could not at the same time patrol the skies over Iraq and not patrol the skies over Iraq. Undoubtedly, some voters prefer more military involvement and some less, but this is the nature of the beast. There is no way to avoid the problem any more than there is a way to mine for diamonds without digging up a lot of dirt. But this is not a failure; rather, it is a challenge.[1]

Turning to voter lack of information, I again see the arguments raised by Niskanen as challenges rather than failures. He demonstrates that there is little reason for most voters to invest in political information. I agree. But institutions arise to mitigate this problem. An important reason for the existence of political parties is to reduce the cost to voters of obtaining political information. Once a voter knows the political party affiliation of a candidate, the voter knows a considerable amount about the candidate. So the problem posed by Niskanen is to some degree solved by the existence of political parties. On a slightly different track, it is true that some groups will provide information that is self-serving, but voters can discount self-serving statements, just as consumers can discount self-serving statements by sellers of used cars. Alternatively, voters can listen to trusted friends and groups on how to vote. In the end, elections are determined by majority rule and the law of large numbers, which means that correct decisions are likely to be made despite the fact that much of the voting is random and based on poor information. For example, if 30 percent of the voters are knowledgeable and vote correctly and 70 percent just flip an honest coin, then the correct decision will be made with an extremely high probability. And even if the wrong decision has been made, that does not mean that there has been a failure if the cost of gaining the requisite information is greater than the benefit of making the correct decision.

Both political parties and the organization of the legislature are responses to the challenge of district self-interest and the potential for negative-sum pork-barrel policies. A political party is a coalition that creates positive-sum gains for its members. The more a political party can create a set of policies that avoid inefficient shifting of costs on to other members of the coalition, the more likely its members will win in an election. Furthermore, legislatures are relatively small, enabling efficiency-enhancing trades (that include the minority). If there are inefficient pork-barrel projects, then there exists an alternative arrangement that can make all the legislators and their constituents better off. That is what logrolling is all about – creating Pareto-improving trades.

The final prong of Niskanen's theoretical attack is that governments are monopolists and that monopolists may choose the easy life over efficiency. But this is the problem that democratic elections eliminate. Governments are monopolists, but elections for the control of the government are relatively low-cost arenas for competition (involving much lower cost than armed struggle, for example). It is this competition for political power that destroys the 'easy life'.

2.   Evidence of Government Failure

The second part of Niskanen's chapter is devoted to providing evidence of government failure. Once again I do not disagree with what is said. It is truly a matter of perspective, which I believe is the fundamental explanation for our differing conclusions.

To illustrate, consider the following quote: 'A recent study of 17 US federal agencies and departments ... identifies about $220 billion of questionable spending, about 12 percent of the total budget'. Niskanen is very upset about this, and perhaps he should be. After all $220 billion is a lot of money. But I say: 'Only 12 percent. That's great. It could have been 70 percent or even higher'.

So I think this is the key to our differences. I judge democracy from the perspective of how bad things could be and are under alternative methods of governance. By this measure, democracy as practiced in the USA is close to being efficient.[2] In contrast, Niskanen compares what is to the best of all possible worlds and finds the reality of democratic politics lacking. We are both right. There is room for improvement, but, measured on the scale of possibilities, democracy is very close to being efficient.

3. Violation of the Social Contract

And much the same holds for the third prong of his chapter. In this part, Niskanen argues that the government of the USA has violated the original constitution (the social contract) by increasing the federal budget from 2.9 percent of GDP in 1929 to 18.2 percent today without benefit of a constitutional amendment. I can understand why he is bothered by this. But from my viewpoint, the twentieth century is marked by genocide, enforced famine and extreme restrictions on human rights. From this perspective, the US Constitution is still a vital force in the USA, and the social contract has been upheld.

Thus, I come back to my opening statement. I agree with almost everything Niskanen says in his chapter and I recommend that everyone read it. It is perceptive and eloquently argued. He and I just have different perspectives. He is upset that democracies do not perform better; I am relieved that we do not have another form of government that would perform much worse.

NOTES

1. Of course, it would be a failure if there were uniformity in policy when none was called for, for example, if public universities required students to take identical courses, the benefit of free choice would be lost. But we do not observe this to be the case. It would also be a failure if governments undertook activity in areas better served by the private sector. This particular failure has been subsiding.
2. See my chapter (Chapter 6) for an extended explanation of why efficiency is the most predictive theory of democracy that we have.

COMMENT ON WITTMAN

William A. Niskanen

Don Wittman should relax. There is no reason for those who practice normative public finance to feel guilty about their specialty. Normative public finance provides a valuable role even if only as a standard by which to evaluate the actual behavior of governments. Moreover, as Wittman has demonstrated, normative public finance provides some guidance about the roles that governments are most likely to perform. The primary problem of Wittman's distinctive professional perspective is that he is inclined to jump from an observation that governments do some things moderately well (such as the distribution of traffic lights from his home to the airport) to a sweeping conclusion that democratic governments do almost nothing wrong.

Wittman specializes in models of rational behavior by political actors and is 'very skeptical about the research demonstrating government failure', so it is necessary to engage him on his own grounds. The type of model outlined in the chapter develops the effects on candidate issue positions of the role of pressure groups and of voter concerns about candidate quality, important effects that have not been incorporated in simpler prior models. I have two primary concerns, however, about this sort of model.

First, the model seems to depend on the assumption that there is only one pressure group on which all voters effectively rely. Since the pressure group is effective in shifting the issue position of the candidate that it endorses toward its preferred position, however, the equilibrium number of pressure groups must be more than one. In that case, surely more consistent with political reality, the effects of pressure groups on candidate positions and of endorsement on voter responses are much less clear.

Second, the type of model Wittman is using is more clearly dependent on the assumption that candidates are both willing and able to shift their issue positions during the campaign some distance, regardless of what position they may have taken in the past or promised to various pressure groups; this seems to imply that candidates have no political history, no ties to sponsors or a party with an issue position, and no political preferences other than to maximize the votes in their favor. Surely, Wittman is more realistic and less cynical than is implied by this assumption.

For all that, I agree with his conclusion that campaign finance limits would be welfare-reducing, but that is a much more complicated story.

PART IV

What Have we Learned about the Theory and
Practice of Public Finance from Three Decades
of Empirical Research on Public Choice?

8. Interest groups, redistribution and the size of government

Dennis C. Mueller

One of the noticeable differences between the USA and Western Europe is the greater amount of and emphasis placed upon redistribution in Europe. Transfers are the single biggest item in most European countries' government budgets, even exceeding *all* of government consumption. It is largely the size of government transfers which explains why the government sector is so much larger in most European countries than in the USA.

Since the USA and all West European countries are democracies, an explanation for these dramatic differences must be found in the political process. Democratic politics in Europe simply results in greater amounts of governmentally driven redistribution. Why?

One possible answer is that Americans are more mean spirited than Europeans. Well-to-do Americans are more willing to see their neighbors living in poverty, more willing to allow their fellow workers to suffer when they become unemployed, more willing to see their parents slide into indigence when they enter old age. University students in Europe seem particularly quick to offer these sorts of explanations for why the public sector is so much larger in Europe than in the USA, but similar utterances are often also heard from European politicians as they defend the size of their welfare states. This explanation for the greater size of government in Europe presumes that European citizens – implicitly all European citizens – demand more redistribution from their governments.

Public choice scholars have offered a second explanation for differences in the size of government sectors across countries which is less benign. Government transfers do not come about to satisfy the will of *all* the people, but only of some of them – those who are members of well-organized and powerful interest groups. This explanation for the differences in the size of government between the USA and Europe would imply that interest groups are better organized and more powerful in the latter than in the former.

In this chapter I shall examine some of the implications of these two explanations for differences in the size of government sectors, and some of the empirical evidence that bears on these explanations. I begin with the essentially normative argument that governmental redistribution programs arise because of citizens' concern about their neighbors.

1.   NORMATIVE ARGUMENTS FOR REDISTRIBUTION

A normative *raison d'être* for the state commonly invoked by public finance and public choice scholars is that the state exists to provide goods and services to its citizens that they cannot obtain in Pareto-optimal quantities without the state. Any state-provided good or service must, therefore, have the potential of making *all* citizens better off. By implication any state redistribution programs must have the potential of making all citizens better off. In this section we discuss three such normative arguments that have been put forward to justify state redistribution programs.

1.1   Redistribution as Altruism

Our normative criterion is that the state should undertake only those activities that benefit all citizens. Redistribution from one group, say the *R*s, to another called the *P*s is consistent with this normative criterion only if the *R*s also benefit from the redistribution. One way in which this might come about is that the *R*s get utility out of seeing the *P*s made better off, and are willing to have their own incomes reduced to bring this about. This sort of *Pareto-optimal redistribution* is quite plausible if the *R*s are richer than the *P*s, and have altruistic preference functions (Hochman and Rodgers, 1969).

Let U_R be the utility of an R, $U_R = U_R (Y_R, Y_P)$ where Y_R and Y_P are the incomes of an R and a P, and U_P be the utility of a P, $U_P = U_P (Y_P)$. An R experiences a utility gain from seeing P have a higher income, and can bring this about by transferring a sum, T, to P. R's optimization problem is then to maximize

$$U_R = U_R (Y_R - T, Y_P + T) \qquad (8.1)$$

with respect to T, which yields as a first-order condition

$$\partial U_R / \partial Y_R = \partial U_R / \partial Y_P \qquad (8.2)$$

The rich transfer money to the poor until the marginal utility that a rich person gets from keeping an extra dollar just equals the utility she gets from giving it to the poor.

One obvious question to ask is why the state must intervene to bring about these transfers. Why cannot the rich simply give money to the poor without the state? The usual answer given to this question is that a rich person does not want to see just one poor person made better off, but rather all poor persons. To accomplish this all rich persons must give to the poor, and a potential free-rider problem arises. State intervention is needed to solve this free-rider problem.

It is reasonable to assume that a rich person gets more utility from giving to someone whose income is one-tenth of the rich person's income than to someone with half of her income. Giving to the poorest person in the community provides a rich person with the highest utility. These considerations lead to the following two predictions with respect to state-induced redistribution for altruistic purposes: (1) both the rich and the poor benefit from and support such redistribution; and (2) transfers are first targeted to the lowest-income people in the community. When their incomes have been raised to that of the second-poorest group, transfers are made to both bottom-level groups and so on until a level of income below that of the rich is reached such that eq. 8.2 is satisfied.[1]

1.2 Redistribution as Social Insurance

All insurance programs involve redistribution of one form or another. Individuals voluntarily enter such programs to avoid certain risks. When they do, they (unanimously) agree to engage in *ex post* redistribution. All purchasers of fire insurance agree to a redistribution from those who do not have fires to those who do.

Although the market is capable of providing many sorts of insurance – like that against fires – optimally, in some cases there may be market failures of one sort or another that justify state provision of the insurance. For example, if it were possible while we were still ensconced in the womb to purchase insurance against our having future physical or mental handicaps that would cause us to be poor, we might all voluntarily sign the insurance contract. Such contracts are as yet infeasible, however, and by the time we are able to join such contracts our physical or mental handicaps are often already apparent, and those who need the insurance most cannot acquire it. Thus state-run involuntary programs of redistribution can be justified on market failure grounds.

Rawls (1971) argued that every adult *ought* to undertake the *Gedankenexperiment* of pretending he might be rich or poor, and that the proper amount of redistribution in a society would be that amount that was unanimously agreed to behind such a veil of ignorance. Thus we can again justify some forms of state-provided rich-to-poor redistribution as being consistent with the criterion that everyone is made better off by them. In addition to using income as a criterion for whether a person is badly off or not, we might also think of using other criteria. Blindness or other physical handicaps, mental deficiencies, sickness and unemployment are all obvious candidates. As with redistribution as altruism, redistribution as social insurance leads to the prediction that the recipients of state transfers are disadvantaged in some way.

2.   REDISTRIBUTION IN PRACTICE

These normative arguments for state-sponsored redistribution are quite compelling. Unfortunately the patterns of redistribution observed in most countries do not correspond to those that these theories predict.

As a first example consider Table 8.1. It presents a summary of the major components of the EU's budget in 1985 and 1995. Almost 90 percent of the EU budget in 1985 went into redistribution programs, almost 80 percent in 1995. In both of these years and in every other year in the EU's history, the largest single item in its budget has been transfers to the agricultural sector. Neither normative theory of redistribution discussed in the previous section can account for this phenomenon. Farmers are not poor. Indeed, the average income of a farmer in the EU is slightly *above* that of the average taxpayer, and a disproportionate share of EU transfers go to the richest farmers (Koester and Tangermann, 1990). Nor can one defend state subsidies to farmers using a social insurance argument. No blue- or white-collar worker in Europe goes to bed each night wondering whether he will awake the next morning as a sugar beet farmer. If someone were to step behind Rawls's veil of ignorance and contemplate what a just distribution of income in a

Table 8.1   Distribution of European Union expenditures by budget category, 1985 and 1995 (percentages)

		1985	1995
Redistribution	Agriculture and fisheries	72.9	53.6
	Regional policy	5.9	13.6
	Social policy	5.7	11.9
Allocative	Research, energy, transport	2.6	5.6
efficiency	External policies	–	6.2
	Administrative costs	4.6	5.1
	Miscellaneous	4.4	4.5

Source: Goodman (1996), pp. 101, 105–6.

society should look like, it is difficult to imagine why she would single out farmers as the worst-off people in society. Farmers are not in any obvious way disadvantaged.

As a second example consider Table 8.2. It presents figures from the US federal budget for transfers in 1995. Over 90 percent of these transfers go into insurance-like programs, over 50 percent go to retirees. Once again it is not possible to rationalize such transfers using either of the two normative theories for redistribution presented above. Every retiree is not poor and every person working and paying social security taxes is not rich. A McDonald's worker in the year 2020 is unlikely to get any utility out of contributing to Bill Gates's retirement income. The theory of Pareto-optimal redistribution cannot be used to defend the kinds of redistribution that we observe in a typical pay-as-you-go pension system as in the USA, where wage income is taxed and the beneficiaries are identified by age and not by income. The same can be said of those programs that finance social security out of general tax revenue, where the payee is the average taxpayer. Insurance against the risk of growing old must be purchased during an individual's working life, and all of us have the opportunity to buy such forms of insurance. The only exceptions to this occur

Table 8.2   Federal transfer payments in the USA, 1995 (millions of dollars)

	Expenditures	As a percentage of all transfers	As a percentage of total budget
1. Insurance-like programs, total		630 316	90.4	38.7
a. Retirement	357 286	51.2	
b. Disability	49 430	7.9	
c. Unemployment	21 576	3.1	
d. Medicare	180 214	25.8	
e. Veterans' insurance programs	21 810	3.1	
2. Noninsurance transfers		67 271	9.6	4.1
a. Welfare and social services	47 120	6.8	
b. Other	17 981	2.6	
c. Veterans	1 412		
d. Housing	87	< 0.1	
e. Agriculture	90	< 0.1	
f. Labor training	581	0.1	
3. Total transfers net of interest payments		697 587	100.0	42.8
4. Total Federal Budget		1 628 419		100.0

Source: Survey of Current Business, October 1998, Tables 3.16 and 3.17.

when someone during her working life is too poor to purchase retirement annuities. This situation calls for rich-to-poor redistribution, however, not young-to-old. If a society undertakes the proper amount of redistribution to the poor, as justified, say, by Rawlsian-type arguments, there is no reason why the state has to intervene to provide old age insurance.[2] Indeed, if someone at the age of 20 was to engage in a Rawlsian experiment of imagining that she might live to be 80 or live to be 60, she would quite likely decide that it is the person who will die at 60 who is the most disadvantaged of the two. Were it feasible, she would favor taxing the person who will live to 80 during his working life and subsidizing the person who will die at 60 to compensate her for missing out on 20 years.[3] She would *never* favor taxing both persons throughout their working lives and then giving all of the money to the lucky one who lives to be 80, as to some extent happens with state-run pension schemes.

We conclude that it is not possible to rationalize the biggest item in the EU budget and the biggest component of government transfers in the USA using the two normative arguments for redistribution presented above. Farmers do quite handsomely in the USA also, of course, and the elderly are well taken care of in Europe. (In Austria they receive 15 percent of GDP.) Before turning to a *positive* account of why this is so, we shall pause to consider one additional quasi-normative justification.

3.　REDISTRIBUTION AS A MERIT GOOD

In an ideal, individualistic society, the state would redistribute income and wealth from the rich to the poor to an optimal degree and each individual would decide how much to consume during each year of her working life, and how much to save and invest to protect against the possibility that she lives to a ripe old age. Each individual would choose her own lifetime consumption plan based on her own, personal rate of time-preference, expectations about her life expectancy, and so on. A heavy smoker might discount the likelihood that she lives to a ripe old age and consume more during her working lifetime than, say, a non-smoker who jogs every day.

State-provided old age insurance is sometimes justified in such a society by invoking the kind of merit good (wants) argument that Richard Musgrave (1959, pp. 13–14) first developed. Individuals are myopic and irrational and do not make the *optimal* choices about how much to save for their retirement. The state must make these decisions for them.

This justification of state-provided old age insurance is inherently élitist, and thus abandons the kind of *normative* individualism premise upon which the other two justifications for state-provided redistribution rest. Some political élite knows how much each citizen should save during her working life and consume in retirement, and it relieves the citizen of the responsibility of having to make these choices.

Such élitism is not only difficult to reconcile with the kind of normative individualism that underlies much normative theorizing in public choice;[4] its premises run counter to much *positive* analysis in public choice. Behind the state in a democracy stand the citizens, the same group of myopic creatures who fail to save the proper amounts for their retirement. A merit–want defense of state pension systems assumes that the individual *qua* saver and investor is myopic and irrational, but as citizen/voter is far-sighted and rational. The citizen/voter invests more time and energy to decide what the proper consumption pattern should be for society than she does for herself. Such an assumption clearly contradicts the proposition that voters are rationally ignorant, and would not seem to have much empirical justification.[5]

An alternative defense of state-provided old age insurance might be to argue that voters are not better informed or less myopic than the average person in a society, but that they somehow choose representatives that have these characteristics. This defense is also problematic, however, since most work in public choice suggests that elected politicians' time horizons do not extend much beyond the next election, and that voters' memories do not go further back than the last election.[6]

We conclude that it is not possible to obtain a justification for state-provided old age insurance that is consistent with the normative criterion that the state should adopt programs that advance the welfare of all citizens, and that these citizens are rational, utility maximizers.[7] The same arguments hold a fortiori for transfers to farmers and other groups. We turn now therefore to a positive analysis of state-provided redistribution.

4.   INTEREST GROUPS AND GOVERNMENT TRANSFERS

If we cannot account for major redistribution programs as voluntary giving that could even come about under a unanimity rule, then we must explain them as involuntary taking that comes about because countries employ the simple majority rule. In Austria one out of every four citizens has retired. Many of the remaining three-fourths are ineligible to vote (for example children). Of those that are eligible to vote, pensioners have the highest turnout percentages of any age group. If pensioners are not already a majority of those who vote, they soon will be.

Pensioners are able to bring about involuntary taking under the simple majority rule merely because of their sheer numbers. Smaller interest groups must resort to other tactics. French farmers are fond of blocking all of the major highways until the government caves in, but most interest groups employ subtler tactics, like lobbying and contributing to the campaigns of individual candidates and parties. A large literature now exists examining this sort of political behavior.[8] It establishes unequivocally that *money buys votes*.

It does so in two senses. First, the campaign contributions of interest groups influence how Congressmen vote. A contribution from a farm group increases the probability that the recipient Congressman votes for the legislation favoring this group. A contribution from a labor union increases the probability that the recipient Congressman votes for a higher minimum wage. Congressmen's votes can be bought.[9]

The second way in which money buys votes is that when a Congressman turns around and spends the contributions from interest groups, they increase the probability of his being re-elected. Table 8.3 summarizes the main findings of 23 studies with respect to the efficacy of campaign spending. Seldom does the empirical literature produce such consistent findings. With one partial exception, campaign expenditures always increase the probability of a candidate's election in studies of elections outside the USA. Without exception, campaign expenditures increase the probability of a challenger's election in studies of elections inside the USA. The one piece of seemingly contradictory evidence comes from the fact that the coefficient on the incumbents' expenditures is statistically insignificant in some studies. This finding is readily accounted for, however, when one takes into account the investment-like nature of campaign expenditures.

Campaign spending is like the persuasive advertising of certain consumer products in that it builds up a stock of goodwill toward the candidate, which in turn translates into votes on election day (Mueller and Stratmann, 1994). The relationship between votes and campaign spending can be expected to look like that presented in Figure 8.1. At low levels of spending, campaign spending makes a candidate's name known to large numbers of voters, and has a large impact on the probability that they will vote for her. As the candidate and her platform become better known to voters through campaign spending, the increase in votes from additional expenditures declines. Eventually, the candidate is so well known that it is impossible to win any more votes through additional spending. The top of the curve has been reached.

In the USA many challengers for Congressional seats start off as nearly complete unknowns in their districts (states) and thus start near the origin in Figure 8.1. Even those who have some reputation in their districts are likely to be less well known than an incumbent running for re-election. Thus, even a challenger who is fairly successful at raising funds is not likely to reach the top

Table 8.3   *Summary of the main results linking votes for candidates to their campaign expenditures*

(a)

Election	Effect of expenditures by		Study
	Challenger	Incumbent	
US House			
1972	sig.	insig.	Glantz et al. (1976)
1972, 1974	sig.	sig. (1974, OLS)	Jacobson (1978)
1978	sig.	sig., wrong sign	Kau et al.[b] (1982)
1972–82	sig.	insig. (usually)	Jacobson (1985)
1972–90	sig.	insig.	Levitt[c] (1994)
1984	sig.	insig.	Coates (1998)
1980	sig.	insig.	Kau and Rubin[b] (1993)
	Dem.	*Rep.*	
1972	sig.	sig.	Welch (1974, 1981)
1980–86	sig.	sig.d	Snyder (1990)
US Senate			
1972, 1974	sig.	sig. (1972)	Jacobson (1978)
1972–82	sig.	insig. (usually)	Jacobson (1985)
1974–86	sig.	sig.	Abramowitz (1988)
	Dem.	*Rep.*	
1972	sig.	sig.	Welch (1974, 1981)
US Presidential			
1972	sig.	sig.	Nagler and Leighley (1992)

(b)

Election	Effect of expenditures by			Study
	Challenger	Incumbent	Candidate	
Provincial elections				
1966, 1970 Quebec			sig.	Palda[a] (1973, 1975)
1973 Manitoba			sig.	Palda[a] (1975)
California Assembly 1972, 1974	sig.	sig. (1974)		Glantz et al. (1976)
Parliamentary Seats, Scotland and Wales, 1974			mixed	Johnston (1978)
8 Provincial Elections in Canada, 1973–77			sig.	Chapman and Palda (1984)
Canadian Federal Election, 1979 (Ontario)			sig.	Palda and Palda (1985)

Notes:

a Palda (1973, 1975) uses votes for all candidates as dependent variable. Incumbency treated as a dummy variable (significant).

b Kau et al. (1982), and Kau and Rubin (1993) regress winner's margin on winner's and loser's expenditures. Given high success rate of incumbents, I have interpreted their results for winners as pertaining to incumbents.

c Sample restricted to contests in which both candidates faced each other more than once. Coefficient on challenger spending much smaller than in other studies.

d Snyder regresses Democrat's share of vote on Democrat's share of expenditures. Significance of Republican spending inferred from significance of Democrat's spending share.

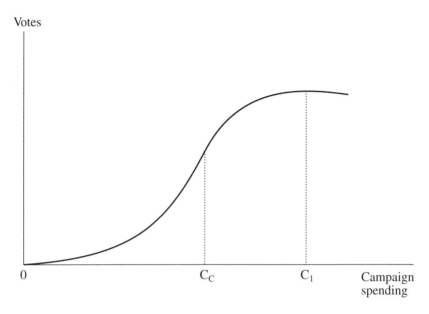

Figure 8.1   Relationship between votes and campaign spending

of the curve in Figure 8.1, but rather some point like C_C. The incumbent, on the other hand, starts the election with a large stock of 'brand recognition' from previous elections, appearances on television and in newspapers during her years in office, mailings to constituents, and so on. Given her high probability of being re-elected, interest groups seeking votes are more likely to give to the incumbent than her challenger. Thus an incumbent can generally outspend her challenger and is quite likely to wind up at the top of the curve in Figure 8.1. This reasoning explains why the estimated slopes of the vote/expenditure lines for challengers are always positive, while for incumbents they are often near zero. Rather than demonstrating that this implies that campaign spending does not help incumbents, it further illustrates its importance.

If members of interest groups are rational actors, they will not contribute to politicians' campaigns unless they expect to get something in return. Rational politicians will not seek donations to their campaigns and spend the donations that they receive unless they believe that they will help them get elected and re-elected. The empirical literature on campaign spending implies that both interest groups and politicians are rational actors. This literature can also explain why certain interest groups are so successful at using the political process to bring about involuntary transfers from the rest of the population to themselves.

5. WHY ARE INTEREST GROUPS IN EUROPE MORE EFFECTIVE THAN IN THE UNITED STATES?

Interest groups exist in Europe and in the USA. Farmers are treated handsomely by European governments; they also do very well in the USA. If interest groups account for a large fraction of the involuntary redistribution that governments undertake, and this redistribution accounts for a significant fraction of the difference in the size of the government sector in the USA and Europe, then it follows that interest groups must be more effective in bringing about involuntary redistribution in the latter than they are in the former. Why might this be so?

Consider an interest group in the USA with a fairly narrowly defined interest, say sugar beet farmers. They can count on the votes of Congressmen and Senators from districts and states where sugar beet farming is important, but these representatives make up a small fraction of the House and Senate. To get a piece of legislation passed that benefits sugar beet farmers and harms the rest of the population, the votes of at least 218 members of the House and 51 Senators are needed and, if the sugar beet farmers want to be sure that the bill is not vetoed, a sympathetic friend in the White House is needed. If this sympathy and these votes are to be won by contributing to the campaigns of the political actors, a great deal of money and organizational muscle is needed. Some interest groups – like the sugar beet farmers – may have what it takes; many will not.

Now consider the situation in a typical European parliamentary democracy. To get a piece of legislation through the parliament an interest group needs the support of the *government*, the party or more often a coalition of parties that effectively selects or supports the cabinet and is capable of passing legislation. The support of at most a few parties is needed. Campaign contributions in Europe go to parties, not to persons. It is most probably the case that an interest group needs to contribute more to a single party in Europe to win its support than an interest group in the USA must contribute to one member of Congress to win her support. It is most certainly the case that an interest group does not have to contribute 50 times as much money to win the votes of a party with 50 seats in the parliament as is needed to win the vote of one member of Congress. Advantage number one for interest groups in Europe is that there are *economies of scale* in winning votes through campaign contributions and other campaign activities.

When a member of the US Congress retires or is defeated in an election, an interest group's investments in that person are effectively wiped out. It must begin anew with one of the candidates from that district in the next election or try to buy the vote of some other member of Congress. Persons can die, retire or suffer defeats in elections; the parties that tend to form governments almost never do.[10] Even when a major party suffers what the newspapers call 'a defeat', it almost always wins enough votes to take seats in the parliament. It lives on to fight another day. Thus a second advantage that interest groups have in Europe is that it is easier for them to form *long-run* linkages to parties than it is for interest groups in America to form long-run relationships with members of Congress.

The proportional representation systems of Western Europe produce both a greater number of parties than exists in the USA, and a greater coverage of the ideological spectrum. Thus it is easy for a European interest group that is either on the right or the left of the ideological spectrum to find a party that comes close to its ideological position. The third advantage that interest groups have in Europe is, therefore, that they are *ideologically closer* to the parties to which they are linked and thus can form closer bonds. The greater importance of ideology in Europe than in the USA is symbolized in the names of parties. The names of the two dominant parties in the USA, Republican and Democratic, reveal nothing about their ideological stance. The names of European parties, on the other hand, often signal their ideological positions – the Conservative Party, the Liberal Party, the Social Democratic Party, the Socialist Party and, of course most vividly, the Communist Party, although this name is somewhat out of vogue now. Some party names in Europe signal direct links to economic interests – the Labour Party, the Farm Party.

For these three reasons we conclude that economic interest groups are more closely linked to political parties in Europe, and thus more effective politically in achieving their goals. Although we believe this to be true across all of Western Europe, it is particularly the case in countries like Austria and Sweden, which have adopted corporatist institutions that formally integrate economic interest groups into the political process, and in which membership in some economic interest group is generally obligatory. In these countries the Olsonian free-rider problem has essentially been solved for economic interest groups.

The two normative theories of redistribution discussed above predict that transfers go from the rich and advantaged to the poor and to those who are disadvantaged in some way. Since all members of society benefit from redistribution of this type, these normative theories can also be treated as positive theories in a democracy. *Some* transfers in every democratic country should be targeted to disadvantaged groups.

Many members of economic interest groups receive transfers or benefit financially in other ways from government programs although they are not disadvantaged. Where economic interest groups are strong, money will flow from the poor to the rich, from one segment of the middle class to another, and so on. The pattern of transfers will reflect the political advantages of different groups, not their economic disadvantages.

Table 8.4 reports the distribution of transfers by income quintile and the average level of transfers as a percentage of median income for 15 countries. Looking first at the last column, we see a great spread of values for the average level of transfers as a percentage of median income, ranging from 7.3 percent of median income in Switzerland to 35.5 percent in Sweden in 1987. Switzerland and the USA are the only two countries with transfer levels that are less than 10 percent of their median incomes. If all redistribution is from the rich to the poor and disadvantaged, then Switzerland and the USA look rather niggardly and mean-spirited in comparison to the 13 other rich countries in the table. If, on the other hand, redistribution largely takes the form of involuntary taking by interest groups rather than voluntary giving by all

Table 8.4   Distribution of transfers by quintile and average transfers as a percentage of median equivalent income

		Bottom	2	3	4	Top	Total	Average transfers as percentage of median equivalent income
Australia	1981	42.8	22.2	13.3	12.5	9.2	100.0	10.8
	1985	40.1	24.6	14.4	12.9	8.0	100.0	11.3
Belgium	1985	22.9	22.5	21.9	16.6	16.1	100.0	33.3
	1988	21.5	23.6	20.1	16.1	18.7	100.0	34.9
Switzerland	1982	38.5	19.2	15.6	13.3	13.3	100.0	7.3
Canada	1981	33.0	22.9	17.9	14.1	12.1	100.0	10.1
	1987	29.5	24.2	19.2	15.0	12.1	100.0	12.4
France	1979	19.7	21.2	18.8	17.7	22.6	100.0	22.2
	1984	17.5	21.8	18.4	17.7	24.7	100.0	25.0
Germany	1984	21.8	22.2	16.7	21.0	18.3	100.0	19.8
Ireland	1987	32.0	21.9	21.3	15.2	9.6	100.0	20.5
Italy	1986	15.6	16.4	19.7	20.7	27.6	100.0	21.4
Luxembourg	1985	17.3	18.3	19.5	22.5	22.4	100.0	23.7
Netherlands	1983	21.8	21.8	18.4	20.4	17.6	100.0	28.5
	1987	24.9	21.3	16.9	17.7	19.2	100.0	28.3
Norway	1979	34.0	20.9	16.4	13.6	15.1	100.0	13.5
Sweden	1981	18.0	23.9	19.8	19.5	18.7	100.0	35.0
	1987	15.2	25.8	21.7	19.9	17.4	100.0	35.5
UK	1979	30.6	20.0	17.4	17.0	15.0	100.0	18.5
	1986	26.7	25.9	19.4	16.1	11.9	100.0	24.3
USA	1979	29.7	21.1	17.4	14.7	17.1	100.0	8.9
	1986	29.2	21.2	17.1	17.5	15.1	100.0	9.4
Finland	1987	25.9	22.6	18.2	15.8	17.6	100.0	27.7

Source: Atkinson et al. (1995), Table 7.5, p. 107.

citizens, then economic interest groups would appear to be much more powerful in countries like Belgium and Sweden than they are in Switzerland and the USA.

Let us look now at the pattern of transfers across the five income categories. The first thing that stands out in Table 8.4 is that *every* income group from the bottom to the top receives a non negligible share of transfers. In only two countries is the share of transfers going to the richest 20 percent of the population less than 10 percent, and then just barely so. In only one country, Australia, does as much as 40 percent of all transfers go to the poorest 20 percent of the population. In France (1984), Italy and Sweden the poorest 20 percent of the population actually received the *smallest* share of the transfers; in France and Italy the largest percentage of all transfers went to the *richest* 20 percent of the population. These patterns clearly do not conform to what we would expect from the two normative theories of redistribution.

Nor do other theories of redistribution find much support in the table. The middle quintile, which presumably contains the median voter in terms of income, never receives the largest share of transfers. A Marxist prediction that the rich take from the poor also fails as a general proposition. Only the interest group hypothesis put forward here seems consistent with the numbers in Table 8.4. In majoritarian democracies economic interest groups at all levels of the income distribution succeed in obtaining transfers. Everyone wins at the redistribution game in a majoritarian democracy; some, however, win more than others.

Although the numbers in Table 8.4 suggest that interest groups are alive and well in all 15 countries, the patterns of transfers come closer to what the normative theories predict in the five countries with the lowest levels of transfers. In all five countries, the bottom quintile receives the highest fraction of transfers, with this fraction being roughly two-fifths in Australia and Switzerland. The bottom two-fifths of the income distribution in these two countries receives roughly 60 percent of all transfers. In Canada, Norway and the USA, over half of the transfers go to the bottom two quintiles. These numbers suggest that interest groups are somewhat less successful in playing the redistribution game in Australia, Canada, Norway, Switzerland and the USA, than they are in the other eight countries in the table.[11]

6.   A PROPOSAL

If the playground pip-squeak asks the playground bully, after the bully has taken the pip-squeak's lunch money from him, 'What right do you have to do that?' and the bully replies, 'Because I'm bigger than you', he will have given an accurate positive explanation for the transfer. Few would regard it as an adequate normative justification, however. By the same token, a transfer of wealth from one group of citizens to another cannot be justified normatively with the argument that the recipients of the transfer were able to form a bigger coalition than the suppliers of the transfer. There are conditions under which the use of the simple majority rule can be justified normatively, but these conditions are *not* satisfied for issues involving pure redistribution.[12] The vast amounts of redistribution that occur in majoritarian democracies as a result of interest group politicking can be *explained* using standard public choice analysis; they cannot be defended by any normative analysis, however.

Suppose one wanted to change things. Suppose one wanted to eliminate, or at least reduce, the amount of redistribution as involuntary taking that takes place in a country, but not the redistribution as voluntary giving, what might one do?

Under the two normative theories of redistribution both the recipients and the payees are willing to vote for the transfers; under involuntary taking most of the recipients can be expected to vote for the transfers; while a large fraction of the payees vote against them. Many redistribution measures that involve only involuntary taking would presumably not succeed without the votes of the takers. With this in mind I make the following proposal for a constitutional amendment, or, where it will suffice, an act of parliament to reduce the amount of redistribution as involuntary taking.

Proposal   Any legislation that involves a direct transfer of income or wealth from one group of citizens to another, or an indirect transfer as through a price ceiling, price floor or some similar device, must be put before the citizens in a national referendum. Only those citizens who will not directly benefit financially from the proposed legislation are allowed to vote in the referendum.

Since the normative theories of redistribution imply that the payees will unanimously support the redistribution, one might in addition require that the transfer legislation receive the support of a super-majority of those voting, as, say, two-thirds. I personally would be happy if the proposal were put into effect and only a mere majority were required to pass it. Even this threshold should be difficult to reach for many forms of redistribution as involuntary taking.[13]

Under the proposal, sugar beet farmers would not be allowed to vote on subsidies, quotas or price supports for sugar beets. Those currently receiving pensions would not be allowed to vote on legislation to extend or increase the payments under the current state pension system. Altruism among those not receiving pensions would undoubtedly result in the current generation of pension recipients still receiving most of, if not all, the payments that they expected. The reweighting of the votes of the young and those active in the labor market that the proposal would bring about would, on the other hand, increase the likelihood that a pay-as-you-go system might be replaced by an intelligently designed fully funded system, which would benefit all future generations of citizens.

One of the likely benefits of the proposal would be to bring involuntary redistribution out into the open. Dairy farmers would have to explain the benefits of higher milk prices for themselves and the rest of the community in trying to win support for them; consumer groups could explain their costs. With full information on the costs and benefits from such programs, citizens might well vote them down. If one believes that democracy is the best form of government, then having decisions made by a better-informed and active citizenry can only improve its outcomes.

Many will regard my proposal as radical and ultra-conservative. It has, however, a liberal pedigree. John Stuart Mill was one of the great thinkers of the nineteenth century. He was perhaps radical, but was no ultra-conservative. He was an early advocate of women's suffrage and favored proportional representation, because he believed that minorities deserved fair representation. Yet Mill felt that it was

> important that the assembly which votes the taxes, either general or local, should be elected exclusively by those who pay something toward the taxes imposed. Those who pay no taxes, disposing by their votes of other people's money, have every motive to be lavish and none to economize. As far as money matters are concerned, any power of voting possessed by them is a violation of the fundamental principle of free government – a severance of the power of control from the interest in its beneficial exercise. It amounts to allowing them to put their hands into other people's pockets for any purpose which they think fit to call a public one ... (Mill, 1865, p. 133)

Most democratic countries did deny those with low incomes or without property the right to vote throughout much of the nineteenth century and in some cases into the twentieth.[14] The US Constitution originally denied US citizens living in the District of Columbia the right to vote for the President, Members of Congress or even representatives to the local government. The logic underlying this provision was a fear that those living in the District would be biased in their views as to the proper scope of and funding for government, since they directly or indirectly obtained their livelihood from it.

My proposal would not target the poor or any other group directly, but would instead prevent *all* interest groups from putting their hands into other people's pockets. As we have seen in Table 8.4, in many countries a disproportionate share of all transfers *does not* go to the very poor. My proposal would force the richest 20 percent of the Italian population to defend why they should receive 27.6 percent of all transfers, and would deny them the possibility of voting for the programs that bring these transfers about. By reducing the amount of redistribution as involuntary taking in a country, the proposal might actually lead to *more* redistribution to the poor, due to the reduction in taxes that accompanies this change and the increase in individual incomes that should result from reducing the deadweight losses that accompany high tax rates.

7. CONCLUSIONS

When the welfare state first came into existence at the end of the nineteenth and beginning of the twentieth centuries, its redistribution programs *were* targeted toward the poor, despite the fact that in many countries the poor had only a limited franchise (Ploug and Kvist, 1997, ch. 2). The theory of Pareto-optimal redistribution can be used to explain why this redistribution took place. Over the course of the twentieth century, the list of recipients of transfers grew along with the size of these transfers. By the end of the twentieth century, almost everyone in some countries was putting their hands in other people's pockets, and having their pockets picked at the same time. My proposal would to some extent put back the clock and limit redistribution to those who are truly deserving because they are poor or disadvantaged in some other way. The USA and Western European countries are much richer than they were 100 years ago; they can afford to be more generous to the poor. But the growth of incomes over the last century has not eliminated scarcity entirely. The high rates of taxation needed to feed huge transfer programs that do not target the poor result in significant deadweight losses that reduce everyone's income.[15] Pay-as-you-go pension systems reduce savings and slow economic growth, thus reducing everyone's income in the long run.[16] In the not-so-long run they threaten to eat up an ever-larger share of national income, and possibly drive out other more worthy social expenditure and transfer programs.

It is worth emphasizing that the gains some interest groups achieve at the expense of the rest of society not only lead to economic inefficiencies; often they also produce significant inequities. And it should also be repeated that benefits for interest groups often come in ways that do not involve direct government subsidies.

French truck drivers got their government to allow them to retire at 55 by blocking all of the major highways in France, thereby bringing auto and truck travel to a standstill. A few years ago, Austrian rail workers went two better. By merely threatening to strike and paralyze the country's rail system, they were able to induce the government to allow them to retire at the age of 53. These interest group victories obviously lower national income by taking people who are able to work out of the workforce prematurely. But they also introduce significant inequities into the state-run retirement system. Shoemakers cannot threaten to bring traffic to a halt; nor can they even make people go barefoot by going on strike. They are powerless compared to truck drivers and rail workers. Shoemakers must work until the mandatory retirement age. Their social security payments help finance the early retirements of those who are politically more powerful, like truck drivers in France and rail workers in Austria, and thus can be viewed as a form of transfer from people who retire at the 'mandatory' retirement age, to those who retire earlier. Neither the inefficiency caused by these early retirements nor their inequity can be discerned from any government statistics on incomes and transfers, however. Once they enter into retirement, the truck drivers and rail workers simply appear as any other retired person enjoying his 'well-deserved and earned' pension.

My proposal would not, of course, prevent Austrian rail workers from striking, if their request for a retirement age of 53 were turned down in a referendum. But it would change the confrontation to one directly involving the citizens who would be hurt by the strike and the rail workers. If a large majority of the citizens thought that the proposed retirement age was unfair, as opinion polls revealed they did, they might be willing to call the rail workers' bluff by rejecting the proposal. A large no vote in a referendum might even give the government the political courage to use whatever means it has at its disposal to end the strike.

Considerable concern has been expressed by political scientists and observers of politics about the dramatic decline in recent years in citizen support for the governments of their countries and for those who serve in these governments. Citizens in the leading democracies favor democracy over other forms of government as much as they ever have, but are disenchanted with those who get elected under the democratic rules operating in their countries.[17] One possible cause for this disenchantment might be that citizens have become unhappy about the scope of government activity in their country and the extent to which this activity serves special interests as opposed to the general interest. Each citizen may be aware that she has her hand in the pockets of other citizens, but that they at the same time have their hands in her pocket. Involuntary taking via the political process is a zero-sum game that all interest groups can play. If the payoffs sum to zero, what is the point in playing the game? Perhaps the growing alienation toward those in government that has been observed in several of the world's leading democracies in recent years has come about because citizens have begun to realize how much of government activity is of a zero-sum nature. In the long run most people's net gains are zero or even negative once the inefficiencies from zero-sum redistribution are factored in, and those who are net winners are not necessarily the most deserving players. Here it is interesting to note the dramatic surge in support for those in government that occurred in the USA after September 11th, 2001. Americans perceived that their government was acting in a way that benefited everyone, and their support for government soared. A reduction of the amount of zero-sum programs in a country might have a similar, although more modest, effect. My proposal would reduce the amount of zero-sum redistribution that goes on in a country, and place control over the redistribution that does take place directly in the hands of the citizens from whom any transfers will flow. Those who vote for redistribution programs must put their hands in their own pockets to pay for them, and all citizens will be able to vote directly against measures that would place other people's hands in their pockets. By reducing the scope for government actions that harm large fractions of the citizenry, the proposal should remove one source of citizen disenchantment. By giving citizens a direct voice in government decisions, the proposal should reduce another source, since each citizen will know that the government redistribution programs that are carried out were not decided by 'them', the politicians, but by 'us, the people'.

NOTES

1. For further discussion and a demonstration of this proposition, see von Furstenberg and Mueller (1971).
2. I do not mean to imply here that the amount of redistribution corresponds to that prescribed by Rawls's difference principle, but rather the amount that rational individuals would select, when uncertain of their future positions including their future incomes. See Mueller (1996, ch. 16).
3. A day may come, and perhaps quite soon, when life expectancies can be accurately predicted by DNA testing, and such forms of redistribution could take place.
4. See, for example, Buchanan and Tullock (1962).
5. The pros and cons of the merit–want justification for state intervention are put forward in a lively series of essays contained in Brennan and Walsh (1990).
6. See, for example, the literature on political business cycles as reviewed by Paldam (1997) and Mueller (2002, ch. 19).
7. For additional discussion and proposals in favor of old age pension systems that are consistent with a principle of *normative individualism*, see Peacock (1997) and Prewo (1997).
8. Most of this literature is concerned with the USA. For a review, see Mueller (2002, ch. 20).
9. See Silberman and Durden (1976), Chappell (1981), Kau et al. (1982), Kau and Rubin (1982, 1993), Peltzman (1984), Frendreis and Waterman (1985), Marks (1993), Stratmann (1991, 1995, 1996), and Kang and Greene (1999).
10. There are, of course, many small parties that enter politics to champion some ideological cause and then depart some time later because their followers have tired of the cause and/or they fail to make some minimum vote cut-off to obtain seats in the parliament. These parties are attached to ideological interest groups, but are not very attractive for the kinds of economic interest groups discussed here, since these parties do not have realistic chances of joining the government.
11. I hasten to add that interest groups can exert their political muscle to benefit their members in other ways than just by securing direct transfers, like minimum wages, agricultural price supports, tax breaks and so on. A full comparison of interest group strengths across countries would need to take these other dimensions of success into account.

12. See May (1952), Rae (1969) and Mueller (2002, ch. 6).
13. Swiss readers of this chapter and those familiar with Switzerland may be surprised by the discussion of the previous paragraph, which seems to imply that interest groups are not politically powerful in this country, given its corporatist institutions. The ability of Swiss citizens to call referenda and reverse government actions that benefit the few at the disadvantage of the many helps protect them against both the actions of their elected representatives and the interest groups that support them, and this helps to explain why Switzerland appears to fall into the weaker interest group category. My proposal is simply to make this happy Swiss institution mandatory for pure redistribution issues. On the important role the referendum plays in Swiss politics, see Kirchgässner et al. (1999).
14. See Ploug and Kvist (1997).
15. On this see Browning (1987).
16. See the various essays in Wise (1997) and Feldstein (1998).
17. See the various essays in Norris (1999).

REFERENCES

Abramowitz, Alan I. (1988), 'Explaining Senate Election Outcomes', *American Political Science Review*, **82**, June, 385–403.

Atkinson, Anthony B., Lee Rainwater and Timothy M. Smeeding (1995), *Income Distribution in OECD Countries*, Paris: OECD.

Brennan, Geoffrey and Cliff Walsh (1990), *Rationality, Individualism and Public Policy*, Canberra: ANUTECH.

Browning, Edgar K. (1987), 'On the Marginal Welfare Cost of Taxation', *American Economic Review*, **77**, March, 11–23.

Buchanan, James M. and Gordon Tullock (1962), *The Calculus of Consent*, Ann Arbor: University of Michigan Press.

Chapman, Randall G. and Kristian S. Palda (1984), 'Assessing the Influence of Campaign Expenditures on Voting Behavior within a Comprehensive Electoral Market Model', *Marketing Science*, **3**, 207–26.

Chappell, Henry W. Jr (1981), 'Campaign Contributions and Voting on the Cargo Preference Bill: A Comparison of Simultaneous Models', *Public Choice*, **36** (2), 301–12.

Coates, Dennis (1998), 'Additional Incumbent Spending Really Can Harm (at Least Some) Incumbents: An Analysis of Vote Share Maximization', *Public Choice*, **95**, April, 63–87.

Feldstein, Martin (ed.) (1998), *Privatizing Social Security*, Chicago: University of Chicago Press, 215-60.

Frendreis, John P. and Richard W. Waterman (1985), 'PAC Contributions and Legislative Behavior: Senate Voting on Trucking Deregulation', *Social Science Quarterly*, **66**, 401–12.

Furstenberg, George M. and Dennis C. Mueller (1971), 'The Pareto Optimal Approach to Income Redistribution: A Fiscal Application,' *American Economic Review*, **LXI**, September, 628–37.

Glantz, Stanton A., Alan I. Abramowitz and Michael P. Burkar (1976), 'Election Outcomes: Whose Money Matters?', *Journal of Politics*, **38**, November, 1033–8.

Goodman, S.F. (1996), *The European Union*, 3rd edn, London: Macmillan.

Hochman, Harold M. and James D. Rodgers (1969), 'Pareto Optimal Redistribution', *American Economic Review*, **59**, September, 542–57.

Jacobson, Gary C. (1978), 'The Effect of Campaign Spending in Congressional Elections,' *American Political Science Review*, **72**, June, 469-91.

Jacobson, Gary C. (1985), 'Money and Votes Reconsidered: Congressional Elections, 1972-1982,' *Public Choice*, **47** (1), 7-62.

Johnston, R.J. (1978), 'Campaign Spending and Votes: A Reconsideration,' *Public Choice*, **33**(3), pp. 83-92.

Kang, In-Bong and Kenneth Greene (1999), 'A Political Economic Analysis of Congressional Voting Patterns on NAFTA', *Public Choice*, **98**, March, 385-97.

Kau, James B. and Paul H. Rubin (1982), *Congressmen, Constituents, and Contributors*, Boston: Martinus Nijhoff.

Kau, James B. and Paul H. Rubin (1993), 'Ideology, Voting, and Shirking', *Public Choice*, **76**, June, 151-72.

Kau, James B., D. Keenan and Paul H. Rubin (1982), 'A General Equilibrium Model of Congressional Voting,' *Quarterly Journal of Economics*, **97**, May, 271-93.

Kirchgässner, Gebhard, Lars P. Feld and Marcel R. Savoiz (1999), *Die direkte Demokratie*, Basel: Helbing und Lichtenhahn/Vahlen.

Koester, Ulrich and Stefan Tangermann (1990), 'The European Community', in F.H. Sanderson (ed.), *Agricultural Protectionism in the Industrial World*, Washington, DC: Resources for the Future, pp. 64-111.

Levitt, Steven D. (1994), 'Using Repeat Challengers to Estimate the Effect of Campaign Spending on Election Outcomes in the U.S. House', *Journal of Political Economy*, **102**, August, 777-98.

Marks, Stephen V. (1993), 'Economic Interests and Voting on the Omnibus Trade Bill of 1987', *Public Choice*, **75**, January, 21-42.

May, Kenneth O. (1952), 'A Set of Independent, Necessary and Sufficient Conditions for Simple Majority Decision', *Econometrica*, **20**, October, 680-84.

Mill, John Stuart (1865) [1958], *Considerations on Representative Government*, Indianapolis: Bobbs-Merrill.

Mueller, Dennis C. (1996), *Constitutional Democracy*, New York: Oxford University Press.

Mueller, Dennis C. (2002), *Public Choice III*, Cambridge: Cambridge University Press.

Mueller, Dennis C. and Thomas Stratmann (1994), 'Informative and Persuasive Campaigning,' *Public Choice*, **81**, 55-77.

Musgrave, Richard A. (1959), *The Theory of Public Finance*, New York: McGraw-Hill.

Nagler, Jonathan and Jan Leighley (1992), 'Presidential Campaign Expenditures: Evidence on Allocations and Effects', *Public Choice*, **73**, April, 319-33.

Norris, Pippa (ed.) (1999), *Critical Citizens*, New York: Oxford University Press.

Palda, Filip and Kristian Palda (1985), 'Ceilings on Campaign Spending: Hypothesis and Partial Test with Canadian Data,' *Public Choice*, **45** (3), 313-31.

Palda, Kristian S. (1973), 'Does Advertising Influence Votes? An Analysis of the 1966 and 1970 Quebec Elections', *Canadian Journal of Political Science*, **6**, December, 638-55.

Palda, Kristian S. (1975), 'The Effect of Expenditure on Political Success', *Journal of Law and Economics*, **18**, December, 745-71.

Paldam, Martin (1997), 'Political Business Cycles', in D.C. Mueller (ed.), *Perspectives on Public Choice*, Cambridge: Cambridge University Press, pp. 342-70.

Peacock, Alan (1997), 'The Future Scope for Self-Reliance and Private Insurance', in H. Giersch (ed.), *Reforming the Welfare State*, Berlin: Springer, pp. 91-108.

Peltzman, Sam (1984), 'Constituent Interest and Congressional Voting,' *Journal of Law and Economics*, **27**, April, 181–210.

Ploug, Niels and Ion Kvist (1997), *Social Security in Europe: Development or Dismantlement?*, The Hague: Kluwer Law International.

Prewo, Wilfried (1997), 'From Welfare State to Social State: Individual Responsibility and Compassion', in H. Giersch (ed.), *Reforming the Welfare State*, Berlin: Springer, 295–309.

Rae, Douglas W. (1969), 'Decision-Rules and Individual Values in Constitutional Choice', *American Political Science Review*, **63**, March, 40–56.

Rawls, John A. (1971), *A Theory of Justice*, Cambridge, MA: Belknap Press.

Silberman, Jonathan I. and Garey C. Durden (1976), 'Determining Legislative Preferences on the Minimum Approach', *Journal of Political Economy*, **84**, April, 317–29.

Snyder, James M. Jr (1990), 'Campaign Contributions as Investments: The US House of Representatives 1980–86', *Journal of Political Economy*, **98**, 1195–227.

Stratmann, Thomas (1991), 'What Do Campaign Contributions Buy? Causal Effects of Money and Votes', *Southern Economic Journal*, **57**, January, 606–20.

Stratmann, Thomas (1995), 'Campaign Contributions and Congressional Voting: Does the Timing of Contributions Matter?', *Review of Economics and Statistics*, **77**, February, 127–36.

Stratmann, Thomas (1996), 'How Reelection Constituencies Matter: Evidence from Political Action Committees' Contributions and Congressional Voting', *Journal of Law and Economics*, **39**, October, 603–35.

Welch, William P. (1974), 'The Economics of Campaign Funds,' *Public Choice*, **20**, 83–97.

Welch, William P. (1981), 'Money and Votes: A Simultaneous Equation Model', *Public Choice*, **36** (2), 209–34.

Wise, David A. (ed.) (1997), *Frontiers in the Economics of Aging*, Chicago: University of Chicago Press, pp. 125–72.

9. The effects of fiscal institutions on public finance: a survey of the empirical evidence

Gebhard Kirchgässner[*]

1. INTRODUCTION

Public choice and especially the economic theory of politics was one of the starting points of the 'New Institutional Economics'. In the beginning, there were two almost contradictory results: in 1948, Duncan Black showed in his paper 'On the Rationale of Group Decision-Making' that with single-peaked preferences the political outcome corresponds to the median voter's preferences, while three years later Kenneth Arrow (1951) proved in his *Social Choice and Individual Values* that there is no political decision mechanism based on ordinal comparisons of the citizens and in addition generally allows aggregation of individual preferences so that the social welfare function satisfies some very simple and plausible democratic and rationality conditions. About ten years later, James M. Buchanan and Gordon Tullock (1962) started with their *Calculus of Consent* what later became 'Constitutional Economics', an economic theory of perhaps the most important formal institutions.

Though it was clear from the beginning that institutions matter, it took quite some time before empirical research was launched that investigated how much they matter. In general, despite the fact that Downs (1957) developed testable hypotheses in his *Economic Theory of Democracy*, during the first two decades of the development of public choice, theoretical work was strongly emphasized, and even today the theoretical work still dominates. Even worse, public choice theorists have been accused by (more traditional) political scientists of ignoring the empirical evidence which is available from other parts of the social sciences and contradicts the theoretical insights of public choice.[1]

The empirical work which is relevant for public finance started from two quite different points. One line of research, starting with Borcherding and Deacon (1972) as well as Bergstrom and Goodman (1973), has taken the

*I thank Lars P. Feld (University of Marburg) for very helpful comments and suggestions.

median voter model as a new basis for explaining the size and development of public expenditure.[2] This has, however, mainly been done in the context of representative democracies. It has been questioned whether this model is really applicable to such systems because it presupposes a direct democracy,[3] and Pommerehne (1978) had already shown in a comparison of Swiss local communities that it is better suited to explain the development of public expenditure in direct compared to (purely) representative democracies.[4] This, however, did not impede its popularity in empirical (and theoretical) research, a development which might be justified in situations of 'divided government', that is, where voters have two independent decisions which have an impact on the political outcome as, for example, in the USA the elections for the president and the Congress or, in Germany, the decisions about the two different chambers of the national parliament. In such situations voters can – and often do – split their vote and – in this way – force the government (parliament) to correct policy outcomes towards the median voter's position.[5]

As long as the median voter model was just employed as a theoretical basis to model fiscal behaviour, institutional factors played at best a secondary role. This changed in the last decade, in which a literature evolved which not only asked whether this model could also be applied to a representative democracy but which explicitly searched for the differences between purely representative democratic systems and democratic systems which have – besides the institutions of the representative democracy – direct political rights of the citizens. Such investigations have been undertaken for the USA and Switzerland.[6] But direct popular rights are not the only characteristic of the political system which shape the institutions of budgetary processes. Another very important one is whether the fiscal system of a country has a federal structure or not.

The second line, particularly following the attack of Buchanan on Keynesian deficit spending policy[7] has been investigating whether (constitutional) balanced budget rules really have an effect on the size of the government and/or the public deficit and debt. The fact that the public deficit and the (rising) public debt were one of the major concerns of this literature can on the one hand be explained by the rising public debt following the acceptance of Keynesian policy prescriptions in the 1950s and 1960s. On the other hand there was (and still is) a strong political belief that a large deficit indicates a mis-functioning of the political system. The share of the government may be high, but as long as the citizens are willing to pay the corresponding taxes there is no reason to be concerned about this.[8] If, however, government spending exceeds tax revenue in the long run, there might be some kind of tax illusion which can be exploited by a Leviathan government. In such a situation it would make sense to search for (constitutional) constraints to tame Leviathan.[9]

However, as will be discussed below, constitutional constraints did not – at least at the beginning – seem to be particularly effective. This was the casual experience, for example, of the Gramm–Rudman–Hollings Act in the USA, but it also showed up in analyses at the state level. Thus people began looking for other institutions which could help to limit the public deficit and – in this way – in the long run also public debt. Such institutions might be included into the budgetary process. It was especially von Hagen who took up this question and showed that budgetary procedures as, for example, the position of the minister of finance or the transparency of the budget, can have a major impact on fiscal performance too.[10]

This chapter is a survey of what we know today from empirical research about the effects of such fiscal institutions. Thus we do not survey the theoretical approaches; neither do we consider other institutions like electoral systems or the differences between presidential and parliamentary systems, even though these can also have (and at least in some cases actually do have) effects on the public budget.[11] We start with a discussion of (constitutional) rules to limit the budget deficit (Section 2). In Section 3 budgetary procedures are considered. Then we ask what is the impact of direct popular rights on the budgetary process (Section 4) and the effect of a federal fiscal structure on the size of the public sector (Section 5). We conclude with a summary and point to some of the interdependencies between the different fiscal institutions (Section 6).

2. RULES TO LIMIT THE PUBLIC DEFICIT

As the recent survey of Poterba (1997) shows, there are not many empirical studies about the effects of constitutional and/or statutory rules which are intended to reduce expenditure and/or the deficit.[12] With one exception of a study on Switzerland, all others are for the USA, some of them for the federal level and the others for the state or local levels.

At the federal level, there are countries which have constitutional restrictions, but with different strength and effects. In Germany, for example, Artikel 115 (1) of the Grundgesetz requires that, except for major macroeconomic distortions, federal net lending must not be higher than investment expenditure on the federal level. This has, however, prevented neither the federal deficit nor the federal debt from rising sharply since the mid-1970s.[13] In the USA, the Gramm–Rudman–Hollings (GRH) Act was enacted in 1985. As early as July 1986 this Act was declared unconstitutional by the US Supreme Court. In 1990, the Budget Enforcement Act (BEA) was passed. The impact of these institutions is not clear. In Switzerland, a similar constitutional amendment, the 'Schuldenbremse' (debt brake), has been accepted by the people in the popular referendum of 2 December 2001.

There are some studies which analyse the US situation at the federal level.[14] According to Gramlich (1990), 'the fact that GRH was instituted just as primary deficits were dropping seems largely incidental – defence spending had lost its political constituency anyway, non-defence spending was drifting down anyway, and taxes were going up anyway. Budget bargaining, or any changes in the process due to GRH, seemed to have little to do with the improvement' (p. 80). Though the results of Hahm et al. (1992) and Reischauer (1990) are somewhat different, the evidence does at least not speak strongly for the effectiveness of GRH. This is somewhat different with BEA, but, as Poterba (1997, p. 71) correctly notes, there might be an endogeneity problem: 'The passage of GRH and later BEA may signal shifting voter preferences, as reflected in the political process. ... If so, then the budget outcomes observed since the enactment of these reforms may not be due to these laws per se but may reflect changing fiscal tastes more generally'. This case is – given the data that are available – observationally equivalent to a situation where these laws really had an effect. Thus, due to this simultaneity problem, it is impossible to distinguish between these two hypotheses.

The natural consequence in such a situation is to look for data samples with more variation, that is, to shift attention from the national to the state and local levels. Some of the first studies to proceed in this way also had no significant impact,[15] while the later studies mostly present positive evidence. One of the first studies which did have a significant impact is Nelson (1986). Using data for the states and the fiscal year 1976/77, he finds a significant effect of borrowing limitations on taxes per capita and (but only at the 10 percent level) on taxes as percentage of personal income. He does not, however, somewhat surprisingly, find a significant impact of tax limitations in his data.

Elder (1992) looks at the effects of state tax and expenditure limitation laws. He uses data from 17 states over the period from 1950 to 1985 which have imposed limitation laws between 1977 and 1982. He does not find a significant effect for the limitation itself, which is measured by a dummy variable equal to one for the period during which the limitation law is in force, but he finds a negative significant effect for the interaction between the limitation variable and real income on state tax revenue, which implies 'that the effective tax rate has fallen by approximately 16 percent compared to the pre-limitation period' (p. 57). On the other hand, while federal transfers had a negative impact on state tax revenue in the pre-limitation period, this effect vanishes in the post-limitation period. Splitting the dummy variable between expenditure and revenue limitations, Elder (1992) finds that only expenditure limits have a significant impact. But according to him this does not necessarily mean that revenue limitations are ineffective; this result might be due to the fact that the four states in his sample which used such limitations did so in an inefficient way.

Using three different measures of fiscal restrictions, Eichengreen (1994) investigates in a panel of the US states and for the years 1985 to 1989 the effect of deficit restrictions on the size of deficits. He finds a significant negative impact on the deficit if a dummy variable is used as indicator for the fiscal restraint which is equal to 1.0 for states prohibited from carrying over a deficit into the next fiscal year or which is equal to 1.0 for states whose governors must sign a balanced budget by statutory or constitutional law (and zero otherwise). In reporting these results, Eichengreen and Bayoumi (1994, p. 786) argue that 'these results uniformly suggest that fiscal restraints affect the size of budget deficits'.

Poterba (1994) asks how states with and without a balanced budget rule react to adverse shocks. He shows that 'states with relatively tight constitutional or statutory rules that make it more difficult to run deficits experience more rapid fiscal adjustments when revenues fall short of expectations or spending exceeds projections' (p. 818).

Using a panel of 49 US states and annual data from 1961 to 1990, Kiewiet and Szakaly (1996) test constitutional limitations on borrowing. They find that revenue-based limitations have no effect at all, but states that prohibit guaranteed debt have less borrowing than if a super-majority of the legislature is required to issue new guaranteed debt. Moreover, the change from a prohibition to demanding only a super-majority for the issue of new guaranteed debt has a highly significant impact. On the other hand, despite the fact that it is not significant in the equation for non-guaranteed debt, it seems to have a positive impact on total state debt. Thus the results reported by these two authors are not consistent.

The most comprehensive study has, up to now, been performed by Bohn and Inman (1996). They use data from 50 states for the period from 1970 to 1991. Their analysis

> leads to four main conclusions: First, balanced-budget constraints that apply to an audited, end-of-year fiscal balance are significantly more effective than constraints requiring only a beginning-of-the-year balance. Second, all state balanced-budget rules are ultimately enforced by a state's supreme court. Those states whose supreme courts are directly elected by citizens have 'stronger' constraints (which lead to larger average surpluses) compared to those states whose supreme court justices are political appointments of the governor or legislature. Third, there is tentative evidence that constraints grounded in the state's constitution are more effective than constraints based upon statutory provisions. Fourth, and finally, budget surpluses in strong balance-rule states are slightly less responsive to cyclical swings in income and unemployment than are surpluses in states with weak requirements. (Ibid., p. 64)

The idea of Poterba (1994, 1995) that tax and expenditure limits are endogenous, that is, that those states of local communities adopt it where voters have a preference for – compared to other states – lower public expenditure and revenue, has been taken up by Shadbegian (1998). Using a panel of local expenditure and revenue data aggregated to the state level over the period from 1972 to 1992, he presents statistical evidence for the endogeneity assumption, and he shows that if this is taken into account one finds in most cases a significant effect of tax and expenditure limitations on the size as well as on the growth of local expenditure and revenue, and on property taxes. Using data for 2955 counties in five-year intervals from 1962 to 1987, Shadbegian (1999a) shows that such limitations induce local governments to shift the revenue structure away from taxes towards other revenue sources. Distinguishing between local governments who face less and those who face more stringent limitation laws, he shows that in the former group this shifting leads to an increase of the revenue from these sources, but only half of the loss of tax revenue is compensated for in this way. For the latter group no such compensation is observed.

The most recent study is by Bails and Tieslau (2000). They use data from 49 states observed at five-year intervals from 1964 to 1994. In their model, expenditure limits, a balanced budget rule in combination with expenditure limits, and a balanced budget rule together with a super-majority requirement for tax increases have a significant negative impact on public expenditure, while neither the balanced budget rule itself nor the super-majority requirement itself nor the line-item veto power has a significant impact.

Another aspect has been considered by Poterba and Rueben (1999). Using a panel of 40 US states over the period from 1973 to 1995, they investigate the effect of state fiscal institutions on state bond yields. According to their estimates, lax anti-deficit rules have a positive, and limits on issuing debt a negative, impact on state bond yields, but neither effect is significant. On the other hand, binding expenditure limits have a significant negative, and binding revenue limits a significant positive, impact on the bond yield.[16]

The effectiveness of fiscal restraints can also be investigated in the Swiss case. While nearly all cantons have constitutional fiscal restraints that demand them to balance their budgets over time in one way or another, only five cantons, Appenzell Ausserrhoden, Fribourg, Graubünden, St Gallen and Solothurn, have statutory fiscal requirements.[17] They require the cantons to increase their tax rates if budget deficits increase above a deficit threshold. In Fribourg this requirement is specified such that local taxes are not covered by it, but a bail-out of the cantonal by the local level is highly improbable. In St Gallen and Solothurn, there is an additional restriction on reductions of the tax rates in order to restrict deficit financing. The requirements are less restrictive in Appenzell Ausserrhoden and much less in Graubünden.

Using a panel of the 26 Swiss cantons and the years 1986 to 1997, Feld and Kirchgässner (2001) show that these restraints have a positive effect on cantonal revenue and a negative one on public expenditure, but neither is statistically significant. On the other hand, the sum of both effects is significant: cantons with such restrictions have significantly lower debts and deficits. The deficit per capita, for example in Fribourg, which is the canton with the strongest requirements, is about SFr 275 lower due to this effect. At the local level the negative and positive effects on expenditure and revenue are again statistically not significant, while the effect on the deficit is significant; it shows that in the case of the strongest restriction deficit per capita is about SFr 245 lower.

If one accepts that in many cases balanced budget rules have been effective, the next questions are what were the reactions of the political bodies and what were – besides lower taxes – the results for the citizens. These problems have been investigated in the USA particularly with respect to the consequences of 'Proposition 13' and the other taxpayer revolts. Especially at the local level, the first reaction to the introduction of constitutional constraints was an escape from the (official) budget and/or increased public debt.[18] In a second step, some tasks have been shifted to the states. The states followed a similar strategy: in doing so, they had little success in shifting tasks to the federal level but more in shifting them to the local level. The local communities changed their revenue structure. They used more charges for specific services, which has regressive distributional consequences, or used more grants from the states.[19] Finally, they found extra-budgetary possibilities to finance their services. One example is the 'Mello-Roos-Financing'. If two-thirds of the electorate in a referendum agree, the local communities have the possibility to erect 'Community–Facilities–Districts', which can collect own taxes and issue own debt to finance several local services. While in 1983 only US$10 million was raised in this way, in 1990 this had risen to US$1 billion.[20]

Taking all results together, fiscal restrictions have had a more restrictive impact at the local than at the state level. Moreover, they had more effect in the short than in the long run, because on the one hand it was tried (with mixed success) to shift tasks to other governmental levels and on the other hand to find other revenue sources, especially fees and charges. It is open to question what the net effect of all this was on the fiscal structure. While Matsusaka (1995) and Rueben (1999) see a significant decentralization, Mullins and Joyce (1996) find evidence for some centralization.

The effect of these limitations on the quality of the services which are provided is also interesting. While the pressure exerted by the limitations might increase the efficiency of the public bureaucracy, the quality of the services might deteriorate. Thus, at least in the long run, such limitations are not necessarily beneficial for the citizens.[21] This can be especially relevant for educational expenditures, because on the one hand this is a large part of local expenditure and on the other hand there have been – at least in the short run – severe expenditure cuts in this area. Moreover, this is an area where quality can be measured quite easily by comparing exam results.

The empirical results are again mixed, but point definitely more in the direction of a deterioration in quality. In a first paper, Downes (1992) concludes that the performance of Californian students has even improved between 1976 and 1985, that is, comparing the situation before and after Proposition 13 was passed. Because the test to measure this performance has been changed during this period, however, this result is rather doubtful. In a second study for about 1500 students in Illinois, Downes et al. (1998) also find no significant reduction in the performance of the students, except in mathematics. However, despite its statistical significance, the authors evaluate this deterioration as quantitatively unimportant.

This is contrary to the result of Figlio (1997) in a study of 5600 students from 49 states for the periods 1987/88 and 1990/91. He comes to the conclusion that students in states with tax or expenditure limitations had – *ceteris paribus* – a worse performance in several areas, among others in core subjects like the sciences and (somewhat less significantly) mathematics. These results have been corroborated by Downes and Figlio (1997, 1999). Comparing the performance of students from the years 1972 (8672 observations) and 1992 (6054 observations), it is shown that students in states with tax or expenditure limitations had significantly worse results in mathematics, but not in English. The reason for this deterioration might be, as Figlio (1998) shows in a study for 305 schooling districts in Oregon and 296 schooling districts in Washington, that the ratio between teachers and students worsened after the introduction of the limitations and that the starting salaries of teachers have been reduced, which – according to Figlio and Rueben (2001) – had the consequence that highly qualified teachers did not want to teach in districts with fiscal limitations.

It is, moreover, highly questionable whether the production efficiency of the publicly provided services really increased. Figlio and O'Sullivan (1997) show for 5150 US local communities and the period from 1975 to 1986 that the expenditure on public security, that is, for police and fire brigades, decreased compared to expenditure for general administration. Similar evidence exists for the relation between teachers and administrative staff in schooling districts.

The distributional consequences were more strongly in favour of the lower income groups. Using five income groups, de Tray and Fernandez (1986) show in a study of four cities each in California and New Jersey that while the average tax burden has been reduced, the lower-income groups benefited more than the average while the top income group even had to accept an increase in the tax burden. Chernick and Reschovsky (1982) derive a similar result with respect to the reduced tax burden of the lower income groups in a simulation model for California. O'Sullivan et al. (1994, 1995, 1999) conclude that the results of Proposition 13 favoured especially immobile households. Because households with low income and/or old people are particularly immobile, they benefited most from the tax limitations. This also explains why these initiatives had a relatively high acceptance from lower income groups and old citizens.

Taking all results together, one can conclude that while not all investigated limitations have been effective, at least at the state and local levels most of them have helped to reduce public expenditure and revenue and the budget deficit. Second, there was a partial shift from taxes to user charges. Third, the quality of the public schools has deteriorated as a consequence of the limitations. Fourth, it is open to question whether the efficiency of the public administration really increased. Finally, the tax reductions favoured especially old citizens and lower income groups. How far the lower income groups have really benefited from the whole process remains to be seen, however, because they mostly depend on the public schooling system and therefore suffer most from the deterioration of the quality of the public schooling system.

3. THE FISCAL EFFECT OF BUDGETARY PROCEDURES

In contrast to the conclusions drawn above, von Hagen (1991, 1992) concludes that 'experience with budget norms in the U.S. suggests that governments find ways to circumvent fiscal restraints in practice, with the result that they are largely ineffective'.[22] Therefore, he looks at the problem of limiting public deficits from quite another perspective. He considers the budgetary procedures themselves and analyses whether they have an impact on the level of government expenditure and budget deficits.[23] In doing so, he distinguishes five dimensions: (i) the structure of negotiations within the government, where the focus is on the position of the minister of finance in the cabinet; (ii) the structure of the parliamentary process; (iii) the informativeness of the budget draft; (iv) the flexibility of budget execution; and (v) a long-term planning constraint. In these dimensions he constructs indicators for several sub-dimensions, and then aggregates them to three different versions of a structural index and an index of long-term planning constraint.

He used these indices to explain public deficits and debts in the European Union, using a panel with annual data from 1981 to 1990 of the 12 member countries. In von Hagen (1992) he showed that there is a strong and significant relationship between the budget deficit and public debt on the one hand and his (first) structural index on the other.

> Specifically, our results suggest that a budgeting process that gives the prime or finance (or treasury) minister a position of strategic dominance over the spending ministers, that limits the amendment power of parliament, and that leaves little room for changes in the budget during the execution process is strongly conducive to fiscal discipline, i.e., relatively small deficits and public debt. (Ibid., p. 53f.)[24]

The index of long-term planning constraint, however, did not prove to be statistically significant. Nevertheless, the results indicate that a hierarchical or top-down budgetary procedure may have advantages over a bottom-up procedure.[25]

Similar studies have been performed by de Haan and Sturm (1994), as well as by de Haan et al. (1999). They get a negative coefficient for this index which is, however, significant only at the 10 percent level in their equation explaining the public-debt-to-GDP ratio. Thus they conclude 'that budget institutions affect fiscal policy outcomes, but the effect is quite small' (1999, p. 284).

Using a cross-section for 1990, Feld and Kirchgässner (2001a) test the hypothesis that these institutional aspects of the budgetary process have an impact on public debt for the largest 134 Swiss local communities. However, due to data limitations only three of the five proposed items are available for Swiss municipalities: (i) the structure of negotiations within the government; (ii) the informativeness of the budget draft; and (iii) the long-term planning constraint. On the other hand, due to the large number of observations, it was not necessary to further aggregate the different indices to save degrees of freedom, as von Hagen (1992) had to do. Thus these items are introduced separately. The estimated coefficients of all three indices have the expected negative sign, but only the coefficient of the index of negotiations within the government is statistically significant, and only at the 10 percent level. Further disaggregation into the different sub-dimensions indicated that the only statistically significant impact is due to the agenda-setting power of the mayor or the head of the finance department. If – besides the other economic and political variables this index is the only one which is included in the equation, then its coefficient is significantly different from zero at the conventional 5 percent level.[26]

Latin America was another field of application of this approach. Alesina et al. (1999), who use a sample of almost all Latin American countries, show that more hierarchical and/or transparent procedures lead to lower primary deficits. The same has been found by Stein et al. (1999), who use a cross-section with up to 26 Latin American countries.

Instead of linearly aggregating the different indicators, Lagona and Padovano (2000) perform a non-linear principal component analysis to aggregate them and use the first two components, which account for about 60 per cent of the overall variance in regressions to explain public deficit, debt and expenditure. As dependent variables they use the ten-year averages of the 1980s and 1990s of the 12 EU member countries; that is they have 24 observations.[27] They consider six groups of indicators: (i) the internal organization of government; (ii) the formulation of the budget proposal within the government; (iii) the discussion and approbation of the budget law in the parliament; (iv) the informativeness of the budget law; (v) the flexibility in the implementation of the budget law; and (vi) the stringency of long-term budget documents.

The first principal component captures the groups of procedures of the structure of negotiations within the government, the structure of the parliamentary process, the informativeness of the budget draft and most of the internal organization of the general government. The authors interpret it 'as a measure of rigidity of the rules for elaborating and approving the budget document, from its birth within the cabinet to its legification in the various government levels' (p. 16). The second principal component explains most of the flexibility in the budget execution, it 'characterises the implementation of the budget law by the bureaucracy' (ibid.). The first component has a significant negative impact on public debt and deficits, but a significant positive one on public expenditure. The second principal component also has a significant positive impact on public expenditure, but no significant impact at all in the other equations. Thus stricter budgetary rules seem to go along with smaller public debt and deficits, but with higher public expenditure.

In a second 'dynamic' model with only 10 or 11 observations, they explain the change of the dependent variables between the 1980s and the 1990s by the distance between the positions of the different countries in those decades in the two-dimensional space which is spanned by the two principal components.[28] This measure of change has no significant impact on public debt, but a significant negative impact on deficits and – contrary to the results of the 'static' model – also on expenditure. Thus, according to this estimate an increase in the strictness of the budgetary procedures between the 1980s and the 1990s reduced the real growth of government expenditure. However, due to the small number of observations, even highly significant t-statistics are to be interpreted very cautiously.

Hallerberg and von Hagen (1999) go one step further.[29] Taking up the 'stylized fact' that electoral systems of proportional representation are more prone to high levels of public debt than majoritarian systems,[30] they distinguish 'delegation states' like Austria, France, Germany or the United Kingdom, where the finance minister has a strong position in the budgetary process, and 'commitment states' like Belgium, Ireland or the Netherlands, where clear budget plans are written into the coalition contract and show that there is some kind of natural connection between the electoral systems and these types of budgetary procedures:

Commitment is appropriate for countries with a proportionality rule, which tends to produce coalition governments. Delegation is the choice for countries with plurality rule or other systems that produce single party governments (or its functional equivalent – governments where the same parties run together election after election, as in France and Germany).[31]

(In between these two types are 'hybrid states', like Denmark or Sweden.) Both strategies can be effective in reducing the deficit, but countries which want to reduce their deficit should – according to these results – choose the appropriate budgetary rules in accordance with their electoral system. Or to state it the other way round: in order to reduce the public deficit it is not necessary to change from a system of proportional representation to a majoritarian system, if the appropriate budgetary rules are implemented. This is contrary to the results of Stein et al. (1999), who in their paper about the situation in Latin America 'do not find evidence that strong budgetary institutions can neutralise the potentially adverse fiscal consequences of proportional representation on fiscal deficits and debt' (p. 105).

Taking all these results together (and accepting them despite the very small number of observations on which some of them are based), it is shown in this literature that budgetary procedures matter, and that the interaction between budgetary procedures and the electoral system matters: not all budgetary procedures have the same effect in all electoral systems. It is not, however, clear that they are more effective than constitutional or statutory balanced budget or tax and expenditure limitation rules. In a situation where it is impossible to introduce such rules they might, however, show a feasible second-best way to reach fiscal sustainability.

4.   THE FISCAL IMPACT OF DIRECT DEMOCRACY

Instead of searching for second-best solutions, one might consider a first-best solution. Such a solution could be to give the citizens direct political rights in the budgetary process by allowing for initiatives and referenda. While referenda can be used to prevent tax increases or to cut down large expenditure programmes, initiatives can not only be used to cut down (or initiate) public projects but also, as has been shown by Proposition 13, to change the budgetary process. According to Feld and Kirchgässner (2000), in more direct democracies, politicians and well-informed specialists in the legislature have less flexibility to pursue their personal interests, and by being able to decide for themselves, citizens might feel more responsible for their community and be more prepared to accept decisions that lead to income or wealth losses for themselves. Both mechanisms are expected to lead to differences in economic policy decisions, especially with respect to the public budget.

To the extent one follows Peltzman (1992) and Moak (1982) in their assessment that voters are fiscally conservative and prefer lower public deficits than representatives, one would expect public deficits to be lower in jurisdictions with deficit referenda than in those without referenda. To the extent one follows Buchanan (1958, 1987) in his assessment of a bias of voters for borrowing, one may expect public deficits to be higher in jurisdictions with deficit referenda than in those without referenda. However, the impact of referenda on budget deficits and public debt does not necessarily have to rely on fiscal conservatism of voters and thus their preferences. In a federal state, the tax base can be seen as a common property resource to which the agents of the different governmental levels, governments and/or parliaments, have access. As Velasco (1999) has formally shown, in such a situation a dynamic problem may arise in analogy to the 'tragedy of the commons' as described by Hardin (1968), which results in overspending and – possibly – also in a too large public debt.[32] However, elements of direct democracy would reduce the danger of different agents overusing the fiscal commons, because the same citizens decide at all three federal levels and not different governments and/or parliaments.

Systematic analyses of the impact of referenda and initiatives on economic policy are available for Switzerland and for the US states.[33] In the first of these papers, using aggregate data on Swiss cities in 1970, Pommerehne (1978) shows that the median voter model performs better in jurisdictions in which political decisions are taken by voters directly in referenda and initiatives.[34] Using data for the year 1990, Kirchgässner et al. (1999, pp. 84f.) show with a simulation that in those cities without budgetary referenda government expenditure would have been about 20 percent less if these cities had had this instrument. Schneider and Pommerehne (1983) show for 110 Swiss cities that expenditure growth in cities with direct democracy was – *ceteris paribus* – almost three percentage points lower than in representative democracies between 1965 and 1975. While expenditure growth was 9.6 percent on average in representative democratic cities (according to simulation results), it would have been 6.8 percent if these cities had been direct democracies. In these analyses, cities are considered as direct democratic if their constitutions contain an obligatory or optional referendum or a local assembly to pass fiscal legislation in the form of changes in tax rates, the budget draft, or budget deficits.

The results of Feld and Matsusaka (2000) for the 26 Swiss cantons during the period 1986 to 1997 point in the same direction. On average, spending in states with a fiscal referendum is SFr 390 per capita lower. The impact of the fiscal referendum on spending can be differentiated according to the spending threshold.[35] Expenditure per capita is SFr 917 lower in cantons with fiscal referenda for the canton with the median spending threshold of SFr 3 million.

The fiscal referendum is still restrictive at a spending threshold of SFr 15 million. It becomes zero at a threshold of SFr 25.8 million.

In a more recent paper, Feld and Kirchgässner (2001) obtain similar results. The estimates show that spending per capita is reduced by 6.5 percent for cantons with fiscal referenda. The estimates of local spending of 132 Swiss local jurisdictions presented in this paper also corroborate these results. Net local public spending is reduced by 20 percent if a referendum on the issue of new bonds is present in a city's constitution.[36]

The corresponding results for the USA are somewhat mixed. In an analysis for the year 1980 for 50 USA states and 1305 local communities, Zax (1989a) found that communities with initiatives have higher public expenditure. Farnham (1990) finds mixed results for 735 US cities in 1981/82. Matsusaka (1995) finds a negative impact of initiatives on expenditures per capita for 49 US states in a pooled cross-section time series analysis for seven years from 1960 to 1990. He reports that spending per capita and year of states with initiatives was US$ 55 to 110 lower (on average about 4 percent) depending on the signature requirement for the initiative. These results are corroborated by Rueben (1999) in a panel data analysis for the same time period[37] and by Bails and Tieslau (2000), who use data from 49 states observed at five-year intervals from 1964 to 1994.[38]

For the period before World War II, Matsusaka (2000) finds, however, higher public spending in initiative states in a similar research design as in his previous study. In a panel of 48 US states in the years 1902, 1913, 1932 and 1942, spending per capita and year of states with initiatives was 11 percent higher. The conclusion Matsusaka provides for the differences in his results for both time periods is that the anti-spending impact of initiatives is not a certain policy outcome. Initiatives serve citizens as instruments to correct policy outcomes in the direction of their preferences if they deviate from them. If citizens are more liberal (in the American sense) than representatives, this leads to higher spending in states in which an initiative is available. If voters are more conservative than representatives, they reduce government spending by the initiative. Interestingly enough, centralization of spending was reduced in the US states with initiatives: state spending was less than local spending in those states, before and after World War II.[39] Since local spending is closer to citizens than state spending and enables them to control spending more strongly, this evidence supports the conjecture outlined that spending outcomes come closer to citizens' preferences in states with initiatives.

While there are also mixed results for revenue of US states for the two periods studied by Matsusaka, the results for Swiss cantons and cities with respect to public revenue are quite strong. The estimates in Feld and Kirchgässner (2001) indicate that cantonal (net) revenue per capita is significantly lower in cantons and cities with fiscal referenda. Quantitatively, the impact is also non-negligible: it is 11 percent lower in the cantonal case and 20 percent lower in the case of the cities. In addition, as Feld and Matsusaka (2000a) have shown, the cantons with direct popular rights in fiscal decisions rely more on user charges than on broad-based taxes. The same holds, as Matsusaka (1995) has shown, for US states with initiatives.

Direct democratic cities in Switzerland also have lower public debt. Feld and Kirchgässner (1999) simulate that in 47 out of the 131 Swiss cities investigated (those where the citizens do not have direct rights with respect to budgetary decisions) public debt per capita would – *ceteris paribus* – have been about SFr 10 000 and thus 45 percent lower in 1990 if these cities had had a corresponding direct democratic organization.[40] These results are again corroborated in different econometric models by Feld and Kirchgässner (2001, 2001a). The cantonal estimates in Feld and Kirchgässner (2001) are, however, less convincing. There is no significant difference in public debt between cantons with and without fiscal referenda, while budget deficits of the cantons with fiscal referenda are even significantly higher than those of cantons without fiscal referenda. The corresponding results of US states are, on the other hand, unambiguous: Kiewiet and Szakaly (1996) provide evidence that US states with a referendum on new bonds had a guaranteed debt per capita between 1961 and 1990 that was 33 percent lower.[41]

The question remains, however, whether the lower level of public spending also leads to a more efficient public sector. Lower public spending could, as Breton (1996) argues, be the result of insufficient vote trading in direct legislation, rendering it inefficient. It is very difficult to make profound statements about empirically measured efficiency. Very few studies attempt to investigate this question.[42] Pommerehne (1983) analysed costs and prices of local garbage collection in 103 Swiss cities in 1970. He found that average refuse collection costs (per household) were – *ceteris paribus* – lowest in cities with direct legislation and private garbage collection. These costs were about 10 percent higher when garbage collection was organized publicly instead of privately. In cities with representative democracy the costs of private garbage collection were about 20 percent higher than in direct democracies. Average costs of garbage collection were highest in cities with representative democracy and public organization (30 percent higher than in the first case). This provides some evidence that direct legislation enhances the efficiency of the public sector. Together with the results on budgetary policy, this is evidence in favour of the hypothesis that direct legislation in Switzerland results in less leeway of representatives to pursue their own interests.

Weck-Hannemann and Pommerehne (1989) derive interesting results with respect to tax morale.[43] They present evidence that tax evasion is lower in those Swiss cantons in which citizens have an impact on budgetary policy in direct legislation. Using data for the years 1965, 1970 and 1978, they show that in those cantons tax evasion is – *ceteris paribus* – about SFr 1500 lower as compared to the average of the cantons without such direct influence.[44] According to Feld and Frey (2001), the higher tax morale in Swiss cantons with direct democracy is also a result of the fact that tax administrations treat their citizens more respectfully than their colleagues in representative democracies. Citizens are seen rather as partners in a psychological tax contract than potential cheaters on the tax code. If, however, the willingness to pay taxes is the higher the more satisfied are citizens with the public services supplied, then these results are evidence of higher satisfaction of citizens and, therefore, of greater efficiency of the provision of public services.[45]

All in all, the evidence regarding the impact of direct popular rights in the budgetary process with respect to public spending, revenue, deficit and debt suggests that citizens demand fewer public services and seem to force a sounder fiscal policy in systems with direct legislation than in parliamentary democracies. This results in a lower public debt per capita under direct democracy. Thus a referendum democracy appears to fit Wicksell's (1896) idea of a link between the tax price and public services better than a purely parliamentary system.

5.   FISCAL FEDERALISM AND THE SIZE OF THE PUBLIC SECTOR

If direct popular rights should have an effect on the budgetary process as well as on the lower governmental levels, fiscal federalism is a necessary precondition. As in Switzerland, Canada and the USA, but contrary, for example, to the situation in Germany, this federalism must include the revenue and not only the expenditure side; that is, it must allow for tax competition as well.[46] Besides this there is, however, another question. Does a federal fiscal structure itself have an impact on the public budget, that is, independent of the additional possibilities it creates to put direct popular rights into practice? In this case, one might think of changing the whole fiscal structure from a more centralized to a more decentralized system as an additional possibility to achieve fiscal sustainability.

The hypothesis that fiscal federalism, that is, a decentralized fiscal structure, might reduce the size of the government was originally stated by Oates (1972, p. 209): 'Centralisation may, for example, lead to a higher level of public spending because of the likely weakening of the link between expenditure and tax payment.'[47] The same idea has been put forward by Brennan and Buchanan (1977, 1978, 1980), who model the government as a Leviathan which maximizes tax revenue. They value fiscal competition as a powerful measure to tame Leviathan, that is, as an effective constraint on the government's power to tax.[48] Thus, while Oates – corresponding to his 'correspondence principle'[49] – considers the closeness between the decision makers and the citizens as the relevant factor, Brennan and Buchanan point to the competitive aspect of fiscal federalism. And while the Oates-hypothesis considers the distribution of tasks between different government levels, the Brennan-Buchanan-hypothesis is more about the fragmentation at lower governmental levels given the distribution of tasks. Thus one can distinguish (i) a decentralization hypothesis and (ii) a fragmentation hypothesis. But both impacts point in the same direction: a federal structure should reduce the tax burden in a country.

This is, however, not the only impact of a federal structure on public expenditure. Oates mentions the possibility 'that decentralization is expensive because of the loss of potential economies of scale' (1972, p. 209).[50] It might also be the case that 'since individuals have more control over public decisions at the local than at the state or national level they will wish to empower the public sector with a wider range of functions and responsibility where these activities are carried out at more localised levels of government'.[51] Thus, even if total government spending is reduced, it might be increased at the lower governmental levels. Moreover, as has been mentioned above, in a federal state the common resource problem might lead to an overuse of the tax base.[52] Therefore fiscal federalism can also have a positive impact on government expenditure, and it is theoretically open whether the positive or negative impact dominates.[53]

It was also Oates (1972) who performed the first tests on these hypotheses. For a sample of 58 countries he found a negative correlation between the size of the public sector measured by tax revenues as a percentage of GNP and the degree of fiscal centralization as measured by the central government share in general government current revenues, but this relation became insignificant as soon as he included GDP per capita in the regression equation. He obtained quite similar results in a later study (1985) with a sample of 43 countries, where he included additional explanatory variables. But when he split this sample into the two sub-samples of industrialized and developing countries, not even the simple correlation coefficients proved to be statistically significant. These results are independent of whether he used the central government share of total government revenue or of total government expenditure as explanatory variable.[54]

In the same paper, he also employed a sample of the US states, and according to the observation of Brennan and Buchanan (1980, p. 185) that 'the potential for fiscal exploitation varies inversely with the number of competing governmental units in the inclusive territory', he additionally used the number of local government units as an explanatory variable to measure the degree of fragmentation. However, looking at the simple correlation only the central expenditure share was statistically significant at the 5 percent level, and in the regression together with other explanatory variables only the revenue share got a coefficient which was significantly different from zero and only at the 10 percent level. Thus he concluded 'that there does not exist a strong, systematic relationship between the size of government and the degree of centralisation of the public sector' (p. 756).[55]

This part of the second study of Oates was the starting point of a series of other studies. Though Nelson (1987) presented evidence similar to that of Oates (1985), but distinguishing between general purpose and single function local units, he was able to show that the average population per general-purpose local government unit has a positive impact on state and local taxes as a fraction of personal income.[56] Similar results have been derived by Eberts and Gronberg (1988). They explain the expenditure of the major local public services as a percentage of personal income on the level of counties and of 280 Standard Metropolitan Statistical Areas (SMSA) and regress it (along with other variables) on the number of local governments, that is, either the number itself or normalized by the size of the population or by the total land area in the county or SMSA. In addition, they find that the number of single-purpose units has a significant positive effect on (local) public expenditure. Performing the same regressions on the state level they obtained the same signs for the estimated coefficients but these did not prove to be significant.

In a similar study, Zax (1989) takes the aggregate county own-source revenues as a share of county income as dependent variable, and regresses them on the county share of local total revenue and two different measures of fragmentation, governments per capita and governments per square mile, both for general-purpose and single-purpose governments. He obtains significant positive coefficients for the county share of local total revenue and for the number of single-purpose governments per capita and a significant negative coefficient for the number of general-purpose governments per square mile. Thus the size of the local public sector increases with increasing centralism and with increasing fragmentation of single purpose governments, and decreases with increasing fragmentation of general-purpose governments. Contrary to these results, Forbes and Zampelli (1989), with data on per capita taxes and revenues for 345 counties in 157 SMSAs, find a significantly positive impact of the number of competing county governments on their size.

Because the data sets which are employed are for different levels of aggregation, these empirical results are not necessarily inconsistent with each other.[57] Nevertheless, the support they provide for the hypothesis that fiscal federalism reduces the tax burden is at best mixed. Moreover, with the exception of Zax (1989), the tests performed are about the fragmentation hypothesis and not about the decentralization hypothesis itself. And those which are directly on the centralization hypothesis in the various papers by Oates are also at best mixed.[58]

There are at least two possible reasons mentioned in the literature for these findings. One is that there might be intergovernmental collusion in the form of intergovernmental grants which reduce competition between lower-level units and – in this way – help to increase the size of the government.[59] Evidence for this hypothesis, that is, that a higher share of federal grants in the receipts of lower-level government increases the total government share, is presented by Grossman (1989) in a cross-section for the US states as well as in a time series analysis with annual data for the USA from 1948 to 1984.[60]

The second reason is that the share of state expenditure (or revenue) of total state and local expenditure might be the wrong indicator because the decentralization hypothesis may still hold even if there is no significant positive relation between this variable and the size of the government as long as federal government expenditure is reduced to such an extent that even an increase of state and/or local expenditure in a federal system is over-compensated. Following this line of reasoning, Joulfaian and Marlow (1991) show for three cross-sections of the US states for the years 1983 to 1985 that in all three years there is a significant negative effect between fiscal decentralization and the size of the government if federal expenditures are included in the dependent variable, but that there is no significant effect if only state and local government expenditures are considered.[61] They also find some (although weak) evidence for the fragmentation hypothesis, but no evidence at all for the collusion hypothesis. This is different in Shadbegian (1999) who – in the most recent study – uses a panel of the US states from 1979 to 1992. He obtains highly significant evidence for the collusion hypothesis, but also highly significant results with respect to the centralization hypothesis: a more decentralized federal system leads to a larger size of state and local govern-ments but to a smaller federal and total government size; that is, the increase of local and state government size is overcompensated by a decrease of the federal government size.

The problem with this study is, however, that the federal government is the same for all US states. It is, of course, possible to disaggregate federal expenditure and grants by states but it is not clear what that means. One possible explanation is that in states with a more pronounced federal structure the demand for federal expenditure is – *ceteris paribus* – lower. This would not, however, necessarily support the Leviathan hypothesis of Brennan and Buchanan (1980). It might only imply a shifting of federal public expenditure from those states with a more pronounced federal structure to those with a less pronounced one, without affecting the total level. Thus the really interesting question of whether the government size of the US would be larger if it had a less pronounced federal fiscal structure remains unanswered. The results do not support (but, of course, also do not contradict) the proposition that countries with a federal fiscal structure have – *ceteris paribus* – a smaller size of the public sector.

To test this proposition one has to perform the analysis at the national level, as did Oates (1972) at the starting point of the whole discussion. There are also some other earlier studies which try to test this proposition and show the expected negative relation,[62] but, as Lybeck (1988, pp. 39f.) correctly states, 'if this is due to the constitutional fact as such or rather to the fact that the included federal states (United States, Canada, Australia and Germany in particular) are fiscally conservative states is a matter for consideration'. Moreover, those studies which not only look at simple correlations but also include other explanatory variables provide mixed results too. Oates (1972, 1985) and Heil (1991) do not find a significant impact. Different results are obtained by Solano (1983), who uses a cross-section over 18 democracies and the fiscal year 1968/69, as well as by Saunders (1988), who uses a cross-section over 22 OECD countries and the average of the years 1978 to 1980. They find a significant negative impact of federalism on government size. Both employ a dummy to characterize federal countries.[63] Moesen and van Cauwenberge (2000), who use a cross-section of 19 OECD countries with data averaged over the years 1990 to 1992, obtain the same result. In all three cases the samples are, however, rather small. On the other hand, because the measure of decentralization employed by Moesen and van Cauwenberge (2000) contains only that part of local government expenditures which is entirely financed through local taxes (in relation to total government expenditure), they might better capture the degree of local fiscal independence than earlier studies. However, this study might be a good starting point for future investigations.

Nevertheless, taking all currently available empirical evidence together on the question of what is the net effect on the size of the government of a federal fiscal system, we might conclude that there is some evidence that fiscal federalism leads – *ceteris paribus* – to a smaller size of the government, but the evidence is far from overwhelming.[64]

6.   SUMMARY AND CONCLUDING REMARKS

What have we learned from the empirical research in public choice in recent years? With respect to the four different kinds of institutions which are considered in this survey, we can summarize the empirical results as follows:

1.   Balanced budget rules and limitations of expenditure, taxes and deficits have in most cases proved to be effective in cutting down public

expenditure, revenue and debt. However, at least in some cases this leads to a deterioration of the quality of the publicly provided services, especially with respect to schooling.

2. Budgetary procedures matter, and the interaction between budgetary procedures and the electoral system also matters: not all budgetary procedures have the same effect in all electoral systems. They might be less effective than constitutional or statutory balanced budget or tax and expenditure limitation rules, but in a situation where it is impossible to introduce such rules they might show a feasible second-best way to reach fiscal sustainability.

3. A 'first-best solution' might be to give the citizens direct political rights in the budgetary process. As has been shown, citizens demand fewer public services and seem to force a sounder fiscal policy in systems with direct legislation than in purely parliamentary systems. This results in a lower public debt per capita under direct democracy.

4. Though it is not overwhelming, there is some evidence that fiscal federalism itself leads – *ceteris paribus* – to a smaller size of the government.

There remain two remarks which must be added. First, these are not the only institutions which have an effect on the fiscal behaviour of the government. Besides fiscal institutions and besides political factors like the ideology of the (leading party of the) government or the number of parties in a coalition[65] there are also political institutions, which can have a considerable impact. At least two of them have also been discussed in the literature to a large extent, and in recent years there has also been some empirical research in this respect. One question is about the impact a presidential system like that in the USA has on public finance compared to a parliamentary system as most European countries have. The second question relates to the electoral system: what is the impact of a majoritarian compared to a proportional electoral system?[66]

Some empirical evidence on this topic has been presented by Persson and Tabellini (2000).[67] Their main results are that presidential regimes lead to a smaller size of the government than parliamentary regimes, and that majoritarian elections lead to a smaller size of the government than proportional elections. Due to some problems with their data, these results must be interpreted very cautiously, however.[68] Nevertheless, this demands further investigations of the impact these political institutions have on the budgetary process.

The second remark is that there are interdependencies between the different institutions. Two of them have already been mentioned: the most obvious one is that direct popular rights in the budgetary processes at the lower governmental levels are only possible if the respective country has the corresponding federal structure. Thus, even if the empirical results leave some doubts whether fiscal federalism really is a constraint on the size of the government, it is a precondition for direct democracy in fiscal matters at these levels, which, according to all that we know, reduces the size of the government. The second one is that budgetary rules have different effects under different electoral systems. But there are other interdependencies as well. Many of the fiscal restrictions in the US states have been introduced by initiatives. And, according to Matsusaka (1995) as well as Schaltegger and Feld (2001), centralization of spending was reduced in the US states with initiatives and Swiss cantons with budget referenda, respectively.

Thus a prudent combination of institutions can help to tame Leviathan; that is to reduce public deficits and debt and also public expenditure and revenue. The problem is similar to many other economic policy problems: we know of possible remedies, but it is difficult to implement them in the political process. Such difficulties are especially severe if the positions of politicians as well as of leading economic interest groups are affected. This should not, however, prevent us from informing the general public about these possibilities. On the other hand, if our proposals do not find a majority in the population, to remain consistent we should not necessarily blame the ignorance of the citizens for this result because we assume in our economic models that the same citizens behave rationally and especially have rational expectations. We should not (always) follow the 'theory of mistakes', as Stigler (1979) has called it, and at least sometimes accept that a majority of the electorate might have different preferences from ours. To accept this is a basic precondition for the functioning of a democratic society.

NOTES

1. See, for example, Green and Shapiro (1994).
2. Another line of empirical research of public choice, the development of 'politico-economic models' or models of the 'political business cycle', respectively, also started at the beginning of the 1970s with the papers by Goodhart and Bhansali (1970), Kramer (1971) and Nordhaus (1975). It consists of an economic theory of voting behaviour which links the decision of voters to the economic development and a theory of government behaviour which assumes vote-maximizing behaviour of the government. (An alternative is ideologically oriented behaviour, as assumed in the partisan model of Hibbs, 1977.) The Frey and Schneider (1978, 1978a, 1979) models in particular used this approach to explain government expenditure and revenue. Models of the political business cycle are still being further developed. The main difference between the earlier and the more recent papers on this topic is that the more recent ones assume rational expectations of the electorate while the earlier ones mostly used adaptive expectations. (See, for example, Lohmann, 1998 or Sieg, 2001 for two recent papers.) However, the only institutional factor in these models is the election or, to state it more precisely, the impact of the coming election on public expenditure. Moreover, there are many surveys of these models available. (See, for example, Paldam, 1997 or Gärtner, 2000.) Thus, we do not discuss them further in this chapter.
3. See, for example, Romer and Rosenthal (1979) or Rowley (1984).

4. See also Megdal (1983), Chicoine et al. (1989) and Santerre (1989, 1993) who use a similar approach for the USA.
5. See, for example, Alesina and Rosenthal (1995) or Kirchgässner (1997).
6. For a review of the empirical evidence see, for example, Kirchgässner et al. (1999) and Feld and Kirchgässner (2000).
7. See Buchanan and Wagner (1977, 1978) or Buchanan (1985).
8. A theoretical basis for this belief can be seen in the fiscal competition model of Tiebout (1956).
9. For Buchanan (1985) this has an important moral dimension: 'Having lived through the destruction of fiscal morality by the Keynesian mind-set, we must make every effort to replace this morality with deliberately-chosen constraints which will produce substantially the pre-Keynesian patterns of results' (p. 5).
10. See, for example, von Hagen (1992a) or von Hagen and Harden (1994, 1995). Empirical analyses of the budgetary process in the USA had been performed at the beginning of the 1970s. (See, for example, Davis et al., 1971.) However, these analyses did not aim to identify institutional aspects which are important for reducing public deficits and debt. Thus they are not relevant for our discussion.
11. For a recent survey about the effects of these political institutions, see Persson and Tabellini (2000). The historical record of political institutions and fiscal policy in the USA, for example, is presented in Inman and Fitts (1990).
12. See also the overview in Bohn and Inman (1996, p. 17).
13. For this, see, for example, von Weizsäcker (1992).
14. See the overview in Poterba (1997, pp. 64ff.).
15. See, for example, Advisory Commission on Intergovernmental Relations (1987), von Hagen (1991) or Alt and Lowry (1994). For a detailed critique of these studies see Bohn and Inman (1996, p. 17).
16. Similar results have already been derived by Bayoumi et al. (1993) and are reported in Eichengreen and Bayoumi (1994). A more thorough analysis about the transmission which leads from balanced budget laws to effects on state government bond rates is given by Lowry and Alt (2001).
17. For a detailed description of these restraints see Stauffer (2001, p. 72).
18. For this, see, for example, Clingermayer and Wood (1995) or King-Meadows and Lowery (1996).
19. For this, see Matz (1981), Mullins and Joyce (1996) as well as Galles and Sexton (1998).
20. For this, see O'Sullivan et al. (1994, pp. 105ff.).
21. For this, see for example, Cutler et al. (1999), who present evidence that in Massachusetts voters in communities with larger initial tax cuts effected by Proposition $2^1/_2$ (which was passed in 1980) supported significantly more overrides in the 1990s.
22. Von Hagen (1992a, p. 1). For a critique of these results see Bohn and Inman (1996, p. 17). Today, the position of von Hagen is somewhat different. See, for example, Strauch and von Hagen (2001).
23. For a description of these institutions see von Hagen (1998).
24. See also von Hagen and Harden (1994, 1995).
25. There is, however, some recent experimental evidence which shows that bottom-up procedures might not be inferior to top-down procedures. See Ehrhart et al. (2000).
26. Using a slightly different specification for the same data, in Feld and Kirchgässner (2001) this coefficient did not, however, prove to be significant. This indicates that the results are not robust against the in- or exclusion of additional variables.
27. They exclude Austria, Finland and Luxembourg.
28. Additionally, they exclude Sweden as an outlier from all equations and Italy as an outlier from the deficit equations.
29. See also Hallerberg et al. (2001).
30. For this, see, for example, Persson and Tabellini (2000).
31. Hallerberg et al. (2001, p. 5).
32. See also Wrede (1999, 2000) as well as Buchanan and Yoon (2000) on fiscal commons.

33. For a more detailed description, especially of the US studies, see Sass (2001) or Kirchgässner et al. (1999, ch. 5).
34. See also Pommerehne and Schneider (1978).
35. In Swiss cantons (and local communities) which have a fiscal referendum in their constitution there is usually a spending threshold: expenditures above this threshold are subject to a (mandatory or optional) referendum.
36. In Feld and Kirchgässner (1999) it is also shown that Swiss cities with budgetary referenda spent less, but had a revenue share from taxes and user charges, as opposed to transfers and subsidies from other government levels, that was 5 per cent higher than in cities without such referenda.
37. These results may not, however, be robust with respect to other political variables such as ideological positions of the electorate. See for this Camobreco (1998). The difference between the results of Zax (1989) and of Matsusaka (1995) may be due to the fact that Zax included Alaska, which is a clear spending outlier.
38. On the other hand, the referendum has a positive but insignificant impact on public expenditure in their model.
39. See also similar results for the Swiss cantons by Schaltegger and Feld (2001).
40. Excluding Zurich, as an outlier with an extremely high debt, the simulated difference was still SFr 4500 or 24 percent, respectively. Neither formal fiscal restraints, nor a budgetary process with a strong role of the mayor or the secretary of finance, succeed in putting such a strong constraint on debt issuing.
41. See also McEachern (1978).
42. An exception is Noam (1980). The efficiency measure used is not, however, very telling.
43. See also Pommerehne and Weck-Hannemann (1996).
44. There are also theoretical arguments why citizens in direct democracies evade less taxes than those in representative democracies. See Pommerehne et al. (1997).
45. In addition to these studies which investigate the impact of direct citizens rights on public finance, Feld and Savioz (1997) study the relationship between budgetary referenda and economic performance of Swiss cantons measured by GDP per employee. In a panel with annual data from 1984 to 1993 for the 26 Swiss cantons, they arrive at the conclusion that GDP per employee is – *ceteris paribus* – by about 5 percent higher in those cantons with budgetary referenda compared to cantons without those referenda. This result is tested in various ways for robustness. In particular, reversed causality is tested under the hypothesis that richer cantons can afford more direct legislation. On the basis of the empirical results, this hypothesis could be rejected. Moreover, the impact of direct democracy is hardly diminished if additional explanatory variables are included in the empirical model. Again there is corroborating evidence for the US states. Blomberg and Hess (2000) report that states with initiatives converged with a growth rate that was 3 percentage points higher than their companion states with no initiative during the period 1969 to 1986. Moreover, in some recent papers, Frey and Stutzer (see, for example, 2000, 2002) present evidence that people in Switzerland perceive themselves as more satisfied with their life as a whole in direct democratic jurisdictions.
46. While the German Bundesländer altogether have a strong impact not only on their own revenue but also on the revenue of the federal government, a single Bundesland does not have any competence to change any tax rate. Thus there is only expenditure (transfer) but no tax competition between the German Bundesländer. For a comparison of the two different kinds of federalism in Switzerland and Germany see, for example, Kirchgässner and Pommerehne (1997).
47. Though Oates (1972) does not refer to it, this idea can already be found in Wicksell (1896).
48. See Brennan and Buchanan (1980, p. 184). For a somewhat less optimistic theoretical analysis in this respect see Apolte (2001).
49. See Oates (1972, pp. 33ff.).
50. According to Lybeck (1988, p. 35), this 'is frequently claimed in Sweden'. The same holds for Switzerland, where the merger of some cantons is demanded with this argument. And it has also been used in Germany in the 1970s when in many of the Länder the number of local communities was strongly reduced.

51. Oates (1985, p. 749). According to him this hypothesis goes back to John J. Wallis, Professor of Economic History at the University of Maryland.
52. This problem is similar to the model of pork-barrel politics of Weingast et al. (1981). See also Inman and Fitts (1990) for an earlier analysis following these lines. Referring to the Swedish situation, this hypothesis has already been stated by Tarschys (1975). Evidence for this effect is claimed by Jones et al. (1999) for Argentina.
53. For a theoretical analysis of why centralization might increase the size of government, see also Persson and Tabellini (1994).
54. It is an open question whether expenditure or revenue is the better measure of the fiscal burden. Marlow (1988) argues in favour of expenditure because – according to deficit spending and the inflation tax – official taxes do not cover the total burden.
55. However, Wallis and Oates (1988), using a large historical panel data set going back to the turn of the twentieth century, find a significantly positive relation between fiscal concentration and the size of the public sector, which contradicts his earlier findings for the US states.
56. Nelson (1986) presents mixed evidence: State and local taxes are significantly higher – *ceteris paribus* – the higher the average population per county, but significantly lower, the higher the state share of total state and local taxes. Thus, while the first result supports the fragmentation hypothesis, the second is contrary to the decentralization hypothesis.
57. For this, see Oates (1989).
58. In addition, Raimondo (1989) presents evidence that the decentralization hypothesis may hold for specific public service areas but not for others.
59. This possibility has already been mentioned by Brennan and Buchanan (1980, p. 185).
60. See also Grossman (1989a), where time series results for the extended period from 1946 to 1986 are presented.
61. See also Marlow (1988) and Joulfaian and Marlow (1990) for studies which show a significant impact of fiscal decentralization on the size of the government including the federal level.
62. See, for example, Cameron (1978) or Lybeck (1986).
63. Solano (1983) additionally includes a variable for the centralization of the tax system. Besides the dummy variable for federalism, this variable has, however, no significant impact on total government expenditure.
64. A similar picture is derived in a study by Hettich and Winer (1999, pp. 221ff.), which shows for the US states that the tax rate in neighbouring states has a significant negative effect on the average personal income tax rate in a state whereas the tax rate in the state with the most similar social conditions has the (expected) significantly positive sign.
65. Roubini and Sachs (1989), for example, report evidence that governments with a short average tenure and with many political parties in the coalition have – *ceteris paribus* – higher deficits.
66. See also Alt and Lowry (1994), who investigate the effect of divided government on US state budgets.
67. See also Persson and Tabellini (1999), Persson et al. (2000) as well as Persson and Tabellini (2000, pp. 245f., pp. 268f.).
68. There are two major problems with their approach. First, they mainly use only the size of the central government as dependent variable. One reason for this might be that as explanatory variables they use political data only from the federal level. However, these results hardly indicate anything about the total size of the government because they do not control for the different fiscal structures. Second, the characterization of the different countries as 'presidential' or 'parliamentarian' is highly debatable. They classify Switzerland, for example, as a 'presidential system', 'since the cabinet – even though chosen by the Assembly – has a life of its own; survival does not depend on majority support in the Assembly' (Persson et al., 2000, p. 1151). This classification not only overlooks the fact that the four parties which formed the government with the same composition during more than forty years always had a majority in the parliament of about or even more than eighty percent, but also that the position of the government in the budgetary process is rather weak; it is much weaker than the governments of most other European countries, as, for example, the German, French or British government.

REFERENCES

Advisory Commission on Intergovernmental Relations (1987), *Fiscal Discipline in the Federal System: Experience of the States*, Washington, DC.

Alesina, A. and H. Rosenthal (1995), *Partisan Politics, Divided Government, and the Economy*, Cambridge: Cambridge University Press.

Alesina, A., R. Hausmann, R. Hommesc and E. Stein (1999), 'Budget Institutions and Fiscal Performance in Latin America', *Journal of Development Economics* **59**, 253–73.

Alt, J. and R.C. Lowry (1994), 'Divided Government and Budget Deficits: Evidence from the States', *American Political Science Review*, **88**, 811–28.

Apolte, Th. (2001), 'How Tame Will Leviathan Become in Institutional Competition?', *Public Choice,* **107**, 359–81.

Arrow, K.J. (1951), *Social Choice and Individual Values*, New York: Wiley (2nd edn 1963).

Bails, D. and M.A. Tieslau (2000), 'The Impact of Fiscal Constitutions on State and Local Expenditures', *Cato Journal*, **20**, 255–77.

Bayoumi, T., M. Goldstein and G. Woglom (1993), 'Do Credit Markets Discipline Sovereign Borrowers?, Evidence from U.S. States', mimeo, Washington, DC: IMF.

Bergstrom, T.C. and R.P. Goodman (1973), 'Private Demand for Public Goods', *American Economic Review,* **63**, 280–96.

Black, D. (1948), 'On the Rationale of Group Decision-Making', *Journal of Political Economy*, **56**, 23–34.

Blomberg, S.B. and G.D. Hess (2000), 'The Impact of Voter Activity on Economic Activity', mimeo, Wesley College.

Bohn, H. and R.P. Inman (1996), 'Balanced-Budget Rules and Public Deficits: Evidence from the U.S. States', *Carnegie–Rochester Conference Series on Public Policy*, **45**, 13–76.

Borcherding, T. and R. Deacon (1972), 'The Demand for the Services of Non-Federal Governments, *American Economic Review*, **62**, 891–901.

Brennan, G. and J.M. Buchanan (1977), 'Towards a Tax Constitution for Leviathan', *Journal of Public Economics*, **8**, 255–73.

Brennan, G. and J.M. Buchanan (1978), 'Tax Instruments as Constraints on the Disposition of Public Revenues', *Journal of Public Economics*, **9**, 301–18.

Brennan, G. and J.M. Buchanan (1980), *The Power to Tax: Analytical Foundations of a Fiscal Constitution*, Cambridge, MA: Cambridge University Press.

Breton, A. (1996), *Competitive Governments: An Economic Theory of Politics and Public Finance*, Cambridge: Cambridge University Press.

Buchanan, J.M. (1958), *Public Principles of Public Debt*, Homewood, IL: Richard D. Irwin.

Buchanan, J.M. (1985), 'Tax Moral Dimension of Debt Financing', *Economic Inquiry*, **23**, 1–6.

Buchanan, J.M. (1987), 'The Constitution of Economic Policy', *American Economic Review*, **77**, 243–50.

Buchanan, J.M. and G. Tullock (1962), *The Calculus of Consent: Logical Foundations of Constitutional Democracy*, Ann Arbor: University of Michigan Press.

Buchanan, J.M. and R.E. Wagner (1977), *Democracy in Deficit: The Political Legacy of Lord Keynes*, New York: Academic Press.

Buchanan J.M. and R.E. Wagner (1978), 'The Political Biases of Keynesian

Economics', in J.M. Buchanan and R.E. Wagner (eds), *Fiscal Responsibility in Constitutional Democracy*, Leiden/Boston: Martinus Nijhoff, pp. 79-100.

Buchanan, J.M. and Y.J. Yoon (2000), 'Majoritarian Management of the Commons', mimeo, George Mason University.

Cameron, D.R. (1978), 'The Expansion of the Public Economy: A Comparative Analysis', *American Political Science Review*, **72**, 1243-61.

Camobreco, J.F. (1998), 'Preferences, Fiscal Policies, and the Initiative Process', *Journal of Politics*, **60**, 819-29.

Chernick, H. and A. Reschovsky (1982), 'The Distributional Impact of Proposition 13: A Microsimulation Approach', *National Tax Journal*, **35**, 149-70.

Chicoine, D.L., N. Walzer and S.C. Deller (1989), 'Representative vs. Direct Democracy and Government Spending in a Median Voter Model', *Public Finance/Finances Publiques*, **44**, 225-36.

Clingermayer, J.C. and B.D. Wood (1995), 'Disentangling Patterns of State Debt Finance', *American Political Science Review*, **89**, 108-20.

Cutler, D.M., D.W. Elmendorf and R. Zeckhauser (1999), 'Restraining the Leviathan: Property Tax Limitation in Massachusetts', *Journal of Public Economics*, **71**, 313-34.

Davis, O.A., M.A.H. Dempster and A. Wildavsky (1971), 'On the Process of Budgeting II: An Empirical Study of Congressional Appropriations', in R.F. Byrne et al. (eds), *Studies in Budgeting*, Amsterdam: North-Holland, pp. 292-375.

Downes, Th.A. (1992), 'Evaluating the Impact of School Finance Reform on the Provision of Public Education: The California Case', *National Tax Journal*, **45**, 405-19.

Downes, Th.A. and D.N. Figlio (1997), 'School Finance Reform, Tax Limits, and Student Performance: Do Reforms Level Up or Dumb Down?', mimeo, University of Florida, Gainsville.

Downes, Th.A. and D.N. Figlio (1999), 'Do Tax and Expenditure Limits Provide a Free Lunch? Evidence on the Link between Limits and Public Sector Service Quality', *National Tax Journal*, **52**, 113-28.

Downes, Th.A., R.F. Dye and Th.J. McGuire (1998), 'Do Limits Matter? Evidence on the Effects of Tax Limitations on Student Performance', *Journal of Urban Economics*, **43**, 401-17.

Downs, A. (1957), *An Economic Theory of Democracy*, New York: Harper and Row.

Eberts, R.W. and T.J. Gronberg (1988), 'Can Competition Among Local Governments Constrain Government Spending?', *Federal Reserve Bank of Cleveland Economic Review*, **1**, 2-9.

Ehrhart, K.-M., R. Gardner, J. von Hagen and C. Keser (2000), 'Budget Processes: Theory and Experimental Evidence', University of Bonn, Center for European Integration Studies, Working Paper No. B 18, November.

Eichengreen, B. (1994), 'Fiscal Policy and EMU', in B. Eichengreen and J. Frieden (eds), *The Political Economy of European Monetary Unification*, Boulder/Oxford: Westview Press, pp. 167-90.

Eichengreen, B. and T. Bayoumi (1994), 'The Political Economy of Fiscal Restrictions: Implications for Europe from the United States', *European Economic Review*, **38**, 783-91.

Elder, H.W. (1992), 'Exploring the Tax Revolt: An Analysis of the Effects of State Tax and Expenditure Limitation Laws', *Public Finance Quarterly*, **20**, 47-63.

Farnham, P.G. (1990), 'The Impact of Citizen Influence on Local Government Expenditure', *Public Choice*, **64**, 201-12.

Feld, L.P. and B.S. Frey (2001), 'Trust Breeds Trust: How Taxpayers Are Treated', forthcoming in *Economics of Governance*, **2**.

Feld, L.P. and G. Kirchgässner (1999), 'Public Debt and Budgetary Procedures: Top Down or Bottom Up? Some Evidence from Swiss Municipalities', in J. Poterba and J. von Hagen (eds), *Fiscal Institutions and Fiscal Performance*, Chicago: Chicago University Press and NBER, pp. 151–79.

Feld, L.P. and G. Kirchgässner (2000), 'Direct Democracy, Political Culture, and the Outcome of Economic Policy: Some Swiss Experience', *European Journal of Political Economy*, **16**, 287–306.

Feld, L.P. and G. Kirchgässner (2001), 'The Political Economy of Direct Legislation: The Role of Direct Democracy in Local and Regional Decision-Making', *Economic Policy*, **33**, 331–67.

Feld, L.P. and G. Kirchgässner (2001a), 'Does Direct Democracy Reduce Public Debt? Evidence from Swiss Municipalities', *Public Choice*, **109**, 347–70.

Feld, L.P. and J.G. Matsusaka (2000), 'Budget Referendums and Government Spending: Evidence from Swiss Cantons', mimeo, University of St Gallen.

Feld, L.P. and J.G. Matsusaka (2000a), 'The Political Economy of Tax Structure: Some Panel Evidence for Swiss Cantons', mimeo, University of St. Gallen.

Feld, L.P. and M.R. Savioz (1997), 'Direct Democracy Matters for Economic Performance: An Empirical Investigation', *Kyklos*, **50**, 507–38.

Figlio, D.N. (1997), 'Did the "Tax Revolt" Reduce School Performance?', *Journal of Public Economics*, **65**, 245–69.

Figlio, D.N. (1998), 'Short-Term Effects of a 1990s-Era Property Tax Limit: Panel Evidence on Oregon's Measure 5', *National Tax Journal*, **51**, 55–70.

Figlio, D.N. and A. O'Sullivan (1997), 'The Local Response to Tax Limitation Measures: Do Local Governments Manipulate Voters to Increase Revenues?', *Journal of Law and Economics*, **44**, 233–56.

Figlio, D.N. and K.S. Rueben (2001), 'Tax Limits and the Qualifications of New Teachers', *Journal of Public Economics*, **80**, 49–61.

Forbes K.F. and E.M. Zampelli (1989), 'Is Leviathan a Mythical Beast?', *American Economic Review*, **79**, 568–77.

Frey, B.S. and F. Schneider (1978), 'An Empirical Study of Politico-Economic Interaction in the United States', *Review of Economics and Statistics*, **60**, 174–83.

Frey, B.S. and F. Schneider (1978a), 'A Politico-Economic Model of the United Kingdom', *Economic Journal*, **88**, 243–53.

Frey, D.S. and F. Schneider (1979), 'An Econometric Model with an Endogenous Government Sector', *Public Choice*, **34**, 29–43.

Frey, B.S. and A. Stutzer (2000), 'Happiness, Economy and Institutions', *Economic Journal*, **110**, 918–38.

Frey, B.S. and A. Stutzer (2002), *Happiness and Economics*, Princeton/Oxford: Princeton University Press.

Galles, G.M. and R.L. Sexton (1998), 'A Tale of Two Tax Jurisdictions: The Surprising Effects of California's Proposition 13 and Massachusetts' Proposition 2½', *American Journal of Economics and Sociology*, **57**, 123–33.

Gärtner, M. (2000), 'Political Macroeconomics: A Survey of Recent Developments', *Journal of Economic Surveys*, **14**, 527–61.

Goodhart, C.A.E. and R.I. Bhansali (1970), 'Political Economy', *Political Studies*, **18**, 43–106.

Gramlich, E.M. (1990), 'U.S. Federal Budget Deficits and Gramm–Rudman–Hollings', *American Economic Review*, Papers and Proceedings, **80** (2), 75–80.

Green, D.P. and I. Shapiro (1994), *Pathologies of Rational Choice: A Critique of Applications in Political Science*, New Haven: Yale University Press.

Grossman, P.J. (1989), 'Federalism and the Size of Government', *Southern Economic Journal*, **55**, 580-93.

Grossman, P.J. (1989a), 'Fiscal Decentralization and Government Size: An Extension', *Public Choice*, **62**, 63-9.

de Haan, J. and J.E. Sturm (1994), 'Political and Institutional Determinants of Fiscal Policy in the European Community', *Public Choice*, **80**, 157-72.

de Haan, J., W. Moesen and B. Volkerink (1999), 'Budgetary Procedures – Aspects and Changes: New Evidence for Some European Countries', in: J. Poterba and J. von Hagen (eds), *Fiscal Institutions and Fiscal Performance*, Chicago: Chicago University Press and NBER, pp. 265-99.

von Hagen, J. (1991), 'A Note on the Empirical Effectiveness of Formal Fiscal Restraints', *Journal of Public Economics*, **44**, 99-110.

von Hagen, J. (1992), 'Fiscal Arrangements in a Monetary Union: Evidence from the U.S.', in D. Fair and Ch. de Boissieu (eds), *Fiscal Policy, Taxes, and the Financial System in an Increasingly Integrated Europe*, Deventer: Kluwer.

von Hagen, J. (1992a), 'Budgetary Procedures and Fiscal Performance in the European Communities', Commission of the European Communities, Economic Papers No. 96, October.

von Hagen, J. (1998), 'Budgetary Institutions for Aggregate Fiscal Discipline', Zentrum für Europäische Integrationsforschung, University of Bonn, Policy Paper B98-01, February.

von Hagen, J. and I.J. Harden (1994), 'National Budget Processes and Fiscal Performance', *European Economy*, **3**, 311-418.

von Hagen J. and I.J. Harden (1995), 'Budget Processes and Commitment to Fiscal Discipline, *European Economic Review*, **39**, 771-9.

Hahm, S.D., M.S. Kamplet, D.C. Movery and T.-T. Su (1992), 'The Influence of the Gramm-Rudman-Hollings Act on Federal Budgetary Outcomes, 1986-1989', *Journal of Policy Analysis and Management*, **11**, 207-34.

Hallerberg, M. and J. von Hagen (1999), 'Electoral Institutions, Cabinet Negotiations, and Budget Deficits in the European Union', in J. Poterba and J. von Hagen (eds), *Fiscal Institutions and Fiscal Performance*, Chicago: Chicago University Press and NBER, pp. 209-32.

Hallerberg, M., R. Strauch and J. von Hagen (2001), 'The Use and Effectiveness of Budgetary Rules and Norms in EU Member States', Report Prepared for the Dutch Ministry of Finance, Institute of European Integration Studies, Bonn, June.

Hardin, G. (1968), 'The Tragedy of the Commons', *Science*, **162**, 1243-8.

Heil, J.B. (1991), 'The Search for Leviathan Revisited', *Public Finance Quarterly*, **19**, 334-46.

Hettich, W. and S.L. Winer (1999), *Democratic Choice and Taxation: A Theoretical and Empirical Analysis*, Cambridge: Cambridge University Press.

Hibbs, D.A. (1977), 'Political Parties and Macroeconomic Policy', *American Political Science Review*, **71**, 1467-87.

Inman, R.P. and M.A. Fitts (1990), 'Political Institutions and Fiscal Policy: Evidence from the U.S. Historical Record', *Journal of Law, Economics, and Organization*, **6**, 79-132.

Jones, M.P., P. Sanguinetti and M. Tommasi (1999), 'Politics, Institutions, and Public-Sector Spending in the Argentine Provinces', in J. Poterba and J. von Hagen (eds),

Fiscal Institutions and Fiscal Performance, Chicago: Chicago University Press and NBER, 135–50.

Joulfaian, D. and M.L. Marlow (1990), 'Government Size and Centralization: Evidence from Disaggregated Data', *Southern Economic Journal*, **56**, 1094–102.

Joulfaian, D. and M.L. Marlow (1991), 'Centralization and Government Competition', *Applied Economics*, **23**, 1603–12.

Kiewiet, D.R. and K. Szakaly (1996), 'Constitutional Limitations on Borrowing: An Analysis of State Bonded Indebtedness', *Journal of Law, Economics and Organization*, **12**, 62–97.

King-Meadows, T. and D. Lowery (1996), 'The Impact of the Tax Revolt Era State Fiscal Caps: A Research Update', *Public Budgeting & Finance*, **16** (1), 102–12.

Kirchgässner, G. (1997), 'Vom Mythos der politischen Führung: Einige Bemerkungen zur gegenwärtigen Diskussion um die direkte Demokratie', in S. Borner and H. Rentsch (eds), *Wieviel direkte Demokratie verträgt die Schweiz?*, Chur/Zürich: Rüegger, pp. 247–57, 363.

Kirchgässner G. and W.W. Pommerehne (1997), 'Public Spending in Federal Systems: A Comparative Econometric Study', in P. Capros and D. Meulders (eds), *Budgetary Policy Modelling: Public Expenditures*, London/New York: Routledge, pp. 179–213.

Kirchgässner, G., L.P. Feld und M.R. Savioz (1999), *Die direkte Demokratie: Modern, erfolgreich, entwicklungs- und exportfähig*, Basel/München: Helbing und Lichtenhahn/Vahlen.

Kramer, G.H. (1971), 'Short-Term Fluctuations in U.S. Voting Behavior, 1986-1964, *American Political Science Review*, **65**, 131–43.

Lagona, F. and F. Padovano (2000), 'A Nonlinear Optimal Scoring Estimate on the Relationship Between Budget Rules and Fiscal Performance in the European Union', mimeo, Center for Economics of Institutions, Università Roma Tre, Rome.

Lohmann, S. (1998), 'Rationalizing the Political Business Cycle: A Workhorse Model', *Economics and Politics,* **10**, 1–17.

Lowry, R.C. and J.E. Alt (2001), 'A Visible Hand?, Bond Markets, Political Parties, Balanced Budget Laws, and State Government Debt', *Economics and Politics*, **13**, 49–72.

Lybeck, J.A. (1986), *The Growth of Government in Developed Economies*, Aldershot: Gower.

Lybeck, J.A. (1988), 'Comparing Government Growth Rates: The Non Institutional vs. the Institutional Approach', in J.A. Lybeck and M. Henrekson (eds), *Explaining the Growth of Government*, Amsterdam: North-Holland. pp. 29–47.

Marlow, M.L. (1988), 'Fiscal Decentralization and Government Size', *Public Choice*, **56**, 259–69.

Matsusaka, J.G. (1995), 'Fiscal Effects of the Voter Initiative: Evidence from the Last 30 Years', *Journal of Political Economy*, **103**, 587–623.

Matsusaka, J.G. (2000), 'Fiscal Effects of the Voter Initiative in the First Half of the Twentieth Century', *Journal of Law and Economics*, **43**, 619–50.

Matz, D. (1981), 'The Tax and Expenditure Limitation Movement', in R. Bahl (ed.), *Urban Government Finance: Emerging Trends*, Beverly Hills: Sage, pp. 127–53.

McEachern, W.A. (1978), 'Collective Decision Rules and Local Debt Choice: A Test of the Median Voter Hypothesis', *National Tax Journal*, **31**, 129–36.

Megdal, S.B. (1983), 'The Determination of Local Public Expenditures and the Principal and Agent Relation: A Case Study', *Public Choice*, **40**, 71–87.

Moak, L. (1982), *Municipal Bonds: Planning, Sale, and Administration*, Chicago: Municipal Finance Officers Association.

Moesen, W. and Ph. van Cauwenberge (2000), 'The Status of the Budget Constraint, Federalism and the Relative Size of Government: A Bureaucratic Approach', *Public Choice*, **104**, 207–24.

Mullins, D.R. and P.G. Joyce (1996), 'Tax and Expenditure Limitations and State and Local Fiscal Structure: An Empirical Assessment', *Public Budgeting & Finance*, **16** (1), 75–101.

Nelson, M.A. (1986), 'An Empirical Analysis of State and Local Government Tax Structures in the Context of the Leviathan Model of Government', *Public Choice*, **49**, 283–94.

Nelson, M.A. (1987), 'Searching for Leviathan: Comment and Extension', *American Economic Review*, **77**, 198–204.

Noam, E.M. (1980), 'The Efficiency of Direct Democracy', *Journal of Political Economy*, **88**, 803–10.

Nordhaus, W.D. (1975), 'The Political Business Cycle', *Review of Economic Studies*, **42**, 169–90.

Oates, W.E. (1972), *Fiscal Federalism*, New York: Harcourt Brace Jovanovich.

Oates, W.E. (1985), 'Searching for Leviathan: An Empirical Study', *American Economic Review*, **75**, 748–57.

Oates, W.E. (1989), 'Searching for Leviathan: A Reply and Some Further Reflections', *American Economic Review*, **79**, 578–83.

O'Sullivan, A., T.A. Sexton and St.M. Sheffrin (1994), 'Differential Burdens from the Assessment Provisions of Proposition 13', *National Tax Journal*, **47**, 721–9.

O'Sullivan, A., T.A. Sexton and St.M. Sheffrin (1995), *Property Taxes and Tax Revolts: The Legacy of Proposition 13*, Cambridge: Cambridge University Press.

O'Sullivan, A., T.A. Sexton and St.M. Sheffrin (1999), 'Proposition 13: Unintended Effects and Feasible Reforms', *National Tax Journal*, **52**, 99–111.

Paldam, M. (1997), 'Political Business Cycles', in D.C. Mueller (ed.), *Perspectives on Public Choice: A Handbook*, Cambridge: Cambridge University Press, pp. 342–70.

Peltzman, S. (1992), 'Voters as Fiscal Conservatives', *Quarterly Journal of Economics*, **107**, 327–61.

Persson, T. and G. Tabellini (1994), 'Does Centralization Increase the Size of Government?' *European Economic Review*, **38**, 765–73.

Persson, T. and G. Tabellini (1999), 'The Size and Scope of Government: Comparative Politics With Rational Politicians', *European Economic Review*, **43**, 699–735.

Persson, T. and G. Tabellini (2000), 'Political Institutions and Policy Outcomes: What are the Stylized Facts?', mimeo, Stockholm University and London School of Economics, November.

Persson, T., G. Roland and G. Tabellini (2000), 'Comparative Politics and Public Finance', *Journal of Political Economy*, **108**, 1121–61.

Pommerehne, W.W. (1978), 'Institutional Approaches to Public Expenditure: Empirical Evidence from Swiss Municipalities', *Journal of Public Economics*, **9**, 255–80.

Pommerehne, W.W. (1983), 'Private versus öffentliche Müllabfuhr: Nochmals betrachtet', *Finanzarchiv*, **41**, 466–75.

Pommerehne, W.W. and F. Schneider (1978), 'Fiscal Illusion, Political Institutions, and Local Public Spending', *Kyklos*, **31**, 381–408.

Pommerehne, W.W. and H. Weck-Hannemann (1996), 'Tax Rates, Tax Administration and Income Tax Evasion in Switzerland', *Public Choice*, **88**, 161–70.

Pommerehne, W.W., A. Hart and L.P. Feld (1997), Steuerhinterziehung und ihre Kontrolle in unterschiedlichen politischen Systemen', *Homo oeconomicus*, **14**, 469-87.

Poterba, J.M. (1994), 'State Responses to Fiscal Crises: The Effects of Budgetary Institutions and Politics', *Journal of Political Economy*, **102**, 799-821.

Poterba, J.M. (1995), 'Balanced Budget Rules and Fiscal Policy: Evidence from the States', *National Tax Journal*, **48**, 329-36.

Poterba, J.M. (1997), 'Do Budget Rules Work?', in A.J. Auerbach (ed.), *Fiscal Policy: Lessons from Economic Research*, Cambridge, MA: MIT Press, pp. 53-86.

Poterba, J.M. and K. Rueben (1999), 'State Fiscal Institutions and the U.S. Municipal Bond Market', in J. Poterba and J. von Hagen (eds), *Fiscal Institutions and Fiscal Performance*, Chicago: Chicago University Press and NBER, pp. 181-207.

Raimondo, H.J. (1989), 'Leviathan and Federalism in the United States', *Public Finance Quarterly*, **17**, 204-15.

Reischauer, R.D. (1990), 'Taxes and Spending under Gramm-Rudman-Hollings', *National Tax Journal*, **43**, 223-32.

Romer, T. and H. Rosenthal (1979), 'The Elusive Median Voter', *Journal of Public Economics*, **12**, 143-70.

Roubini, N. and J.D. Sachs (1989), 'Political and Economic Determinants of Budget Deficits in the Industrial Democracies', *European Economic Review*, **33**, 903-38.

Rowley, Ch. (1984), 'The Relevance of the Median Voter Theorem', *Zeitschrift für die gesamte Staatswissenschaft*, **140**, 104-26.

Rueben, K.S. (1999), 'Tax Limitations and Government Growth: The Effect of State Tax and Expenditure Limits on State and Local Government', mimeo.

Santerre, R.E. (1989), 'Representative versus Direct Democracy: Are there Any Expenditure Differences?', *Public Choice*, **60**, 145-54.

Santerre, R.E. (1993), 'Representative versus Direct Democracy: The Role of Public Bureaucrats', *Public Choice*, **76**, 189-98.

Sass, T.R. (2001), 'The Anatomy of Political Representation: Direct Democracy, Parliamentary Democracy and Representative Democracy', in W.F. Shughart and F.A.P. Barnard, *The Elgar Companion To Public Choice*, Cheltenham, UK and Northhampton, USA: Edward Elgar, pp. 157-79.

Saunders, P. (1988), 'Explaining International Differences in Public Expenditure: An Empirical Study', *Public Finance/Finances Publiques*, **43**, 273-94.

Schaltegger, Ch.A. and L.P. Feld (2001), 'On Government Centralization and Budget Referendums: Evidence from Switzerland', mimeo, University of St Gallen, SIAW-HSG, October.

Schneider, F. and W.W. Pommerehne (1983), 'Macroeconomia della crescita in disequilibrio e settore pubblico in espansione: il peso delle differenze istituzionali', *Rivista Internazionale di Scienze Economiche e Commerciali*, **33**, 306-420.

Shadbegian, R.J. (1998), 'Do Tax and Expenditure Limitations Affect Local Government Budgets? Evidence from Panel Data', *Public Finance Review*, **26**, pp. 118-36.

Shadbegian, R.J. (1999), 'Fiscal Federalism, Collusion, and Government Size: Evidence from the States', *Public Finance Review*, **27**, 262-81.

Shadbegian, R.J. (1999a), 'The Effect of Tax and Expenditure Limitations on the Revenue of Local Government, 1962-87', *National Tax Journal*, **52**, pp. 211-17.

Sieg, G. (2001), 'A Political Business Cycle With Boundedly Rational Agents', *European Journal of Political Economy*, **17**, 39-52.

Solano, P.L. (1983), 'Institutional Explanations of Public Expenditures Among High Income Democracies', *Public Finance/Finances Publiques,* **38**, 440-58.

Stauffer, Th.P. (2001), *Instrumente des Haushaltsausgleichs: Ökonomische Analyse und rechtliche Umsetzung*, Ph.D. Thesis, University of St Gallen.

Stein, E., E. Talvi and A. Grisanti (1999), 'Institutional Arrangement and Fiscal Performance: The Latin American Experience', in J. Poterba and J. von Hagen (eds), *Fiscal Institutions and Fiscal Performance*, Chicago: Chicago University Press and NBER, pp. 103-33.

Stigler, G.J. (1979), Why Have the Socialists Been Winning?', *ORDO*, **30**, 61-8.

Strauch, R.R. and J. von Hagen (2001), 'Formal Fiscal Restraints and Budget Processes as Solution to a Deficit and Spending Bias in Public Finances: U.S. Experience and Possible Lessons for EMU', University of Bonn, Center for European Integration Studies, Working Paper No. B14.

Tarschys, D. (1975), 'The Growth of Public Expenditures: Nine Modes of Explanation', *Scandinavian Political Studies*, **10**, 9-31.

Tiebout, Ch.M. (1956), 'A Pure Theory of Local Expenditures', *Journal of Political Economy*, **64**, 416-24.

De Tray, D. and J. Fernandez (1986), 'Distributional Impacts of the Property Tax Revolt', *National Tax Journal*, **39**, 435-50.

Velasco, A. (1999), 'A Model of Endogenous Fiscal Deficits and Delayed Fiscal Reforms', in J. Poterba and J. von Hagen (eds), *Fiscal Institutions and Fiscal Performance*, Chicago: Chicago University Press and NBER, pp. 37-57.

Wallis, J.J. and W.E. Oates (1988), 'Does Economic Sclerosis Set in With Age? An Empirical Study of the Olson Hypothesis', *Kyklos*, **41**, 397-417.

Weck-Hannemann H. and W.W. Pommerehne (1989), 'Einkommensteuerhinterziehung in der Schweiz: Eine empirische Analyse', *Schweizerische Zeitschrift für Volkswirtschaft und Statistik*, **125**, 515-56.

Weingast, B.R., K.A. Shepsle and Ch. Johnsen (1981), 'The Political Economy of Benefits and Costs: A Neoclassical Approach to Distributive Politics', *Journal of Political Economy,* **89**, 642-64.

v. Weizsäcker, R.K. (1992), 'Staatsverschuldung und Demokratie', *Kyklos*, **45**, 51-67.

Wicksell, K. (1896), *Finanztheoretische Untersuchungen nebst Darstellung und Kritik des Steuerwesens Schwedens*, Jena: Gustav Fischer.

Wrede, M. (1999), 'Tragedy of the Fiscal Commons?: Fiscal Stock Externalities in a Leviathan Model of Federalism', *Public Choice*, **101**, 177-93.

Wrede, M. (2000), 'Shared Tax Sources and Public Expenditure', *International Tax and Public Finance*, **7**, 163-75.

Zax, J.S. (1989), 'Is There a Leviathan in Your Neighborhood?', *American Economic Review*, **79**, 560-67.

Zax, J.S. (1989a), 'Initiatives and Government Expenditures', *Public Choice*, **63**, 267-77.

10. Experimental investigation of collective action

Frans van Winden[*]

1. INTRODUCTION

Politics is about conflicting interests and ,influence backed up by force. Although rooted in individual behavior, it is not a one-man affair. Lack of information and control make social groups important, as they provide the behavioral clues and political clout (van Winden, 1999). Action – in particular, collective action – aimed at shared interests is thereby a key issue in political economics; think of participation in lobbying, riots, voting and the like. Fiorina (1997, p. 402) even speaks of the 'fundamental irrelevance of the individual voter'. Important research topics are related to this observation. They concern the determining factors of shared interests (linked up with a sorting process of individuals into (formal or informal) groups), the way political action is coordinated and organized, decision making regarding the type and level of activity, and the determinants of political influence.

Public choice theory has been very helpful in developing some fundamental insights in this field of research, with seminal contributions by Downs (1957) and Olson (1965). Emphasizing methodological individualism and focusing on self-interest and rationality as behavioral assumptions (*homo economicus*), it was argued that shared interests are not sufficient for collective action, due to a free-riding problem. The usual example is voting in large-scale elections. Why would an individual bother to turn out and vote if the chance of being decisive is negligible? Given some cost of voting one would not expect many people to do so. This is precisely what is predicted by existing voting models applying a purely individual calculus of expected benefits and costs. Unfortunately, often more than 50 percent of the electorate turns out in actual elections. The main theoretical conclusion is that something like an additional benefit derived from voting – such as through the fulfilment of 'civic duty' – is required for an 'explanation' (see, for example, Mueller, 1989; Aldrich, 1997).[1] Or is it non-selfish behavior and/or irrationality that plays a role? Even

*Comments by Arthur Schram and Jens Grosser are gratefully acknowledged.

more qualitative predictions derived from these models, like higher turnout the closer the election, have not found undisputed empirical support. A major problem with the empirical studies is, however, that they have to rely on field data, from elections or surveys that are not particularly tailored to test the theoretical predictions. For example, with surveys it is unclear what motivates the responses that people provide, while election data are typically highly aggregated and violate the *ceteris paribus* condition of theoretical models (is the higher turnout in a closer election due to a larger probability for a voter of being decisive or to a larger effort by candidates to get the vote out?).

Fortunately, an alternative research method exists that allows the investigation of behavior under controlled conditions: laboratory experimentation. In an economic experiment real people make real choices with real (generally, monetary) consequences in a controlled environment. The environment can be linked to a specific theoretical model and attention focused on essential aspects, which can be manipulated (varied) one by one. Moreover, to check the robustness of findings the experiment can be replicated. Control and replication are the major comparative advantages of this relatively new research method (see, for example, Davis and Holt, 1993; Kagel and Roth, 1995). By now, a substantial number of studies exist applying this method to issues of public choice, like electoral competition, committee decision making and principal–agent problems (see Palfrey, 1991; Kinder and Palfrey, 1993; van Winden and Bosman, 1996).

In this survey, attention will be focused on collective action experiments. More particularly, I will discuss three sets of experiments, in three separate sections. Section 2 is concerned with the fundamental issue of free-riding. It considers participation as a contribution to a public good. Section 3 adds an important political dimension by introducing competing groups, while Section 4 focuses on the activity level and political influence of interest groups (lobbying). Implications for theory and practice will be discussed in Section 5. Section 6, finally, concludes with some issues for future research.

2.   PARTICIPATION AS CONTRIBUTION TO A PUBLIC GOOD

The question addressed in this section is whether people will indeed free-ride if participation in the provision of a public good (collective action) is costly to them whereas the benefits are shared by all.[2] Many experiments, using different designs, have been run to study this issue and the precise conditions under which participation takes place (for surveys, see Ledyard, 1995; Offerman, 1997). In the *basic experimental design* each individual in a group has a number of tokens that can be allocated to a 'private account' (private good) or a 'group account' (public good). Group members do not know each other's identity. Each token contributed to the group account leaves the individual a smaller payoff than putting it in the private account. However, the payoff from a token allocated to the group account is enjoyed by all members of the group. Moreover, the total payoff to the group of that token is larger than the payoff the individual would get from the private account.[3] The implication is that a rational own-payoff maximizer (a *homo economicus*) should not contribute to the group account in the experiment. But this would run against the group interest in the sense that all members would be better off by contributing all tokens. Typically, this public-good game is repeated over a number of rounds, to allow for some learning, for example. Variants of the basic design include 'strangers' versus 'partners' (that is, changing instead of constant group compositions over rounds), continuous versus step-level public-good games (in the latter case, contributions have to exceed a certain level before the public good is obtained), opportunities for communication or sanctioning, and different payoff functions. The first results to be presented belong to the strong and replicable effects mentioned by Ledyard (1995).

- Contributions to the public good are substantial (on average, 40–60 percent of the tokens), but decline over rounds (at least, with strangers).
- There is a tendency towards free-riding – zero contributions – in the final rounds (so-called 'end effect').
- Contributions increase with the individual payoff from the public good, relative to the private good.[4]
- Communication positively affects contributions, even if only 'cheap talk'.
- Contributions do not decrease with larger group size (up to a size of 100, at least).

These results are difficult to reconcile with the standard *homo economicus* model, in particular if joined with the following more recent observations.

- There exists clear evidence of reciprocal behavior. In repeated games, contributions adjust to the group average, with contributions higher (lower) than the average showing a tendency to become lower (higher) (Keser and van Winden, 2000). Moreover, if given an explicit opportunity to reward or punish group members, people use the opportunity to do so, where reward and punishment appear to be related to the (average) contributions made by these other members. This happens even if doing so is costly, and even after the final round (see Ostrom and Walker, 1997; Fehr and Gächter, 2000). The presence of such an opportunity turns out to have a significant impact on cooperation; it substantially increases the contribution level. At this stage, it is not completely clear what precisely drives this behavior. It may be due to cognitive deliberations based on norms like fairness ('I should punish unfair behavior'). On the other hand, reciprocal behavior also appears to be triggered by emotions like anger or gratitude (Fehr and Gächter, 2000; Bosman and van Winden, 2002), which over time may generate positive or negative social ties (van Dijk et al., 2002).

- People show different motivations. For example, some individuals free-ride all the time, whereas others appear to be 'conditional cooperators' whose willingness to cooperate depends on the cooperation observed among the other group members (see Schram, 2000).[5] Motivations are also affected by the nature of the environment. Situations where individuals stay together in groups (partners) – in particular, if opportunities for communication exist – appear to be beneficial for fostering cooperation. A sense of group identity affecting beliefs and expectations may play a role here (see, in this context, Brewer and Gardner, 1996).

The picture that emerges from the experimental studies is the following. First, the free-riding problem for collective action is not as bad as the *homo economicus* model suggests. Second, motivational factors other than own (monetary) payoffs, like norms and emotions or identification with a group, are important. Third, and related to the previous point, the smaller the 'social distance' – as determined by factors like social mobility (cf. partners versus strangers) and opportunities to communicate or to reward and punish – the greater the likelihood that collective action succeeds.

In this section we have focused on the collective action problem within a social group. The next section is concerned with the politically highly relevant issue of the impact of competition between groups.

3. PARTICIPATION WITH COMPETITION AMONG GROUPS

Politics is about conflicting interests, in particular between social groups. Does intergroup conflict affect the participation in collective action? If so, what are the consequences? Since government policies will be influenced by the relative participation of social groups, a competitive aspect is now added to the (within group) cooperative 'team' aspect of collective action (see Palfrey and Rosenthal, 1983). The latter is again related to the fact that the political outcome of collective action is like a public good within the groups concerned (for example, a service, tax rate, or subsidy). The *basic experimental design* of such 'team games' is as in the single group case discussed in the previous section, with the exception that there are now two (equally sized) groups and the individual payoff decreases with the participation level of the other group (resembling proportional representation in politics).[6] Although it is easy to see that, again, a rational own-payoff maximizer should free-ride (contribute nothing to the group account) – whereas it is in the interest of each group separately that people participate (contribute tokens) – this behavior is now in line with the collective interest of the groups taken together. The reason is that the competitive and symmetric nature of the situation causes cooperation by group members to lead to the same result as when all free-ride (namely, a tie). Thus it is in their collective interest not to participate in collective action (like voting, pressure group activity, or a war against the other group). It is important to note, however, that own-payoff maximization can lead to a completely different outcome in the case of a winner-takes-all situation (where a zero payoff is obtained from the group account if total contributions fall short of those in the other group), which resembles majority rule in politics. It is readily seen that in such a situation, with equally sized groups, it would be individually rational for all to participate. Although there are not many experimental studies, some interesting results can be reported (see the survey of Bornstein, 2000; Schram and Sonnemans 1996a, 1996b). The findings reported below relate to the basic design and some variants thereof, concerning partners instead of strangers, communication, and winner-takes-all instead of proportional influence.

- Contributions within groups are higher than with one group (no competition).
- Again, contributions are higher when group composition is constant (partners), and with communication among group members.
- Again, there appears to be no (clear) effect of changes in group size.
- Again, motivational heterogeneity is observed.
- Contributions are higher in the case of a winner-takes-all situation, compared to proportional influence.

Thus it appears that competition between groups stimulates participation in collective action within groups, and the more so in the case of a winner-takes-all type of situation (note the similarity with a step-level public good). As discussed above, this behavior runs counter to the collective interest of the groups, which would now be furthered by less collective action (on both sides). This, as well as other important issues, needs further investigation. For example, what are the effects of strong asymmetry (highly unequal group sizes) or of different decision-making procedures within groups (for some first results, see Bornstein et al., 2002)? Regarding the latter, experimental evidence exists showing that so-called unitary groups, where group members can make (costless) binding agreements, are more competitive than individuals (see Insko and Schopler, 1998). This is an important result because it is common in economics to model groups – like firms, unions, or political parties – as individuals.

4.   LOBBYING

In the previous two sections attention was focused on the collective action issues of participation and coordination. We will now report on experimental studies concentrating on the costly endeavors of interest groups to influence policy making. Three types of models dealing with this topic are investigated: rent-seeking, common agency, and signaling models (for a discussion and references, see van Winden, 1999). In contrast with the other models, in rent-seeking models the benefits from lobbying are not determined by an actual policy maker (player) but by an assumed mechanism, that is, a function mapping rent-seeking expenditures into a probability of success for each interest group. The main difference between common agency and signaling models is that the latter are concerned with the (strategic) transmission of information and the influence thereof, whereas the former (as yet) focus on the influence of contributions to a policy maker under perfect information. Further details are given below when we discuss the experiments for each type of model. All of these theoretical models employ the *homo economicus* assumption that players aim at the maximization of their own payoff (net of lobby costs).

Rent-seeking

In view of the huge number of publications concerning theoretical rent-seeking models, it is quite remarkable that there are only a few experimental studies. In the *basic experimental design* there are two players, each having an identical number of tokens, which they can use to bid (simultaneously) for a given 'prize'. The probability of winning the prize, and thereby the (expected) payoff, depends on the player's bid relative to the other player's bid; in the case of a tie, this probability is assumed to be $1/2$.[7] The starkest contrast is between the case where the probability of winning equals the ratio of the bid and the sum of the bids (proportional probabilities) and the case where the highest bidder wins (perfect discrimination). Note that the importance of relative bids implies that there is a public-good (bad) aspect to lobbying in these models, in the sense that players might benefit if they could restrain themselves from lobbying. In fact, they would get the highest payoff if they did not bid at all. However, the theoretical prediction is that players will bid. And, if bids stand for the use of resources that could otherwise be productively employed, this means that behavior would be inefficient. Put differently, the rent represented by the prize would be more or less dissipated by the rent-seeking expenditures. The experiments show the following findings (see the survey and results of Potters et al., 1998).

- The rent-seeking model has predictive power. Rent dissipation (inefficiency) is observed, and, at least for the two starkest cases, the results are in line with the theoretical predictions.
- There is some evidence of less dissipation if players stay together over rounds of play (partners situation).
- Players are of different types. Some play like 'gamesmen': they appear to understand the strategic nature of the game and behave accordingly. Others seem simply confused and just randomize, while a substantial proportion of players adapts behavior to the outcomes in earlier rounds.

In an interesting variant of the basic model, Weimann et al. (2000) have players make sequential instead of simultaneous bids. Theoretically, this two-stage game gives the first mover the opportunity to make a pre-emptive bid, leaving the second player with at best a zero payoff. So, what is observed?

- No support is found for the theoretical first-mover advantage. Rather, a second-mover advantage is observed.
- The driving factor appears to be the opportunity for second movers to punish first movers, which is costly to the former but even more costly to the latter. Moreover, they exploit cooperative (efficient or 'fair') behavior by first movers.
- Emotions, rather than strategic behavior, appear to play a role because second movers still intensively punish in the last round (and they do not seem to be motivated much by norms like fairness; see the previous point).

Thus, with this variation of the rent-seeking model little support for the theory is found. Interestingly, as with the public-good experiments, the opportunity to punish appears to be used in a non-strategic way but plays an important role in producing the results. The fact that second movers are better off shows that the 'irrationality' of this kind of behavior can be questioned (cf. Frank, 1988).

Common Agency

In common agency game models multiple lobbyists (principals) offer contributions to a policy maker (agent) in the form of a schedule, where contributions are contingent on the policy chosen by the policy maker (see Bernheim and Whinston, 1986). For example, think of campaign contributions offered to political candidates in exchange for policy promises (which are assumedly kept), where the more is offered, the better the promise. As yet, we only know of one experiment investigating this type of model (Kirchsteiger and Prat, 2002). In the experiment the game is between one player (the agent) who has to choose between a number of alternatives of no direct interest to himself and two other players (the principals) with conflicting interests. The latter simultaneously choose a contribution schedule, promising a non-negative contribution (here, an amount of money) for each alternative. Then, the first player chooses between the alternatives and collects the contributions. Assuming rational own-payoff-maximizing behavior, theory predicts that the agent will maximize the sum of the contributions and that the principals will spread their contributions in a specific way.[8] The main findings are the following.

- Little support is obtained for the theoretical equilibrium predictions.
- Players only make serious contributions to the most preferred alternative.

According to Kirchsteiger and Prat, an important reason for these findings may be the complexity of the theoretical equilibrium strategies.

Signaling

An important reason for lobbying, neglected by the previous models, is the lack of information on the side of policy makers concerning the consequences of policies. Interest groups are likely to be better informed, either because the policies affect them directly or because of their better contact with those who are concerned. The problem for the policy maker, of course, is the possibility of strategic information transmission by the lobbyists representing these interest groups. They may not (always) provide all of the information they have or may not transmit it in a truthful way. Signaling models of lobbying try to formalize such a situation, without assuming that those involved can make binding contracts as in common agency models (for a basic model, see Potters and van Winden, 1992). Again, only few experiments have been carried out to date. In the experiments of Potters and van Winden (1996, 2000) there are two players. One of the players (the policy maker) has to choose between two alternatives. The alternative chosen determines the payoffs of both players, given the 'state of the world'. The second player (the interest group) is informed about the actual state, while the policy maker only knows the likelihood of the possible states. The distribution of the states is such that the alternative that is least preferred by the interest group (whatever the state is) gives the higher expected payoff to the policy maker. Before the policy maker decides, the interest group has the option to send a costly message to the policy maker concerning the actual state. For illustration, think of a policy maker who is uncertain about the benefits of subsidizing a firm, where the benefits depend on the competitiveness of the firm. Theoretically, in this situation, rational own-payoff-maximizing interest groups should more often send messages if the state is such that there is no conflict of interest with the policy maker; otherwise, the latter would not risk changing the policy that is believed to be best in the absence of a message. In equilibrium, then, both the interest group and the policy maker can expect to benefit from the possibility of lobbying (sending costly messages). The experimental results show the following.

- Information transmission benefiting both the interest group and the policy maker occurs.
- However, the predictive power of the theory is rather weak. Players focus (too much) on their own payoffs and adapt (beliefs) to the observed actions of the opponent.
- Professional lobbyists – compared to students – earn more money and behave more like gamesmen. Professional rules of conduct (like 'avoid conflicts of interest', 'focus on win–win situations', and 'never cheat or misinform') may explain.

Taking stock, the conclusion should be that experimental studies, generally, only find weak support for the models of lobbying that are proposed in the literature. On the other hand, there are as yet very few studies. Furthermore, many aspects are still left to be explored, like the group (decision-making) aspect of interest groups, (financial) constraints on contributions, or the entry and exit decisions of interest group members.

5.   IMPLICATIONS FOR THEORY AND PRACTICE

What can we conclude from the experimental findings concerning collective action obtained so far? Let us start with some policy implications and then look at the findings from a more theoretical perspective.

Implications for Practice

In my view, there are at least three major policy implications.

- *The rationale for government intervention needs to be revisited.* Although free-riding occurs, and quite a few people free-ride all the time, the experiments show that on average people make substantial voluntary contributions to public goods. They also use (costly) opportunities to communicate and sanction, even when this runs against their self-interest. Thus the textbook *homo economicus* rationale for government interference with the supply of public goods does not get much support. Note, however, that from a collective welfare point of view this is not always good news. There are circumstances where collective action may lead to welfare losses. Experiments showed this for intergroup conflicts, where collective action (being a group-specific public good, in that case) may trigger a detrimental escalation. Another well-known example is collusion among firms.

- *Lobbying is important for informed policy making.* Once we step back from the rent-seeking and common agency models of lobbying where the information problem for policy making is neglected, and acknowledge the lack of information confronting policy makers in practice, the opportunity to transmit policy-relevant information through lobbying becomes extremely important. The signaling model experiments showed that people use such a (costly) opportunity and that it can be beneficial to all concerned. This is not to say, of course, that there are no potential welfare losses that have to be taken into account, which may be due, for example, to an unequal access to lobbying or an excessive spending of resources.

- *We know substantially more now about how to enhance collective action.* Options for people to communicate, to apply sanctions, and to stay together (with the prospect of future interaction and the possibility of social ties) appear to be important. Note that mobility and government intervention may be two-sided swords in this respect, because of their impact on the possibility to apply sanctions and form social ties (for example by breaking up or diminishing the relevance of the social network established through collective action). Also, norms and values that people internalize through the interaction with educators, teachers and others play a role. Culture matters (see also Ockenfels and Weimann, 1999; Henrich et al., 2001). This includes what we learn to attribute to other people in this respect. For example, it seems that training in the *homo economicus* model of behavior encourages the view and expectation that others are motivated primarily by self-interest, and thereby increases the likelihood that people will defect in social dilemmas (Frank et al., 1996; Blais and Young, 1999). Finally, the experimental results point at paying heed to collective choice procedures, such as proportional representation or winner-takes-all, because they can affect collective action.

Implications for Theory

The evidence surveyed in this chapter only adds to a great deal of other experimental evidence (see Kagel and Roth, 1995; Camerer, 1998) in support of the following conclusion.

- *The* homo economicus *model fails as a generally applicable model to explain economic behavior.*

First, we have seen that many people do not seem rationally to pursue their economic self-interest alone. For instance, they punish or reward other people even if this is only costly to themselves. Behavior is shaped by different social norms and values, as well as psychological traits (ways of thinking and feeling). People often do care about the well-being of other people or the appropriateness of their behavior. Moreover, the experimental evidence indicates that individuals have feelings that motivate them. They get angry, and feel urged to retaliate if an opponent defects from cooperative behavior, for instance. Whereas it may be obvious to any casual observer of politics in practice that emotions count, these are completely neglected in our economic models. Where's the heat? Substantial evidence exists showing that emotions are an important motivational factor and, in addition, may in fact be crucial for rational decision making. In the next section, I will return to these issues. Another important implication of the experimental results is that models should allow for adaptive and mostly backward-looking behavior. It would help in understanding the dynamics of collective action – a neglected area of research – such as the gradual tendency towards free-riding among 'strangers', and the different pattern displayed by 'partners' (see Keser and van Winden, 2000). And, finally, it is to be acknowledged that the usual single-player assumption for interest groups is not innocent. Even so-called unitary groups (making jointly binding decisions) appear to behave differently in comparison with an individual. In the next section, I will elaborate on some important topics for future research that are linked to these observations. I expect that the necessary enrichment of our formal conception of economic behavior will have the following more general implication.

- *Specific models for specific classes of cases will have to be developed for generating further insights.*

It is only by going through a phase where solid evidence is collected for models focusing on particular behavioral settings (in terms of cognition and emotion) that we can hope to arrive at a powerful more general model at some later stage. *Homo economicus* may very well survive in a more restricted habitat, like certain markets, as suggested by the experimental literature (see Davis and Holt, 1993; Kagel and Roth, 1995).

6.   FUTURE RESEARCH

In the Introduction, the following major issues concerning collective action were distinguished: the nature of the interests shared by those (potentially) involved in the collective action; the way the action is coordinated and organized; the type and level of an interest group's activity; and the determinants of its political influence. The laboratory experiments discussed in the previous sections have generated some important insights, but they have also raised many new interesting questions, and much is left to be (further) explored. In this section I will focus on some important issues dealing with individual behavior, organization, and the role of laboratory experimentation.

Behavior

Individual behavior is determined by interests, cognition (reasoning) and emotions. Although economists – as in fact psychologists, up to about the mid-1980s – have neglected emotions as a motivational factor, there exists substantial evidence now that they should be taken into account to understand and predict behavior. Let me start, however, with the following statement regarding interests.

● *People are groping for political interests; they do not just have them*   I guess some introspection will make it clear that we often do not know what precisely are our interests in the political sphere. Take the interests of a worker in the taxation of wages and profits. At first glance, one might perhaps think that a worker would prefer profit taxation. However, confronted with statements about capital flight, a worker may become convinced that wage taxation is to be preferred. In a world with severe uncertainty about what is right or wrong in terms of policy, one cannot simply take the interests of political agents as given. But, then, how do they develop? As I have discussed more extensively elsewhere, we have to pay much more attention to the social embeddedness of behavior and take a group frame of reference (van Winden, 1999). People interact, which affects their beliefs and preferences. In this way they sort themselves into (informal) social groups, the members of which are characterized by similar behavior. There are many concepts related to this phenomenon, like social norms, conformity, imitation, contagion, herding, bandwagons, neighborhood effects, and peer influences (see Manski, 2000). As yet there are hardly any collective action models which allow for such dynamic aspects (see, however, Lohmann, 1994; Sadiraj et al., 2002), and almost no experiments (an exception is Ehrhart and Keser, 1999).

● *Bounded rationality: cognition*   In contrast with the usual assumption in economics, the rationality of individuals – in terms of capacity and skills of reasoning – is clearly bounded (see Camerer, 1998; Rabin, 1998).[9] People find it hard to look ahead (do backward induction or exponential discounting), to reason strategically (put themselves in the position of others), or to deal with probabilities (apply Bayes's rule). It is, therefore, important to investigate, for example, non-expected-utility models like prospect theory. The risk-seeking in the domain of losses predicted by this theory may help explain, for instance, why political movements against incumbents and in favor of challengers stand a better chance in case of economic adversity (Quattrone and Tversky, 1993).

● *Bounded reasoning: emotions*   Our economic decisions are not only affected by cognitive limitations but also by the impact of emotions. I will elaborate somewhat more on this issue, because I think it is important and refers to a relatively much less familiar aspect of behavior. An emotion arises when an event is appraised by an individual as relevant to an important concern or interest (see, for example, Oatley and Jenkins, 1996). If the interest is advanced (impeded) a positive (negative) emotion is generated which is experienced as pleasurable (painful); consequently, they have a direct hedonic effect. The occurrence of an emotion cannot be chosen, because the underlying mental processes are unconscious and not cognitively penetrable. Emotions have a dual nature: they entail benefits or costs (hedonic impact), but also affect the decision-making process as such (for example via attention and memory). Central to an emotion is an action tendency, an urge to execute a particular action, which may be regulated by further appraisals. If the intensity of an emotion is sufficiently strong, however, it surpasses a regulation threshold, leading to a mode of operation where we just react rather than think. This implies that emotions may lead to less-reasoned decisions, and in this sense contribute to bounded rationality (Kaufman, 1999). On the other hand, many arguments and substantial evidence exist pointing to beneficial effects; according to some scholars emotions are even necessary for cognitions to have an influence on behavior (see Elster, 1998; Loewenstein, 2000). In any case, emotions would seem to play an important role in politics. There are not only many statements by professional and academic experts bearing this out, but also some empirical studies. Regarding the former, De Tocqueville and Schumpeter, for example, pointed to the role played by emotions in determining political behavior (see the quotes in Mueller, 1989, pp. 348–9). And many politicians and commentators have referred to hatred as a motivation for political violence, on the occasion of the terrorist attacks of 11 September 2001. According to Roemer (1979), collective action in the form of demonstrations or riots may often be the expression of bottled-up anger with no instrumental purpose. In a similar vein, Romer (1995) sees political participation related to anger induced by the perceived negation of entitlements. As regards the empirical evidence, Abelson et al. (1982), for instance, find that affect scores of presidential candidates are highly predictive of political preferences, adding significantly to the explanation offered by trait scores and party identification (see also Rahn et al., 1990). Marcus and Mackuen (1993) provide empirical evidence indicating that anxiety stimulates voters to pay attention to campaigns, to learn policy-related information about candidates, and to rely to a lesser extent on habit in voting decisions. Furthermore, some political psychologists have speculated that anxious people are more susceptible to the influence of leaders who are adept at discovering 'enemies' as the 'cause' of their anxiety (Barner-Barry and Rosenwein, 1985). Also, it is to be expected that emotions like guilt and shame – which may be triggered by peer influences or internalized norms (for example that it is one's civic duty to vote) – can help explain political participation. Emotions are not just random and transitory events that are of no political economic significance. They are very systematic in character, and some first economic experiments point at a significant behavioral impact in a politically relevant setting of appropriation and retaliation (see van Winden, 2001; Bosman and van Winden, 2002). The waiting is now for models of collective action allowing for emotions, and for experiments to explore their importance in such a setting.

Organization

So far, experimental studies of collective action – as, in fact, theoretical studies of interest groups – have either focused on the contributions of members of a given group to some (group-specific) public good or on the lobbying by single-player interest 'groups'. The way that such groups get started and develop as well as their decision-making structure have been neglected.

● *How do formal (organized) interest groups get started and how do they develop?* We need to know much more about the initiative takers (political entrepreneurs), and the determinants of why people join, stay with and leave interest groups – in short, the dynamics of interest groups. Political economic outcomes can be very different once these dynamic aspects are taken into account (Sadiraj et al., 2001, 2002). More knowledge is also required about the choice and impact of means of communication and sanctioning. Moreover, how are the decision-making procedures and rules actually determined? Experiments can be very useful here, because such issues may be difficult to investigate systematically in the field. The same holds for the next question.

- *What is the impact of decision-making structures?* For example, does it matter for a group's decisions whether these are taken in a democratic or dictatorial way? And, if so, how would that affect the outcome of intergroup conflict? The little experimental evidence that exists suggests that it does make a difference which of these collective choice rules are used by interest groups (Bornstein et al., 2002), but more research is needed. Another interesting issue would be whether there are any interaction effects between the choice rules employed by (competing) interest groups and their use of communication and sanctioning mechanisms (for example the choice between 'words' and 'deeds').

Laboratory Experimentation

Laboratory experimentation has proved to be a useful research method for the study of collective action problems. As regards the kinds of problems that are investigated, however, it is now time to move on to topics other than free-riding in social dilemma situations. It is hoped that the previous paragraphs show that there is much left to be researched. In addition to the topics already mentioned, I would like to point to the importance of executing experiments with very large groups. So far, group sizes up to about 100 participants have been studied. With the use of modern technology, like the Internet, it should be possible to go much further. Laboratory experimentation is no substitute for other research methods, however. First, there are other forms of experimentation that may be fruitfully used. Apart from field experiments, which are typically difficult (and costly) to organize, one should in particular think of computer experiments (simulations), because of the opportunity it gives to study complex interactions (see, for example, Sadiraj et al., 2001, 2002). Second, there are other empirical research methods (like questionnaires or case studies). And, third, we should try to relate our findings to theoretical models. There is a need for problem-driven models (focusing on classes of cases first), which are tested and improved through the use of the afore-mentioned research methods, and take the findings from the other (social) sciences seriously.

NOTES

1. According to the 'rational voter hypothesis', people will vote if: $PB + D - C > 0$, where P stands for the perceived probability that the vote is decisive, B denotes the benefit from changing the election outcome, D the benefit from voting *per se* (like civic duty), and C the cost of voting. The main conclusion is that D is necessary to explain the substantial turnout levels observed in practice.
2. Of course, the public good may also consist of the prevention of a public bad like the excessive use of fishing grounds, deforestation, and the like.
3. Formally, the payoff to an individual i from a group with n members is given by: $payoff_i = p(z_i - x_i) + g \Sigma_j x_j$ $(j = 1, \ldots, n)$, with z the total number of tokens (endowment), x the number allocated to the group account, and p (g) the return on a private (group) account token. Moreover: $ng > p > g > 0$.
4. In case of a step level, this is relative to the required sum of contributions (Croson and Marks, 2000).
5. Fischbacher et al. (2001) find about 20–30 percent free-riders and about 50 percent conditional cooperators among their subjects.
6. Formally: $payoff_i = p(z_i - x_i) + g (\Sigma_j x_j - \Sigma_j y_j) + t$, with x (y) indicating the tokens allocated to the group account by a member of group X (Y), t denoting the payoff from the group account in case of a tie (that is, $\Sigma x = \Sigma y$), and again $ng > p > g > 0$. Alternatively, the payoff from the group account may be related to the relative level of contributions.
7. Formally, letting x and y denote the respective bids, and P the prize, then the payoff to the player with bid x equals: $payoff = [x^r/(x^r + y^r)].P - x$, with $[.] = \frac{1}{2}$ if $x = y = 0$. The higher r, the more discriminatory the game becomes (with $r = \infty$, the highest bidder wins). The basic model is due to Tullock (1980).
8. In the experiment the first player was actually substituted by a robot.
9. See in this context also the critical study of Green and Shapiro (1994) regarding applications of rational choice theory in political science.

REFERENCES

Abelson, R.P., Kinder, D.R., Peters, M.D. and S.T. Fiske (1982), 'Affective and semantic components in political person perception', *Journal of Personality and Social Psychology*, **42**.

Aldrich, J.H. (1997), 'When is it rational to vote?', in: D.C. Mueller (ed.), *Perspective on Public Choice*, Cambridge: Cambridge University Press.

Barner-Barry, C. and R. Rosenwein (1985), *Psychological Perspectives on Politics*, Englewood Cliffs, NJ: Prentice-Hall.

Bernheim, B.D. and M.D. Whinston (1986), 'Menu auctions, resource allocation, and economic influence', *Quarterly Journal of Economics*, **101**, 1–31.

Blais, A. and R. Young (1999), 'Why do people vote? An experiment in rationality', *Public Choice*, **99**, 39–55.

Bornstein, G. (2000), 'The intergroup prisoner's dilemma game as a model of intergroup conflict', mimeo, Hebrew University, Jerusalem.

Bornstein, G., A. Schram and J. Sonnemans (2002), 'Do democracies breed chickens?', in R. Suleiman, D.V. Budescu, I. Fischer and D. Messick (eds), *Contemporary Psychological Research on Social Dilemmas*, forthcoming.

Bosman, R. and F. van Winden (2002), 'Emotional hazard in a power-to-take experiment', *Economic Journal*, **112**, 147–69.

Brewer, M.B. and W. Gardner (1996), 'Who is this "we"? Levels of collective identity and self representation', *Journal of Personality and Social Psychology*, **71**, 83–93.

Camerer, C. (1998), 'Bounded rationality in individual decision making', *Experimental Economics*, **1**, 163–83.

Croson, R.T.A. and M.B. Marks (2000), 'Step returns in threshold public goods: a meta- and experimental analysis', *Experimental Economics*, 239–59.

Davis, D. and C. Holt (1993), *Experimental Economics*, Princeton, NJ: Princeton University Press.

van Dijk, F., J. Sonnemans and F. van Winden (2002), 'Social ties in a public good experiment', *Journal of Public Economics*, **85**, 275–99.

Downs, A. (1957), *An Economic Theory of Democracy*, New York: Harper and Row.

Ehrhart, K.-M. and C. Keser (1999), 'Mobility and cooperation: on the run', Working Paper, CIRANO.

Elster, J. (1998), 'Emotions and economic theory', *Journal of Economic Literature*, **36**, 47–74.

Fehr, E. and S. Gächter (2000), 'Fairness and retaliation', *Journal of Economic Perspectives*, **14**, 159–81.

Fiorina, M.P. (1997), 'Voting behavior', in D.C. Mueller (ed.), *Perspectives on Public Choice*, Cambridge: Cambridge University Press.

Fischbacher, U., S. Gächter and E. Fehr (2001), 'Are people conditionally cooperative? Evidence from a public good experiment', *Economics Letters*, **71**, 397–404.

Frank, R.H. (1988), *Passions within Reason*, New York: Norton.

Frank, R.H., T.D. Gilovich and D.T. Regan (1996), 'Do economists make bad citizens?', *Journal of Economic Perspectives*, **10**, 187–92.

Green, D.P. and I. Shapiro (1994), *Pathologies of rational choice theory*, New Haven: Yale University Press.

Henrich, J., R. Boyd, S. Bowles, C. Camerer, E. Fehr, H. Gintis and R. McElreath (2001), 'In search of homo economicus: behavioral experiments in 15 small-scale societies', *American Economic Review*, **91**, 73–8.

Insko, C.A. and J. Schopler (1998), 'Differential distrust of groups and individuals', in C. Sedikides, J. Schopler and C.A. Insko (eds) (1998), *Intergroup Cognition and Intergroup Behavior*, Mahwah, NJ: Erlbaum.

Kagel, J.H. and A.E. Roth (eds) (1995), *The Handbook of Experimental Economics*, Princeton: Princeton University Press.

Kaufman, B.E. (1999), 'Emotional arousal as a source of bounded rationality', *Journal of Economic Behavior and Organization*, **38**, 135–44.

Keser, C. and F. van Winden (2000), 'Conditional cooperation and voluntary contributions to public goods, *Scandinavian Journal of Economics*, **102**, 23–39.

Kinder, D.R. and T.R. Palfrey (1993), *Experimental Foundations of Political Science*, Ann Arbor: University of Michigan Press.

Kirchsteiger, G. and A. Prat (2002), 'Inefficient equilibria in lobbying', *Journal of Public Economics*, forthcoming.

Ledyard, J. (1995), 'Public goods: a survey of experimental results', in J.H. Kagel and A.E. Roth (eds), *The Handbook of Experimental Economics*, Princeton: Princeton University Press.

Loewenstein, G.F. (2000), 'Emotions in economic theory and economic behavior', *American Economic Review, Papers and Proceedings*, **90**, 426–32.

Lohmann, S. (1994), 'The dynamics of informational cascades', *World Politics*, **47**, 42–101.

Manski, C.F. (2000), 'Economic analysis of social interactions', *Journal of Economic Perspectives*, **14**, 115–36.

Marcus, G.E. and M.B. Mackuen (1993), 'Anxiety, enthusiasm, and the vote: the emotional underpinnings of learning and involvement during presidential campaigns', *American Political Science Review*, **87**, 672–85.

Mueller, D.C. (1989), *Public Choice II*, Cambridge: Cambridge University Press.

Oatley, K. and J.M. Jenkins (1996), *Understanding Emotions*, Oxford: Blackwell.

Ockenfels, A. and J. Weimann (1999), 'Types and patterns: an experimental East–West-German comparison of cooperation and solidarity', *Journal of Public Economics*, **71**, 275–87.

Offerman, T. (1997), *Beliefs and Decision Rules in Public Good Games*, Dordrecht: Kluwer.

Olson, M. (1965), *The Logic of Collective Action*, Cambridge: Harvard University Press.

Ostrom, E. and J. Walker (1997), 'Neither markets nor states: linking transformation processes in collective action arenas', in D.C. Mueller (ed.), *Perspectives on Public Choice*, Cambridge: Cambridge University Press.

Palfrey, T.R. (ed.) (1991), *Laboratory Research in Political Economy*, Ann Arbor: University of Michigan Press.

Palfrey, T.R. and H. Rosenthal (1983), 'A strategic calculus of voting', *Public Choice*, **41**, 7–53.

Potters, J., C.G. de Vries, and F. van Winden (1998), 'An experimental examination of rational rent-seeking', *European Journal of Political Economy*, **14**, 783–800.

Potters, J. and F. van Winden (1992), 'Lobbying and asymmetric information', *Public Choice*, **74**, 269–92.

Potters, J. and F. van Winden (1996), 'Comparative statics of a signaling game', *International Journal of Game Theory*, **25**, 329–53.

Potters, J. and F. van Winden (2000), 'Professionals and students in a lobbying experiment: professional rules of conduct and subject surrogacy', *Journal of Economic Behavior and Organization*, **43**, 499–522.

Quattrone, G.A. and A. Tversky (1993), 'Contrasting rational and psychological analyses of political choice', in D.R. Kinder and T.R. Palfrey (eds), *Experimental Foundations of Political Science*, Ann Arbor: University of Michigan Press.

Rabin, M. (1998), 'Psychology and economics', *Journal of Economic Literature*, **36**, 11–46.

Rahn, W.M., J.H. Aldrich, E. Borgida and J.L. Sullivan (1990), 'A social–cognitive model of candidate appraisal', in J.A. Ferejohn and J.H. Kuklinski (eds), *Information and Democratic Processes*, Urbana: University of Illinois Press.

Roemer, J.E. (1979), 'Mass action is not individually rational: reply', *Journal of Economic Issues*, **13**, 763–7.

Romer, P. (1995), 'Preferences, promises, and the politics of entitlement', in V. Fuchs (ed.), *Individual Social Responsibility*, Chicago: University of Chicago Press.

Sadiraj, V., J. Tuinstra and F. van Winden (2001), 'A dynamic model of endogenous interest group sizes and policymaking', Working Paper, University of Amsterdam.

Sadiraj, V., J. Tuinstra and F. van Winden (2002), 'Interest groups and social dynamics in a model of spatial competition', Working Paper, University of Amsterdam.

Schram, A. (2000), 'Sorting out the seeking: the economics of individual motivations', *Public Choice*, **103**, 231–58.

Schram, A. and J. Sonnemans (1996a), 'Voter turnout as a participation game: an experimental investigation', *International Journal of Game Theory*, **25**, 385–406.

Schram, A. and J. Sonnemans (1996b), 'Why people vote: experimental evidence', *Journal of Economic Psychology*, **17**, 417–42.

Tullock, G. (1980), 'Efficient rent-seeking', in J.M. Buchanan, R.D. Tollison and G. Tullock (eds), *Toward a theory of the rent-seeking society*, College Station: Texas A&M University Press.

Weimann, J., C.-L. Yang and C. Vogt (2000), 'An experiment on sequential rent-seeking', *Journal of Economic Behavior and Organization*, **41**, 405–26.

van Winden, F. (1999), 'On the economic theory of interest groups: towards a group frame of reference in political economics', *Public Choice*, **100**, 1–29.

van Winden, F. (2001), 'Emotional hazard, exemplified by taxation-induced anger', *Kyklos*, **54**, 491–506.

van Winden, F. and R. Bosman (1996), 'Experimental research in public economics, in *Experiments in Economics - Experimente in der Ökonomie*, Ökonomie und Gesellschaft, Jahrbuch 13, Frankfurt: Campus Verlag.

PART V

A Practitioner's View of the Political Economy
of Redistribution

11. Equity policy and political feasibility in the European Union

Aníbal Cavaco Silva[*]

1. INTRODUCTION

Over the past 20 years, many European countries have experienced increases in income inequality, in the number of people suffering from poverty, and in social exclusion. In general, governments are criticized for their lack of equity concern and accused of being ineffective in reducing income inequality and, perhaps, of having adopted policies that even contributed to greater income inequality.

In most of the European Union (EU) countries the disposable income shares for the higher income groups have increased while the lower income groups have lost share in disposable income (Atkinson et al., 1995; Forster, 2000).

By the mid-1990s 18 percent of the population in the EU (65 million) had an income below the poverty level (percentage of persons with an income less than or equal to 60 percent of the median in their own country[1]), a proportion that had remained broadly unchanged over the past ten years. In the European Union 14 million (8.3 percent of the labour force) are unemployed, of whom 50 percent are long-term unemployed; and 2.5 million are homeless. This situation is a matter of growing concern to political and social actors, at both the national and EU levels.

However, there is no indication that individuals' preferences for less income inequality and for living in a fairer society have diminished over the past two decades. Inquiries made in the European Union show that 80 percent of the population want the fight against poverty and social exclusion to rank among the highest government priorities.

The discussion and analysis of the factors and strategies underlying the design of government policies that, in practice, can lead to reduced income inequality and a more equitable society are issues of the greatest importance. Political factors that may influence policy choices and their implementation must be taken into account. Economic policy advisers, mainly those who

[*] This paper is an extension of the one presented at the IMF conference in June 1998 on economic policy and equity. The author wishes to thank Miguel Gouveia for his useful suggestions.

provide direct advice to the head of the government and ministers and whose recommendations may influence their decisions, should try hard to understand the elements that determine politicians' behaviour. The focus of their advice should be on those inequality-reducing measures that politicians can embrace, rather than on those that may be theoretically more correct but not politically feasible. This does not mean that a policy adviser who is especially concerned about income inequality should not care about the eventual efficiency costs of the proposed measures.

What is a politically realistic equity policy agenda for European governments? I shall discuss the priority areas that, in the international environment of globalization and associated technological developments and of economic integration, European policy makers can be persuaded to include in their agendas, so that distributive equity will be better over the next 20 years than in the past 20 years.

2.   POLITICAL FEASIBILITY

Political feasibility has to do with the politicians' willingness to take policy actions to achieve desirable goals. In the current stage of the EU it is useful to think that, in member states, given ideological preferences, politicians' willingness to take a certain economic decision is determined by three main interdependent forces.

First is the short-run reaction of the public opinion to the envisaged policy measure, as expected by the politicians. The reaction of interest groups, like employers and trade unions, may be particularly important.

Second is the effect of the policy measure on the rate of approval of the government by the electorate at the election time, as expected by the politicians. Politicians' expectations may be influenced by their advisers' technical analyses.

Third is the international pressure on the policy makers to adopt or not to adopt specific policy actions. This pressure may be in the form of a simple suggestion, a public recommendation or a quasi-imposition. Generally, international pressures reflect the technical analyses made by international organizations' experts.

The political feasibility of a policy measure will depend on the weight that the policy maker attaches to each of these three forces. Each of them may be neutral (without effect on the policy choice), or point in a positive direction (adoption) or a negative one (rejection) and in different degrees (strong/weak). The age of the government may affect the weight that the politician places on each force. The short-run reaction of interest groups tends to become more important as election time draws near. The recognition of the relevance of these three forces does not mean that European politicians are driven just by a desire to stay in office, and in no way by a desire to pursue the social good.

Those forces may interact with one another. The policy maker may invoke international pressure to mitigate the domestic negative reaction to a certain policy measure. And the opinion of an international organization about a policy action may change the politicians' expectations on its effect on voter approval.

Pressures arising from the European integration process have an increasing influence on the political feasibility of specific economic decisions in EU member states. The single currency has led to the reinforcement of the European coordination of economic policies, thus enlarging the national policy areas which are subject to EU recommendations and increasing the costs on the governments that do not comply with them. Thus monetary union is likely to raise the political feasibility of some economic measures that otherwise European politicians would not be willing to take.

Until recent years the EU institutions have shown little or no concern about income inequality in member states compared to unemployment, inflation and efficiency. Pressures on governments to adopt equity-enhancing measures were practically non-existent until the end of the 1990s. Only in the year 2000 was the question of poverty and social exclusion considered important enough to be discussed by the heads of government and included in the conclusions of the European Council. It is likely that improving distributive equity in the EU over the next 20 years will require that Community institutions pay more attention to inequality and put stronger pressure on governments to frame their policies to reduce it. The decision of the Nice European Council of December 2000 to implement a two-year action plan for combating poverty and social exclusion is a move in the right direction.

3. CHANGE IN POLITICIANS' ATTITUDES

In the 1960–90 period European governments were deeply engaged in policy actions aimed at improving equity in income distribution. Social protection systems covering pensions, health care and unemployment compensation were significantly strengthened. Consequently, public social spending increased substantially in European countries (Tanzi and Schuknecht, 2000). Politicians responded to the social pressures for a fairer society and were convinced that their choices would increase their chances of being kept in office.

By the end of the 1980s social security systems reached a mature stage in most EU countries. However, income inequality continued to be an important political issue. The objectives of reducing income inequality and combating social exclusion are usually given a high priority in politicians' electoral campaigns. Political electoral speeches generally give at least equal emphasis to equity as to economic growth and employment. When political proposals put greater emphasis on economic growth, it is usual to underscore its contribution to an improvement of social justice. European politicians seem to be convinced that voters dislike large income and wealth inequalities as well as profound poverty. They consider that reflecting a strong concern for social injustice is important in winning voters' support. Politicians' behaviour is influenced by the attention paid by media to inequality, poverty and social exclusion.

However, a change in politicians' attitudes towards redistributive policies is taking place because of globalization and deeper European integration. It appears that European politicians are now less willing to take specific measures to reduce income inequality. If this is the case, while at the same time globalization increases income inequality, as some economists argue, then much imagination on the part of economic policy advisers will be required to influence the policy makers to follow a path that can lead to a more equitable society.

The observation of European governments' behaviour in recent years reveals that once in office, they give a lower priority to reducing income inequality, in contrast with the priority assigned to this goal in electoral campaigns. Assuming that politicians want to be re-elected, it seems strange that they would downgrade the equity objective once they take office. One explanation may be that policy makers are becoming more pessimistic about the possibility of achieving improvements in equity during their terms that are visible enough to offset such potential negative side effects as lower growth, higher unemployment and higher inflation. Such an attitude may be stimulated by the disappointing performance of economic growth and employment in EU countries during the last decade and by the increased awareness that in a globalizing world the high levels of social protection that exist in EU countries are negative for job creation and output growth. This is an idea that OECD and the European Commission have persistently spread in recent years.

Another explanation may be that politicians are increasingly convinced that the budgetary costs of a comprehensive policy designed to achieve a socially fair distribution of income would be unsustainable and would crowd out financial resources from the pursuit of other goals. Since the approval of the Maastricht Treaty, European governments have been under increasing pressures to reduce and eliminate public deficits through current primary expenditure restraint. On the other hand, the European Commission has called governments' attention to the effect of the demographic trends on public expenditure growth.

Globalization may also influence the voters' valuation of the politicians' performance, as far as the equity objective is concerned. The idea that globalization imposes additional constraints on national policies and makes income inequality and poverty more difficult to solve leads the electorate to forgive incumbent politicians for weak results. On the other hand, given the improvement in social protection in the 1960–90 period, voters have greater difficulty in detecting changes in the overall state of income distribution, and increasing inequality is not always evident during a government's term. The information about income distribution available to voters is more incomplete than that about unemployment, inflation or economic growth. Because politicians enjoy considerable discretion once in office, equity is likely to be an area where, from an electoral point of view, political speeches and promises are more important than concrete results.

When policy makers realize that economic growth, employment, or price stability are below target, they tend to react by announcing additional measures. However, when an income distribution target is missed, policy makers do not react. This is a behaviour that economists seem to accept as rational. The literature on political business cycles hypothesizes that politicians adjust economic policies to show a positive performance in economic growth, employment and inflation as re-election nears. However, income distribution results are not viewed as a determining factor for the behaviour of politicians once in office.

4. GLOBALIZATION AND TAX AND TRANSFER POLICIES

With globalization and economic integration, European policy makers tend to consider the traditional income distribution mechanisms as infeasible. It is unlikely that an effective improvement in income distribution in the EU member states can be achieved in the future through progressive taxation and transfers.[2]

Although fairness continues to be an important goal of tax systems, tax progressivity is no longer viewed by European politicians as the key means to change the distribution of disposable income. Three factors may explain this attitude.

First is the increasing international mobility of capital and highly skilled workers arising from globalization. High tax rates provide a strong incentive for tax bases to move abroad to lower-tax countries. European governments have responded to growing capital mobility by reducing capital income taxation, whereas labour income, which is less mobile, is relatively burdened with taxation.

Second is the need for more efficiency. The increasing competition brought about by globalization and economic integration puts pressure on governments to reduce the inefficiency costs of high taxes and other public policies.

Third, a great demand has been placed on the role of the tax system to achieve objectives other than equity. European decision makers have been receptive to granting various tax incentives aimed at stimulating savings, new investment, competitiveness, technological development and other goals.

The current political debate within the EU on the question of tax competition illustrates the declining role of the tax system as a redistributive instrument. Although tax competition has led to high taxation of labour compared with more mobile factors,[3] the European Commission has emphasized their negative effects on economic efficiency and job creation rather than the effects on equity in income distribution. To mitigate the problems of 'harmful' tax competition, the EU has been discussing the introduction of greater coordination – if not harmonization – of corporate taxes and savings taxes in the framework of the monetary union.

Tax competition helps explain the reductions seen in several European countries since the mid-1980s in the tax rates on corporate profits, the special tax concessions granted to new investments, and the cuts in the marginal tax rates on personal income.

In the 1960–90 period European politicians revealed a high preference for increasing social security benefits. For certain, they were convinced that such a policy had a positive effect on the political support from important social groups, at least in the short run. Thus governments made their best efforts to give high visibility to their decisions.

Although social security transfers have made an important contribution to a fairer European society over the past 40 years, it is politically unrealistic to think that further progress in income distribution can be achieved by increasing social security benefits. The reduction of the European governments' ability to increase tax revenue and the increasing pressure on them to reduce their public spending, brought about by globalization and economic integration, have convinced politicians that the increase in social security benefits is a policy that is no longer available to them. Besides, politicians are now less convinced than in the past that an increase in social transfers will improve their chances of being kept in office. This attitude has been stimulated in recent years by the widespread idea that social security systems are, to some extent, in crisis in most of the EU member states and should be reformed.

The OECD and European Commission have insisted that in most countries the social security systems which cover pensions and health insurance are financially unsustainable owing mainly to demographic changes (higher life expectancy) and that the prevailing high social security contributions strongly discourage investment and job creation. European governments are under strong pressure to reform their social security systems by cutting benefits and thus the growth of public expenditure. On the other hand, Community institutions and the OECD have emphasized that in several countries unemployment benefits are too generous and discourage work effort.

Thus a strategy to improve equity based on the traditional tax/transfer system does not appear politically feasible. In the near future, income inequality will probably not be reduced through changes in the tax system or in the state social security system. The exception lies in possible improvements in administration. A significant improvement in equity could be achieved in some countries by efficient measures that reduce tax fraud and evasion.

5. UNDERSTANDING POLITICIANS' BEHAVIOUR

European policy makers seem to be increasingly convinced that globalization and economic integration constrain redistributive tax/transfer policies. But this does not mean that they do not care about taking measures to reduce income inequalities. Economic policy advisers, whose recommendations influence policy makers, should try to determine which policy measures are effective to achieve a more equitable society and that politicians are willing to adopt. What the global economy has changed fundamentally is the effectiveness of the instruments through which EU countries may pursue desirable social objectives rather than the scope of social choice.

In the current international and technological economic environment it is unlikely that European politicians will make major efforts to reduce income inequality if they are convinced that competitiveness and economic growth will be negatively affected. Programmes that promote the reduction of income inequality and also benefit economic growth and employment are more likely to be adopted by politicians than are those that only aim at reducing income inequality.

Globalization and budgetary constraints have contributed to convince European politicians that without sustainable economic growth it is difficult to achieve a significant reduction in social inequalities. Though mainstream economics emphasizes that redistributive policies may have negative effects on economic growth, there are policy measures that suit both the equity and growth objectives. Tanzi (1998) asserts that many of the policies that benefit the lowest income groups are often those with the highest social rate of return.

Besides, a more equitable income distribution may also favour growth, as underscored by Chenery et al. (1974) and as emphasized more recently by others (Persson and Tabellini, 1994; Alesina and Rodrik, 1994; Bardhan,

1996; Aghion et al., 1999). Perotti (1996) summarizes the channels through which income distribution can affect growth. However, this linkage, running from equity to growth, is unlikely to be relevant for European politicians' decisions.

Visibility is also important for politicians. It is quite normal for them to prefer programmes that have high visibility and media impact, produce short-run results, and fall within budgetary limits. Consequently, in a globalizing environment policy makers will tend to prefer expenditure programmes targeted to specific groups or situations, instead of global income redistribution policies through the tax and transfer system, and non-cash subsidies tend to be preferred to cash transfers. The idea that it is politically infeasible to move from universal to targeted programmes, because the political support of middle income classes is seriously eroded, may no longer be valid in the new European context.

Generally, European politicians believe that, as far as equity is concerned, voters' attention is mainly on specific vulnerable groups and the programmes adopted by the government to assist them. It is easier for voters to see the 'beneficial' effects of targeted expenditure programmes. Thus targeting society's most vulnerable elements and focusing on specific poverty problems may be more popular with the electorate than programmes that involve the whole population.

In the global economy it is more difficult to persuade European politicians to take measures aimed at reducing income inequality if the equity goal is defined in terms of dispersion throughout the income scale, because the results of government policy could be disappointing. Generally, they are more willing to adopt a less ambitious equity goal and adhere to a concept of absolute poverty, thereby focusing on the lowest income groups and social exclusion. It seems realistic to assume that politicians consider poverty a more serious problem than wide dispersion of the overall income distribution.[4] Focusing on the poorest groups might produce better equity results and will mitigate the tension between redistribution and growth objectives. Just in the case in which income disparities above the poverty line – measured as a percentage of national median income – are socially unacceptable or jeopardize other policy goals, the policy maker should be persuaded not to ignore distributional developments affecting non-poor groups.

Regulatory measures that aim at the distribution of market earnings, such as minimum wages and job protection legislation, are also attractive to politicians. This is because these measures enjoy a high public profile, worker and trade union support, and low direct budgetary costs. Economic advisers should, however, remind politicians that market-distorting measures have a negative effect on both efficiency and equity in the long term. Although these measures are likely to benefit current workers, they are detrimental to the unemployed, the less skilled, and younger people. The severe criticism by international organizations of regulatory measures, in attempts to enhance the efficiency of the economy, has played a key role in reducing politicians' attraction for those measures.

The constraints that globalization and economic integration impose on governmental policies make more complex the government internal decision-making and coordination process aimed at improving equity. This objective is no longer a clear job of two ministries: the Ministry of Finance, which is responsible for tax policy, and the Ministry of Social Affairs, which is responsible for the policy of social transfers. The participation of other ministries is required to achieve a given equity goal.

Thus improving income distribution requires clear and strong government leadership – and the commitment of the head of government and his or her inner cabinet. Because the necessary measures have to be prepared by several ministries, the head of government will have to supply the impetus to policy action and ensure the coordination and consistency between economic policy and sectoral social policies. On the other hand, the government inner cabinet is in a better position than the Council of Ministers to reconcile discipline on social spending with distributive equity. Strong government leadership is also important for the adoption of policy measures that have a positive effect on income distribution in the long run but which may generate a negative social reaction in the short run.

6. STRATEGIC PUBLIC INTERVENTIONS

To the extent that globalization and economic integration are changing politicians' attitudes towards redistributive policies, economic policy advisers with an equity concern should exploit more complicated channels to affect income distribution in EU countries than social transfers and progressive income taxation. One possibility is to adopt strategies based on other policies which can be appropriately adjusted to a concern for social justice. That is the case of government policies in the interrelated areas of employment and human capital formation.

A more equal society in European countries may be achieved giving priority to equity-adjusted policy interventions aimed at reducing unemployment and improving human capital. These are strategic interventions that, in the long run, should improve growth and equity and have a good chance of being accepted by European politicians.

These areas for policy action are not new. However, their significance for the purpose of improving income distribution has changed as well as the environment in which policy measures in those areas can now be implemented. Some of them appear today to be much more politically viable than they were in the past. Therefore, a new emphasis is justified.

In many countries, unemployment is a main factor of income inequality, and it hits poor people especially hard. The social security system does not cover all the unemployed, the benefits do not always provide an acceptable standard of living, and unemployment also negatively affects a person's well-being, beyond the loss of income. Long-term unemployment has spread considerably during the 1990s and is a major cause of poverty and social exclusion in the EU. In general, a job is considered to be the best safeguard against social exclusion. Thus the fight against unemployment should be viewed by economic and social policy advisers as a strategic step to promoting a more equitable distribution of income. Moreover, an increase in employment would ease budgetary pressures by increasing tax revenue from the new workers and reducing the amount of unemployment compensation.

European governments are concerned about their high levels of unemployment. Moreover, pressures arising from economic globalization and monetary union are increasing the political feasibility of more effective measures to fight the structural component of unemployment.

Since 1994, the OECD has advanced a set of policy recommendations aimed at reducing unemployment – known as 'the OECD Jobs Strategy' (OECD, 1994) – and by the end of 1997 it was decided, at the highest level of the EU, to develop a strategy to coordinate employment policies with a view to increasing the employment level and to lowering unemployment rates in member states.

In recent years OECD and EU official documents have strongly recommended greater flexibility in the labour market for EU member states, mainly with a view to promoting economic efficiency and competitiveness. Labour market flexibility refers not only to labour cost flexibility, but also to mobility, flexibility of working time and work organization, adaptability, and less strict employment protection legislation. Because this may widen wage dispersion and, in the short run, low-skilled workers may be hit, this policy is often regarded as being adverse to equity, engendering a negative reaction from social agents. Thus European politicians delayed the approval of measures to increase labour market flexibility because they were afraid that voters' approval would be negatively affected. However, their attitude is changing.

In a globalizing world, policy advisers should include structural reforms that create jobs in their policy proposals to improve equity. The policy makers should be persuaded that maintaining current European labour market rigidities in the new global economy might increase unemployment, social exclusion and consequently create a more unfair society in the long run.

If equity improvement policies are focused primarily on the poorest groups, labour market flexibility can contribute to a less unequal society. Improving labour market performance would create more employment opportunities for jobless and socially excluded individuals to work and earn wages. From this equity perspective, the employment effects of labour market flexibility are viewed as more important than the potential widening of wage distribution. However, greater flexibility must be accompanied by appropriate and well-targeted social safety nets that protect the consumption levels of those whose well-being is negatively affected. In-work benefits may also be required to ensure that low-income families are above poverty levels. This would ease workers' concern and help minimize negative social reactions to labour reforms, thus increasing the politicians' willingness to implement them.

The increasing international pressure on European politicians seems to have convinced them that labour market flexibility is an important factor in improving competitiveness. Consequently, they are now more willing to implement the necessary measures and face possible negative social reactions in the short run, in the expectation that their effects on economic growth and employment will be positive, thus regaining voter approval. However, it is most unlikely that a radical change in European labour markets in the direction of the US model is politically feasible. European politicians are convinced that some use of labour market regulation is indispensable to preserve social cohesion.

Social partnership institutions, including government, employer associations and trade unions, can create more favourable conditions for implementing labour reforms. Social partners are supposed to press the government to take the complementary actions required by an equity concern, thereby preserving social cohesion. Economic advisers should encourage policy makers to introduce accompanying programmes designed to cushion the costs on those workers who lose their jobs, including training to acquire new skills. The risk of the social dialogue lies in the trade unions demanding compensations that benefit those workers who are and will continue to be employed, but not those who lose their jobs.

Other job creation incentives should also be viewed as equity-enhancing measures, for example, targeted tax cuts at the lower end of the wage scale or on consumer services, a sector that makes intensive use of low-skilled labour, or even selective subsidies for marginal job creation, targeted to the young and long-term unemployed. Daveri and Tabellini (2000) have found empirical evidence that high taxes on labour are a main cause of unemployment in EU countries. Employment promotion measures should include reinforcing entrepreneurship, reducing administrative costs for small and medium-sized enterprises, and promoting local employment initiatives. In the EU, two-thirds of jobs are created by firms with fewer than 250 employees.

Improving human capital is another area of strategic public intervention to reduce income inequality in a globalizing world. It has been widely recognized that persons with low levels of education and skills face higher risks of unemployment and social exclusion. Policy advisers should give special priority to the measures that improve human resources through education, vocational training, and apprenticeships – particularly measures that help those at the lower level of income distribution. This is a policy concern that goes beyond the positive externalities associated with education, thereby justifying government action. Equality of opportunities, which is normally associated with access to education, is extremely important for the distribution of income.

Given rapidly changing technology, one of the most appropriate policies for promoting greater equality of income is that which increases the income-earning capacity of the poor by promoting their human capital formation.

Such policies also have a positive effect on employment and productivity and are economically and politically recognized as key factors in enhancing competitiveness and economic growth. This area for governmental intervention as a means to achieve a more equitable income distribution has gained an increased importance in the knowledge-based society that is being created by the information and communications revolution.[5]

Because capital market imperfections are a severe constraint on human capital investment by poor individuals, government intervention is justified. Various governmental measures are important: free basic education, and even secondary education; education subsidies directed toward low-income families; programmes to prevent school failure or dropouts; and programmes to integrate truant children. Governments should also provide training programmes for the unskilled, unemployed and socially excluded; social integration programmes for single parents; and work and apprenticeship programmes. The central importance of education and training in pursuing social equity is reviewed, for example, in OECD (2001a). In recent years, the European Commission has stressed the importance of strengthening education and training efforts in member countries in order to fight unemployment and social exclusion due to lack of skills. In some countries, improving access to basic health care and government assistance for housing and rehabilitation for low-income families in urban areas are also needed to enhance human capital and equity.

The above-mentioned priority areas for government action may lead to a more equal European society in the long run. This does not, however, diminish the importance of specific transfer programmes targeting vulnerable groups. In a globalizing world, equity in income distribution does not dispense with special social assistance programmes designed for those living in conditions of deep poverty and for the unemployable; for example, programmes targeting poor pensioners, the homeless, drug addicts, the disabled, ethnic minorities, or even those who have lost their jobs – and retraining them is problematic because of their age.

Because in-kind or quasi-in-kind benefits – such as housing, food, transportation and health-care benefits – are more visible and can have an immediate impact, they may be more politically attractive than cash benefits. Some economists criticize the paternalism toward the poor which underlies non-cash subsidies, but voters, like the politicians, seem to prefer them. Moreover, in-kind benefits may produce better results in terms of well-being, as they are easier to target. They induce self-selection that removes the need for means-testing and stigma.

The budgetary constraints imposed on EU governments by monetary union have made European politicians more receptive to reform their public assistance programmes and even reduce the share of social expenditures. These reforms are not necessarily anti-equity. On the contrary, they may reduce unjustified benefits and free up money for job creation and human capital formation.[6]

The fight against poverty can be more effective by cutting universal benefits provided without means-testing and concentrating benefits on those truly in need. Policy advisers should persuade politicians to implement a more effective targeting of benefits toward the most disadvantaged groups. It is widely recognized that transfer programmes are not well targeted in EU countries.

Empirical evidence suggests that a higher share of public transfers goes to lower income groups in those countries where means-tested elements play a stronger role (Forster, 2000).

Social protection schemes in some European countries also need to be reformed because they are too generous, encourage a culture of dependency, and discourage work effort. Policy advisers with an equity concern should support, not oppose, the reform of social policies aimed at making work pay and giving individuals an incentive to enhance their competencies and job skills and thereby improve their employability. This concept has been increasingly emphasized in the EU, where it is now generally felt that passive social policies, which provide cash benefits to the unemployed and socially excluded, lone parents, and other needy groups, should be replaced by a more active social policy. Under the latter, approved beneficiaries should be required to learn new skills and be advised on job search and social integration. Eligibility criteria should be strengthened and those who refuse to improve their skills should be penalized with a reduction in social benefits.

In some countries an improvement in the efficiency of public service agencies responsible for the administration of redistributive programmes is also indispensable. Poverty alleviation programmes targeted to more vulnerable groups tend to produce better results, at a lower cost, if implemented by local authorities – with the active involvement of private social organizations. The decentralization of social policy tends to increase local responsibility in decision making and produce more active policies. Individuals can be better oriented and encouraged to return to work and thus to escape social exclusion. At the same time, local authorities have better information on the individual situations, which can help ensure that benefits reach those who really need them, reduce fraud, and lower administrative costs. The involvement of private, non-profit and voluntary institutions in the implementation of welfare programmes helps improve their quality and cost-effectiveness, mainly programmes targeted to children, the elderly, the disabled and drug addicts.

7.   CONCLUDING REMARKS

A change in the attitude of European politicians towards redistributive policies is taking place because of globalization and deeper economic and monetary integration. They seem to be now less willing to undertake specific policy actions to reduce income inequality.

It is politically unrealistic to think that an effective improvement in income distribution in the EU member states can be achieved in the future through the traditional tax/transfer system. To help governments design policies that, in practice, can lead to reduced income inequality, economic policy advisers should try to understand better politicians' behaviour and identify those policy actions which are politically feasible. Globalization and monetary union are likely to raise the political feasibility of some economic measures. In EU countries, channels to affect income distribution which are more complicated than social transfers and progressive income taxation will have to be exploited.

If the focus is primarily on the poorest groups, equity-adjusted policies aimed at reducing unemployment and improving human capital seem to be strategic public interventions that, in practice, can lead to better results in improving equity in the long term. Job creation widens the employment opportunities of the poor groups and of those who complete training programmes and acquire new skills, while their improved employability allows for a better adjustment of labour supply to market needs. In the knowledge-based economy and society the policy measures that help those at the lower level of income distribution by promoting their human capital formation are particularly important as a means for achieving a more equitable society.

Public assistance programmes and social security systems will have to be reformed in several European countries. These reforms are not necessarily anti-equity. The fight against poverty can be more effective by confining assistance programmes to those truly in need. A reduction of the share of social expenditure through a reform of social policies aimed at making work pay and giving individuals an incentive to improve their employability is not adverse to equity. On the contrary, it may be indispensable to making budgetary room for policies that are more effective in reducing income inequality and in increasing employment.

Given the budgetary constraints imposed on EU governments by monetary union, the financing of job creation incentives and human capital investment directed to the lower income groups will have to rely mainly on the change in the composition of public expenditure and allow for an increase in user fees in the financing of tertiary education, health care and other public services.

It is my impression that an equity policy agenda such as that outlined above now has a good chance of being accepted by politicians in the EU.

NOTES

1. EUROSTAT definition.
2. Tanzi and Schuknecht (2000) pointed out that in OECD countries relatively little improvement in income distribution is actually caused by taxation and by tranfer programmes.
3. The overall tax burden on labour in the EU increased by one-third over the last 30 years (European Commission, 2001).
4. 'Helping the poor, the truly poor, is a much worthier goal than merely narrowing inequalities' (*The Economist*, 16–20 June 2001).
5. Citing OECD (2001): 'Increasing inequalities in income in many OECD countries in recent decades may be further compounded as new forms of learning and technology develop.'
6. Citing Tanzi and Schuknecht (2000, p. 140): 'Over the years, some of the greatest crimes in economy policy, in terms of resource waste and welfare costs, have been committed and justified in the name of income redistribution.'

REFERENCES

Aghion, P., E. Caroli and C. García-Peñalose (1999), 'Inequality and Economic Growth: The Perspective of the New Growth Theories', *Journal of Economic Literature*, **4**, December.

Alesina, A. and D. Rodrik (1994), 'Distributive Politics and Economic Growth', *Quarterly Journal of Economics*, **109** (2), May.

Atkinson, A.B., L. Rainwater and T.M. Smeeding (1995), *Income Distribution in OECD Countries: Evidence from Luxembourg Income Study*, OECD Social Policy Studies no. 18, Paris: OECD.

Bardhan, Pranab (1996), 'Efficiency, Equity and Poverty Alleviation: Policy Issues in Less Developed Countries', *Economic Journal*, **106**, September.

Chenery, Hollis et al. (1974), *Redistribution with Growth: Policies to Improve Income Distribution in Developing Countries in the Context of Economic Growth: A Joint Study* (commissioned) by the World Bank's Development Research Center and the Institute of Development Studies, University of Sussex, London: Oxford University Press.

Daveri, F. and G. Tabellini (2000), 'Unemployment, Growth and Taxation in Industrial Countries', *Economic Policy*, **30**, April.

European Commission (2001), *European Economy*, Supplement A, no. 1, January.

Forster, M. (2000), 'Trends and Driving Factors in Income Distribution and Poverty in the OECD area', *Labour Market and Social Policy Occasional Papers* no. 42, Paris: OECD.

Organization for Economic Cooperation and Development (1994), *The OECD Jobs Study*, Paris: OECD.

OECD (1996), *The OECD Jobs Strategy: Technology, Productivity and Job Creation*, Paris: OECD.

OECD (2001), *The Well-being of Nations; The Role of Human and Social Capital*, Paris: OECD.

OECD (2001a), *Education Policy Analysis*, Paris: OECD.

Perotti, Roberto (1996), 'Growth, Income Distribution, and Democracy: What the Data Say', *Journal of Economic Growth*, **1**, June.

Persson, Torsten and Guido Tabellini (1994), 'Is Inequality Harmful for Growth? *American Economic Review*, **84**, June.

Tanzi, Vito (1998), 'Macroeconomic Adjustment with Major Structural Reforms: Implications for Employment and Income Distribution', in Vito Tanzi and Ke-young Chu (eds), *Income Distribution and High-Quality Growth*, Cambridge: MIT Press.

Tanzi, V. and L. Schuknecht (2000), *Public Spending in the 20th Century,* Cambridge: Cambridge University Press.

PART VI

Where Do We Go From Here?

12. Directions for future research

Eugene Smolensky[*]

My assigned task is to point to future directions for research from a rather practical perspective. In thinking about future directions, I asked myself: what was omitted from this conference? If there are some apparent omissions, do they point the way to a future research agenda?

Omissions were not only inevitable, but their bias was predictable, a priori. A conference relying primarily on self-selection into the ranks of presenters is likely to tilt heavily toward what was currently fashionable. This was no doubt worth doing, but it also seemed plausible that what was not fashionable might not only be worth doing but might suggest a whole domain of profitable work. A review of a large segment of the recent work in the field by Persson and Tabellini is about to appear in the next *Handbook of Public Economics*. I began the search for unfashionable omissions, therefore, with their taxonomy of the political economy literature that has appeared since the previous *Handbook*. (The Persson and Tabellini review is of the micro-side of political economy only, and I will confine myself to the same half of the field.)

To Persson and Tabellini, three features characterize the political economy literature that has emerged since the previous volumes of the *Handbook*. Public policy is now modeled as an equilibrium outcome of purposeful, rational actors in an explicitly modeled political process. (No hypothetical benevolent planners, thank you very much.) These exercises generate behavioral predictions, which, despite being highly contingent on the assumptions of the models, should in their view attach to real, although often stylized, data. As Table 12.1 shows, Persson and Tabellini divide this literature into three types. I have labeled them: unidimensional policy issues (Type 1); interest group politics (Type 2); and comparative (constitutional) politics (Type 3). The search for omissions, then, can be made operational as, 'Was one or another of the three types of papers under-represented?' If so, why? Are we to presume that the under-represented categories are in need of further research? To anticipate: yes, there is an under-represented category, and yes, it is in need of further research. In fact, the line of argument we are about to pursue, which proceeds from identifying the under-represented type

*I am very much indebted to Theresa Wong for her very careful editing.

Table 12.1   Political economics and public finance: three classes of models

Type 1	Type 2	Type 3
Unidimensional policy issues	Interest group politics	Comparative (constitutional) politics
• Redistribution in the modern welfare state • Median voter models	• Legislative bargaining • Lobbying • Electoral competition	• Allocation of control rights • Contingent promises • Agency problems – Leviathan

Source: Abstracted by the author from Torsten Persson and Guido Tabellini, 'Political Economics and Public Finance', mimeo 15 March 1999. Forthcoming in Alan Auerbach and Martin Feldstein (eds), *Handbook of Public Economics*, vol. III.

of analysis to a conjecture as to its cause, points the way to a large research agenda, but not one that has gone out of fashion. Rather, it's an opportunity to move political economy research into a whole new and promising domain.

IDENTIFYING THE UNDER-REPRESENTED TYPE

Moving across Table 12.1 from left to right, the individual voter becomes less salient while the institutional structure grows more salient. The economics becomes less complicated, and the politics of voter demographics also becomes less salient. In the Type 2 models the emphasis is on agency problems associated with legislators. Concentrated benefits and dispersed costs are residually financed out of a common pool of tax revenues. In the Type 3 models, the analytic focus is on incomplete contracts and constitutional issues. For each model in each type, an equilibrium is defined, a set-up described that captures the motives of the actors, often the sequence of moves is detailed, and the political process specified by which equilibrium is to be reached. Ideally, evidence of a connection to observed behavior is also provided.

Before turning to the remainder of my remarks, it will be useful to compare Type 1 and Type 2 models further (Table 12.2). In Type 1 models, the general question is: how do voters' preferences shape programs? The equilibrium is from a median voter model with a Condorcet winner. That is, equilibrium reflects only the distribution of individual preferences. The politics is

Table 12.2 Comparing representative models: Types 1 and 2

	Type 1	Type 2
Question	How do voters' preferences shape programs?	How do political institutions confer power on particular groups?
Equilibrium	Median voter Condorcet winner	Hotelling
Politics	Downsian	Voters trade ideological preferences against promised economic gains

Downsian: politicians care only about winning elections. The issues, therefore, are those where disagreement among voters is one-dimensional – that is, voters reasonably can be aligned in a continuum – for example, from left to right, and a stable Condorcet equilibrium is attainable. Contenders include: rich and poor, young and old, employed and unemployed, labor and capital.

In contrast, Type 2 models are of electoral competition. The general question is: how do political institutions confer power on particular groups? The equilibrium is Hotelling, or Nash. Voters have ideological preferences that they trade off against promised economic benefits. Legislators concentrate their attention on those who represent the voters most likely to be swayed by economic promises. It will turn out that Type 2 models are quite underrepresented in this conference, so that further understanding of electoral competition will be one distinguishing characteristic of the proposed research agenda.

To determine how the papers in this conference were distributed across the three types of models, I asked Stanley Winer to pull a roughly 10 percent sample of the papers. These are not a random sample, by any means, but they serve. As long as I was willing to waive the explicit equilibrium requirement, it did not prove difficult to code the papers by type. Of the 20 plus papers that Winer dispatched, 60 percent were of Type 1, 30 percent of Type 3 and only two papers were – and then only in something of a stretch – of Type 2.

YOUNGER AMERICAN ECONOMISTS ARE UNDER-REPRESENTED

Why is it that Type 2 models are relatively under-represented? I offer the conjecture that at least part of the reason may be that younger American economists are under-represented at this conference. The representative institutions under scrutiny in Type 2 papers are not those of parliamentary governments. Lobbyists, the powers of chairs of legislative committees, allocations of agenda-setting procedures in the legislature and so on are not issues of great interest in parliamentary democracies. In the USA, which is the exceptional case, these institutions receive considerable theoretical, and even greater empirical, attention. (Of course, these activities take place in parliamentary governments too, but their locus is different.)

The under-supply of American papers contributes to the shortage of Type 2 papers in a second way. Americans and Europeans differ on what the key question is. The fundamental question being addressed by the PE (public economics) micro-theorists is: 'Is government too large?' Interest persists in this now hoary (Type 3) question on the Continent for a counter-intuitive reason. The many demonstrations that government is too large are, with increasing frequency, being shown to lack robustness. In those European countries with a lingering affection for the welfare state, these demonstrations have more resonance than in the USA where, at the level of abstraction of the PE theorists, the issue is moot – government may be too large, but government is not the meaningful unit of analysis. The micro-public economists in the USA are obsessed with a different question: 'Given that the government has decided to achieve a particular objective, have they chosen the best available alternative to achieve that objective?' In these analyses, goals are multiple, a dominant solution rare, and Type 2 considerations at one step removed. American economists have thus far been unwilling to extend Type 2 analyses to their cost-effectiveness analyses.

Both questions sound as if they are questions of facts and data, but as we well know, whether government is too large in the aggregate is a question of theory almost entirely. The American question (Boadway would call it the Anglo-Saxon question, perhaps) calls for detailed, intricate measurement of the programs as they are. The emergent frame of mind is that whether government is doing good or not is highly dependent on the precise parameters that characterize each program separately. The European political economists are studying government from the heavens; the American micro-public economists are down in the intestines. Type 2 analyses in the USA are primarily by political scientists.

That leads to a further difference between the two cultures. With important exceptions evident enough in this conference, continental Europeans do theory and Americans empirical analysis. Of course, each is as worthy as the other, but the disconnect between what continental Europeans and Americans do feeds into a disconnect between political economy and public economics more generally. Take it that each *Handbook* defines the field as it stands at the moment it appears. To the extent that view is justified, the forthcoming

Handbook is a vivid illustration of that disconnect. With one exception, the literature reviews in the *Handbook* that might have been expected to at least touch on the political economy literature do not do so: not Auerbach on taxation policy, nor Feldstein and Liebman on social security, not Cutler on health care, and not Lans Bovenberg and Lawrence Goulder on environmental taxation. Yet all these authors were represented at a seminar (where I too was present) in which Persson presented the PT review. And the purpose of that seminar was to promote integration of the various chapters! This is essentially a European conference and the *Handbook* is a largely American enterprise (86 percent of the 28 authors in it are American). It follows that this conference is short on empirical studies of particular program areas, while the *Handbook* is short on equilibrium political theory. It is true that Poterba in his chapter on risk-taking makes a brief reference to the PE literature and Scotchmer and Hanushek each indicate that it would have been a good idea to take account of the PE literature; they just didn't. Obviously, the important direction for the future research that comes out of this conference is to bridge these two cultures. More particularly, those who are committed to PE will serve themselves and the profession by taking a genuine interest in the design of particular public programs. The Americans get up to the door and stop while the Europeans stay as far from the door as they can.

Many PE papers assert in their titles a connection to particular public programs: social security, education, military spending and the environment are examples. These papers, however, do not contribute to the literature on those important government programs; they are relevant only to the extent that they provide some highly aggregated data useful for testing a finding of PE theory. Of course, such research is important and in short supply, but forging connections to the rest of public economics is at least as important.[1]

One obvious place to forge connections between political economy and public economics is in program evaluation – that is, within the American preoccupation. In that literature a subsidiary question is almost always present: as these programs have actually been implemented, who wins and who loses? As a Type 1 question, distributional effects are widely examined in theory and practice and with real live data and in many countries, but particularly the USA. As a Type 2 question, however, it is rarely examined, and almost never in real time with real data.

An area in which evaluation research could benefit from the exercise of Type 2 theory and measurement is in social protection programs. As Silva has told us earlier in this volume (Chapter 11), what programs do for the poor has emerged as a crucial question for politicians of the EU. That question is generally not asked by the modern micro-political economists who meet the Persson and Tabellini attributes with which I began: equilibrium, rational actors, well-specified political behaviors. Macro-economists, and the earlier generation of Type 1 micro-theorists often ask, even if public finance economists do not: is redistribution compatible with goals like maximizing growth? Neither micro- nor macro-theorists often ask, with real data and in real time, about how the poor will fare over different equilibria. My conjecture is that political economy will make contact with the rest of the field of public economics and with practicing politicians most quickly if it shifts its focus from the aggregate size of government to how the distributional consequences of the design elements of government's constituent components could be altered in the political process. It seems an obvious and very short next step.

What too frequently happens now in cost-effectiveness studies is that the programs are found to be barely cost effective (Don Wittman is right again), but that their distributional consequences are not as anticipated or intended. Both findings are attributed to politics and the analysis terminated. I propose that it is at that stage that the PE economists enter, to make positive, institutional-affecting proposals to remedy the results. It is in the programmatic details that policy analysts and legislators fight the propensity for government to be too large. And it is the occasional demonstration that policy analysts and legislative tacticians are sometimes successful that is undermining the general consensus that government will always be too large.

It may seem here that Boadway, in his chapter (Chapter 4), has argued against the position I have taken here. If so, I surrender, because I found Boadway's argument to be entirely persuasive. But, Boadway does say, 'I suppose that ... at least those normative analysts who advise political parties must necessarily take political consequences into account'. While most American economists are not formally advising political parties, it is increasingly the case that they nevertheless are anxious to affect short-run policy choices. Consider Professor Silva's chapter once again. To my American ears, Silva reads a great deal like an urbane US President Lyndon Johnson, or perhaps his economist, Walter Heller, circa 1964. A hand-up not a handout. Targeted, cost-effective, investments promoting human capital and social inclusion. Work first.

But it cannot be said that President Johnson's war on poverty proved to be good politics. Nor can the record of the past 35 years of US policy support Silva's expectation that human capital and labor market policies acceptable to politicians will lower wage inequality in the long run. The US record even bodes poorly for Silva's hope that offsetting inequality caused by market liberalization with social safety net policies will constrain poverty from increasing in the short term. Quite paradoxically, one contributor to the sorry record in the USA may be a conscious decision taken in the USA to ignore inequality so as to concentrate on poverty. It is now well established that it is technically more difficult to reduce poverty through social net programs when inequality is increasing. More to the point for this volume, to ignore inequality is also to ignore the political feedback from increasing inequality in determining the level of spending on particular public programs, their composition, and their design elements. Would Lyndon Johnson have launched the war on poverty as he did, if he were advised by a Walter Heller steeped in political economy? I suggest that he would not and that the EU countries may make a similar mistake unless the PE club turns to helping them get it right.

What I am suggesting is that PE suggests that the EU not take its eyes off inequality altogether – the endogenous political response may undo their hopes. So, here's a paradox. To efficaciously reduce poverty through public programs will require reducing income inequality more generally. But passage of poverty reducing programs can't get initial passage by appealing to a reduction in income inequality. Solving such conundrums is what political scientists call political engineering.

Those who work in PE as espoused by Persson and Tabellini, I would urge, should believe in their theories and turn to their application in the real world, in real time, with real data, so as to promote better programs, as opposed to better theory. That is, turn to political engineering. The theory will inevitably get better too.

NOTE

1. Macro-PE has clearly connected to one other branch of economic research – endogenous growth theory. I don't know why it is that integration with growth theory is proceeding apace, while it seems not to have had much of an impact even on that part of public finance that addresses political business cycles.

13.   Where do we go from here?

Heinrich W. Ursprung

Where do we go from here? This innocent question is a very nice example of the ambiguity and subtlety for which the English language is so well suited. Am I supposed to develop a theory explaining the advance of economic research, and then derive some predictions about the future role of political economy in the theory and practice of public finance? Surely, if Stanley Winer had wanted me to do that, he would have asked: where *shall* we go from here? Or, am I supposed to tell you what you had better do with your valuable time after your return to whatever august institution of scholarship and higher learning you may come from? In this case Winer would certainly have asked: where *should* we go from here? He may have settled for the implied ambiguity, which hints in a subtle manner at the complex relationship between positive and normative analysis underlying the general theme of this conference, to give me the opportunity to indulge in a more personal reflection which transcends these categories. And this is exactly what I intend to do.

Some ten years ago I had the honor of presiding over the European Public Choice Society. In my presidential address I chose to speculate about the future development of modeling and analyzing political processes. Looking back, I realize now that in my youthful enthusiasm – remember, I am reminiscing about 1991 – I took it for granted that what will happen also should happen – and vice versa. Nevertheless, my endeavor was, in principle, to answer a positive question and my predictions actually proved to be quite accurate. The gain in insight and the true intellectual satisfaction which I thought the anticipated progress would entail did not, however, materialize.

This is all the more distressing since another development, which I did *not* anticipate would gain as much momentum as it did, should make any political economist of long standing rejoice. I am referring to the fact that the public choice viewpoint, which for a long time was denied access to the traditional mainstream of economic policy analysis, became in the 1990s not only generally accepted but even one of the hot topics in the profession. What a difference as compared to the late 1970s, when I was involved in organizing some of the first public choice meetings in Europe! At that time public choice scholars were marginalized academically and their core ideas met with incomprehension if not outright enmity. Today the most prestigious journals of our profession publish the research output of political economists, even those journals which 20 years ago would not have touched endogenous policy questions with a ten-foot pole. What a glorious academic victory! But why then do I derive so little satisfaction after having ridden such a great academic bandwagon – why do I sometimes even feel depressed when looking back at the progress of my discipline?

Of course, there is a fly in the ointment. There always is, isn't there? I begin with a minor issue which I could have skipped; but I simply cannot resist the opportunity to poke some fun at those of my colleagues who make a very clever and calculating distinction between *public choice* and *political economy*. If we define political economy with Allan Drazen as the *study of how political constraints explain the choice of policies and thus economic outcomes*,[1] then – to give you just one personal example – Peter Bernholz's public choice lectures,[2] which I had the privilege to attend as an undergraduate student in Basle in the early 1970s, already represented what is nowadays so often called 'new' political economy – a description which is probably supposed to suggest that this line of research was initiated in the 1990s by the author using this term or maybe the author's venerable supervisor. Political economy does not, as Persson and Tabellini's textbook insinuates, draw – *among other traditions* – on the public choice tradition.[3] Political economy, for all practical purposes, *is* public choice, and vice versa. It is also not fair to claim that 'researchers in the public choice tradition were reluctant to use formal game-theoretic tools or to impose strong notions of individual rationality'.[4] A close look at the back issues of the journal *Public Choice* will reveal that public choice scholars have used all the analytical techniques that were available at the time. I admit that the analytical techniques employed in any discipline do change as time passes, but to construe a whole new discipline on the basis of these changes, which, after all, do not concern a matter of principle but rather of analytical convenience, is an insolence. The 'new' political economists would benefit from a little bit of academic restraint and integrity by admitting that the term 'new' refers to their being relatively new in the field because it took them some time to realize and admit that, to paraphrase Nietzsche, the benevolent dictator is dead. As I said before, for me, having no claim whatsoever to anything close to a founding father status, all this is just a minor source of irritation; after all, this kind of posturing is not at all uncommon in academia, which lacks direct measures of personal success; and I have no doubt that those of you who really *were* instrumental in initiating the public choice bandwagon can live with it, too. What counts, in the end, are the tangible results, and history will deal with allocating the slots in the hall of fame – for what it's worth.

The roots of my dissatisfaction thus reach deeper than personal sensitivities. The truth of the matter is that I am often bored with what I hear and read and, to be frank, sometimes also with what I am doing myself. I certainly had more fun with political economy at the beginning of my academic career, and I do not think that the absence of excitement is solely due to old age. Public choice used to be exciting because it came with a vision, a soul if you want, and this vision constituted a refuge from the traditional mainstream of economic policy analysis which was unattractive for the public choice scholars because it was tainted with two crucial shortcomings.

The traditional mainstream of economic policy analysis was, in principle, based on the implicit assumption that social interactions are always in need of constant and far-reaching planning from above, an assumption which may ultimately be traceable to some deeply rooted craving for security and salvation, the obvious analogy between the concepts and the general reception of the invisible hand and biological evolution, at least, seems to support such a speculative interpretation. In any case, Adam Smith's vision of spontaneous order emerging from the interaction of free individuals in a market system was replaced by the socialist paradigm of a paternalistic social planner. The *desirability* of a social planner was, of course, the first tenet which the public choice scholars could not accept. It is worthwhile to point out, however, that the objection to the benevolent dictator presumption derived not so much from the obvious fact that the portrait of the political process was inadequate, but rather from the implications of this portrait for social engineering and the resultant loss of individual liberty.

The second unacceptable view which traditional mainstream economists held was their abhorrence of redistributional conflicts. The root of this uneasiness was probably the desire to become a generally acknowledged science, and the messiness and inherent unresolvability of the redistribution conflicts fought out via the political process represented a permanent source of embarrassment for a discipline seeking universal acceptance. But, as Robin Boadway pointed out in his chapter (Chapter 4), 'governments are not primarily involved in exploiting gains from trade arising from free-riding and market failure; instead, like it or not, government is primarily an institution for redistribution'. The only route of escape which offered itself to the mainstream was to separate efficiency from distribution considerations with the help of lump sum compensations. And these lump sum compensations, I think, were the original sin of the traditional mainstream; this concept – in a much more subtle manner than the benevolent dictator presumption – introduced a perfectly fictitious element which led normative policy analysis on the slippery road leading to a complete withdrawal from reality.

Traditional normative policy analysis, in a sense, thus abandoned its own socialist vision of social engineering and began to analyze perfectly fictitious problems of efficient policy design in a fairy-tale world which was not tainted by interpersonal welfare comparisons. The early advocates of the public choice school refused to settle into this kind of intellectual boredom and insisted on a research program which was not only firmly based on a realistic representation of the political process but, more importantly, was to address the topical economic policy problems of its time.

As I mentioned before, we all seem to be political economists now; the topic of this conference, if anything, documents the victory of endogenous policy theory. What made this tidal shift in paradigms possible? I am not sure that I have a good answer. Disenchantment with social engineering after the collapse of the communist world may have contributed; the parallelism in time, at least, seems to suggest that. Another contributing factor may have been that economics as a science has become much more accepted, with the consequence that mainstream economists can now acknowledge that controversial interpersonal welfare comparisons are a necessary ingredient of any interesting economic policy analysis.

Whatever the reasons for the dismantling of the benevolent dictator presumption might be, subscribing to the endogenous policy viewpoint does not necessarily imply that the whole public choice program has been adopted by the mainstream. As a matter of fact, I would like to propose that the ongoing process of 'supersession', the replacement of public choice by political economy, is about to kill the true soul of the original research program. Mainstream economic policy analysis has not become more realistic by endorsing utility-maximizing political agents, and the former advocates of the public choice school, because the endogenous policy viewpoint is no longer their exclusive property, feel hard pressed to play along with the crowd.

Why is it that the adoption of a more realistic portrait of the political process does not automatically give rise to deeper insights into economic policy making? What went wrong since I predicted ten years ago that the 1990s would see a refinement of our good old public choice models by incorporating more and more transaction costs accruing in the political process, thereby increasing the accuracy and realism of our analytical tools? My prediction was fine as far as predictions go: the standard arsenal which at that time basically consisted of the simple unidimensional median voter approach, the probabilistic voting or political support function approach, and the lobbying approach, has been augmented in the meantime to include the electoral competition approach, the Helpman/Grossman type models of political corruption, the agency or incomplete-contract models, and the citizen candidate models. All of these top of the line modeling approaches focus on transaction costs whose formal representation has been neglected up to now: monitoring costs underlie the corruption approach, costly disclosure of competence the career-concern models, entry costs the citizen candidate models, and so on. However, as a rule, the models based on these approaches do nothing more than highlight one type of transaction cost, one characteristic of the political process; and the profession jumps from one approach to the other, driven by fads (and sometimes also by a calculating attempt to please the self-declared forerunners), not by analytical necessity. By doing so, we certainly did not make our models more realistic; at most we can claim to have captured different aspects of reality.

There is nothing wrong, of course, with extending our models to portray aspects of the political process which have not been dealt with so far. But the search for new ways of portraying economic policy making should be guided by the idiosyncrasies of the analyzed subject matter, a specific policy area or a specific political institution, and not, as is so often the case, by some arbitrary standard of intellectual gamesmanship. The assimilation of public choice into the mainstream appears to have contaminated endogenous policy theory with the self-centered striving for analytical refinements and the disregard for practical applicability which characterized so much of the traditional mainstream. In other words, political economy now suffers from the very same shortcoming that made the early advocates of public choice theory look for new avenues of analysis.

The victory of public choice over the traditional mainstream thus turns out to be a Pyrrhic victory. The original research agenda of the public choice school has only partially been adopted by what we now call political economy: nobody seems to object any more to acknowledging that the agents operating in the political domain can be portrayed with the economic model of behavior; but, nevertheless, much of what is now advertised as political economy does not yield any genuinely interesting insights into the burning problems of political interaction.

At a conference like this one, discussants often claim to have enjoyed reading the assigned paper, and I ask myself whether these otherwise level-headed colleagues may not suffer from some kind of hidden masochism. It is, of course, just possible that these colleagues simply have a very strong preference for beautifully crafted intellectual edifices or an unusually high regard for the structural coherence of our discipline. It is more likely, however, that the reason for their willingness to accept perfectly useless intellectual games is more urbane. We usually like a paper if it allows us to pick up some cute technical trick that may embellish our own work. After all, nobody terribly minds acquiring some additional academic brownie points in an easy manner. Moreover, a paper that meets the generally accepted standards seemingly justifies our own struggles, and does not disturb the established scholars' comfortable environment in which they can set their own rules without the potential interference of unsettling external demands.

I know, of course, that I am not the only one who suffers from nagging doubts. Critical comments on the state of economics as a science are not in short supply. The academic literature is full of pertinent admonitions. What I would like to point out here is simply that public choice theory – which was conceived as an antidote to ivory-tower sophistry – is in the process of being contaminated with the bacillus of intellectual boredom. We are in real danger of losing the anchor which ties our intellectual efforts to the actual working of the institutions that guide social interaction. This de-coupling is liable to undermine the respectability of our discipline and – worse – it will eventually erode our self-respect.

I am not a preacher, even though I might now make this impression. I do not really believe that I can convert anybody who is dancing to the tune of the siren songs of the ongoing intellectual rent-seeking game. Only in game theory can the subtle move from public to common knowledge change the world. I thus realize that my statement that some boring papers have been presented at this conference will not give rise to the celebrated unraveling process, and everything will be fine in Helsinki next year. I rather want to ask *myself*, a fellow sinner no doubt, what routes of escape I can conceive.

First of all, it seems to me more important than ever to stick to whatever vision we have in pursuing our work. The public choice school has its roots in the philosophy of classical liberalism. I do not think that this philosophic foundation is the only one that supports endogenous policy theory, but for a classical liberal, public choice certainly represents a natural approach to analyzing economic policy issues. Since I happen to subscribe to this philosophy, I ask myself why contemporary political economists have so little to say about personal freedom in social interactions. After all, even economists who are not classical liberals do, at least in principle, assign personal liberty one of the top ranks in the hierarchy of economic policy objectives. In analyzing specific policy issues and political institutions most political economists do, however, disregard personal liberty to focus entirely on efficiency – and now and then on justice in distribution. This omission may well be a metastasis of the traditional mainstream's paternalism; it might, however, also reflect the unfortunate consequentialist defense of personal liberty employed by many influential economists such as Friedrich Hayek and Milton Friedman. Whatever the true cause may be, designing political institutions with a view to providing the individual citizens with a maximum of personal liberty in political–economic interactions appears to be a worthwhile research program; it is not a new program, but one that has been sadly neglected by the 'new' political economy school. Moreover, this program appears to me to be of utmost importance for the political reforms which are so much discussed in Europe these days.

Constitutional reform in Europe has, by the way, not been an official topic at this conference. Isn't it a shame that political economists are so much detached from what is hotly debated in the political arena that whoever is interested in this core subject of our discipline needs to consult a traditional political scientist, for example Larry Siedentop whose book *Democracy in Europe* is widely discussed these days?[5]

This brings me to the crucial point. If we are at all willing to address economic policy issues which are ultimately relevant, we need to be knowledgeable about these issues; more, we need take a truly scholarly interest in them. This is something that is lacking in much of our work. Gene Smolensky was absolutely right in pointing out (Chapter 12) that our work's connection to particular public programs is quite often to be found only in the titles of our papers. A political economist who is not really deeply interested in the human condition, which means in our case in the relationship between the individual and the state, be it an interest in ultimate objectives such as personal liberty, distributional justice, values of community, or even policy efficiency, that is, the creation of wealth, or be it a derived interest in some specific kind of public program or political institution (social security, education, federalism, direct democracy, and so on), a political economist who is driven by academic rent-seeking and peer recognition (for what little it's worth), will finally lose the attention of students and peers. The attention of the general public we have lost already.

At the risk of annoying the guardians of the holy grail of public choice, I admit that these days I prefer being entertained by a knowledgeable old-school social welfare maximizer who may even conjure up Walter Hettich's chariot-propelled gods for all I care (Chapter 5), than to endure a talk about a theoretical model which has no relevance for suffering humankind, an empirical study proving a perfectly obvious fact, or an experiment which demonstrates a truism.

If anybody has a right to be a little boring, it is the Ph.D. students. At the beginning of an academic career, one could argue, it is legitimate to demonstrate one's analytical prowess and not to care too much about the social value of one's work. On the other hand, I ask myself whether some of the young technical wizards are at all capable of relating to the real world. As a graduate dean I tend to admit those students to our graduate program who can document superior mathematical skills. But is it really a good idea to choose our incoming graduate students according to their ability to excel in using the analytical techniques of our trade? By disregarding intrinsic motivation to undertake meaningful social research, we may well create a severe selection bias. It is true that this bias might provide us, in the short run, with a distinguished record as academic teachers, but I fear that this short-run satisfaction comes at a high external price: this strategy is liable to further estrange political economy from anything that remotely resembles the real world, with the consequence that it will become increasingly difficult for us to take our own subject seriously.

To summarize: Stanley Winer has organized a fine conference which impressively documents the fact that endogenous policy theory is here to stay. Moreover, the conference gave us all a good impression of what leading-edge political economy looks like today. Who can ask for more? We can now all make an informed decision about where we want to go from here. I have elected to give you a very personal answer, which is predicated on how I see the status quo. I see a discipline dear to my heart in danger of losing its soul. The embrace of public choice by the mainstream of economic policy analysis has led many political economists to succumb to playing the kind of intellectual games which have brought economics as a science into disrepute. As much satisfaction as I derive from the demise of the benevolent dictator, I deplore even more that the second part of the public choice paradigm, the analysis of actual or potential real-world institutions, has not been part of the take-over. In a sense, I thus arrive at the same evaluation as Smolensky in Chapter 12.

What change of the rules of our trade is likely to curb the observed intellectual rent dissipation? Smolensky recommends turning to applications of our theories in the real world. I could not agree more! How do we know that we are dealing with the real world? The praise of our peers is not a good indicator. On the other hand, if the number of our students drops and government support for our research dries up, we know that there is still room for improvement. A more practical guideline might be to see whether a serious newspaper is willing to carry an article summarizing our research output. In the end, however, the only standard is really our own self-esteem, which probably depends on how much our work is in line with whatever vision concerning the relationship between the individual and the state we may have. I wish that you will succeed in mustering the intellectual strength to adhere to whatever vision you may have. Good luck to you!

NOTES

1. Allan Drazen, *Political Economy in Macroeconomics* (Princeton: Princeton University Press, 2000, p. 7).
2. Published as *Grundlagen der Politischen Ökonomie*, Band 1–3 (Tübingen: UTB, Mohr, 1972, 1975 and 1979).
3. Torsten Persson and Guido Tabellini, *Political Economics* (Cambridge, MA: MIT Press, 2000, pp. 2–4).
4. Ibid., p. 3.
5. Larry Siedentop, *Democracy in Europe* (New York: Columbia University Press, 2001).

COMMENTS ON SMOLENSKY AND URSPRUNG

Stanley L. Winer

In this final comment I reflect briefly on how the remarks of Eugene Smolensky and Heinrich Ursprung relate to some of the broader issues raised in this book.

Eugene Smolensky's contribution ends with a call for more 'political engineering' by public finance experts. I shall begin by raising some questions about the normative foundations upon which this engineering is to be based.

Giving advice about the public finances requires a well-defined standard of reference, but the nature of this standard is ambiguous even within the traditional social planning framework used by authors such as Robin Boadway (Chapter 4). Public finance economists often point to the fact that governments must act in the absence of perfect information and with the recognition that lump sum taxation is not feasible. This requires that a constraint be added to the social planner's problem to reflect the costliness of information and that lump sum taxation be excluded from the available set of policy instruments. Setting up the planner's problem in this manner, however, prejudges the type of policy that is politically as well as economically feasible. The extent to which knowledge of individuals is acquired and the ability to levy quasi-lump sum taxation is just a matter of choice about how much to spend on uncovering the personal characteristics of citizens and about how to deal with the ethical and political problems that arise (even with perfect information) when people cannot or will not pay their taxes.[1]

Similar ambiguities arise in other approaches to welfare economics. For example, those adopting a transactions cost perspective insist that all prospective allocation mechanisms, including those that involve collective choice, entail various types of transactions costs. They argue that a standard of reference defined without taking such costs into account, such as the allocation chosen by an omniscient social planner, is both unreasonable and unrealistic. What the (non-zero) transactions cost standard should be, however, is by no means a settled issue, in part because there is no widely accepted definition of the relevant transactions costs.

Several contributors to this volume have argued that it is essential to take collective choice into account when designing or assessing *public* policy. Presumably, then, it is reasonable to compare what actually happens with the allocation of resources and the level of welfare that could be expected in an ideal democracy. Again, it is not obvious how this sort of standard of reference is to be operationalized.

Some of the authors in the book have, directly or indirectly, suggested that an ideal democracy would place limits on the extent to which individuals can be coerced as a result of the operation of majority rule (see the contributions by William Niskanen and Dennis Mueller, Chapters 7 and 8 respectively), a position that has a long tradition in political economy. Here one can ask what the right degree of coercion would be, and what the answer to that question would imply for the day-to-day life of the public finance practitioner asked for advice about, say, the structure of the value-added tax.

Without a well-defined standard of reference, the social engineer is in danger of advocating reforms that would lead us in the wrong direction. The development and operationalization of a standard that is cognizant of democratic choice, one that is shared by a substantial subset of economists and public finance practitioners and that can inform the daily activity of professionals, is one of the big challenges that faces political economy today.

A second problem concerning 'political engineering' that I want to point to has not received direct attention in this volume, though it is related in a general way to many of the approaches advocated by this volume's contributors. The problem is this: once political behavior and the determination of policy instruments are brought within the combined economic and political framework of analysis, where does the policy analyst stand when giving advice? Can he or she continue to advise politicians whose actions are described by the model and used as a basis for understanding what governments do?

Perhaps it will be necessary to refine the analysis of fiscal institutions, and to confine one's advice to issues of process and institutional design. That is the route that appears to have been taken in the field of industrial organization, and perhaps this is also the future of public economics. In my view, however, a retreat to the institutional level can only serve as a partial answer in the field of public finance, for two reasons. First, there is no democratic alternative to having self-interested politicians themselves alter existing institutional arrangements. And second, in the likely event that the political process remains imperfect, some concern with policy outcomes as well as with process seems prudent.

It should be noted that the problem of where to stand remains, though it has a different form, even when the 'engineer' uses the traditional social planning model as a basis for giving advice. For, as Carl Shoup once pointed out (1991, personal communication), 'any policy framer who adopts an "activist" approach puts himself outside the scope of [the] welfare analysis, for he becomes then just one of the combatants in the struggle to get for himself the most with the least pain'.

Smolensky's political engineer could use a firmer conceptual framework as a basis upon which to act.

Despite the problems or challenges pointed to above and elsewhere in this book, I am much less worried by the current state of political economy than is Heinrich Ursprung. It is the nature of scientific inquiry that any new set of ideas, such as those associated with the Virginia School of public choice, be exploited quickly. It is also normal for the period of rapid progress to gradually transform itself into something more ordinary, as the most important applications are drawn out first and the myriad of lesser discoveries left to those who come later. Perhaps we are now in such a period of 'normal science' in political economy, which is a valuable stage in any scientific enterprise, though one can never be sure.

Another reason that I am not as pessimistic as Ursprung is that I never thought of public choice in the same monolithic way as he appears to see it. In my view, there have always been other important lines along which public choice developed besides those advocated by the Virginia School (a school that has contributed greatly to political economy), so that the playing out of this particular set of ideas, if that in fact is what has happened, is of less concern. A partial and far from comprehensive list of related but distinct approaches includes: the study of group formation started by Olson; the use of experimental methods to study behavior under alternative institutional arrangements pioneered by Smith, Plott and others; the construction of various models of political equilibrium at Carnegie-Mellon by Epple, Meltzer, Romer, Rosenthal and others; the political economy of the Chicago School associated with Stigler, Becker, Peltzman and others; and the transactions cost approach to institutional design of Coase, North and others. All these approaches point in different complementary directions, so that younger academics interested in public finance and in the integration of economics and politics now have several flourishing lines of inquiry among which to choose.

Most contemporary public finance textbooks still relegate public choice to one or two chapters and do not integrate this large body of work in a substantial manner. For this and the other reasons discussed in this volume, there remains much to do before political economy, or public choice, or whatever one wants to call it, becomes an integral part of the study of the public finances. Why isn't this an exciting time to be at work?

NOTE

1. Other critiques of social planning are found in the Introduction and in the chapters by Brennan, Breton and Hettich.

Index

235